M000114915

Tina,
I hope to one
day chat with you
about these ideas.
Best,
Louis Chude-Sokei

THE LAST "DARKY"

A John Hope Franklin Center Book

THE LAST "DARKY"

Bert Williams,

Black-on-Black Minstrelsy,

and the African Diaspora

Louis Chude-Sokei

Duke University Press

Durham and London 2006

© 2006 Duke University Press

All rights reserved

Printed in the United States of

America on acid-free paper ∞

Designed by Amy Ruth Buchanan

Typeset in Quadraat by Keystone

Typesetting, Inc.

Library of Congress Cataloging-in-

Publication Data appear on the last

printed page of this book.

Frontispiece: photo of Bert Williams by

Samuel Lumiere, c. 1921. Courtesy

Library of Congress Prints and

Photographs Division.

For Shirley Chude-Sokei.

Responsible for this Diaspora,

the only center possible.

CONTENTS

Introduction 1

1. Black Minstrel, Black Modernism 17

2. Migrations of a Mask 46

3. Theorizing Black-on-Black Cross-Culturality 82

4. The Global Economy of Minstrelsy 114

5. *In Dahomey* 161

6. Claude McKay's Calypso 207

Notes 249

Bibliography 263

Index 273

The masks alone occasionally suggest a correspondence
to the chthonic realm and hint at the archetypes of transition, yet even the majority of them flee the full power of
cosmic vision, take refuge in deliberately grotesque and
comic attitudes. Such distortions are easily recognized as
the technique of evasion from numinous powers. Terror
is both contained by art in tragic form and released by
art through comic presentation and sexual ambience.
The tragic mask, however, also functions from the same
source as its music—from the archetypal essences whose
language derives not from the plane of physical reality or
ancestral memory (the ancestor is no more than agent or
medium), but from the numinous territory of transition
into which the artist obtains fleeting glimpses by ritual,
sacrifice and a patient submission of rational awareness
to the moment when fingers and voice relate the symbolic language of the cosmos.
—Wole Soyinka, "The Fourth Stage"

From the left, from the right, from the South, and from the North,
there rises the wall impassive
to the mole and the needle of water.
Do not seek, Negroes, for the cleft to find the infinite mask . . .

Ah, masqueraded Harlem!
Ah, Harlem, threatened by a mob wearing clothes without heads!
Your rumour reaches me,
your rumour reaches me, crossing tree trunks and lifts,
across the grey plates
where your cars float covered with teeth,
across the dead horses and the minute crimes,
across your great despairing King,
whose beard reaches the sea.

—Federico García Lorca, "The King of Harlem"

INTRODUCTION

Although his name has faded into near-utter obscurity, Egbert Austin—"Bert"—Williams was arguably the first black performer who could be described as an international pop star. He was acknowledged as the greatest stage comedian in late-nineteenth- and early-twentieth-century America, and his success in England guaranteed there a legacy almost as popular, but no less significant. By the time he integrated Broadway in 1910 via his controversial yet highly successful stint with the Ziegfeld Follies, his influence, his voice, and his image had already circulated throughout much of the world from late in the previous century. Indeed, Williams was one of the earliest black starring performers in two media which would prove decisive in the century of "pop" itself, which is to say, the century of America's imperial coming of age: film and sound recording.

Decades before the explosion of "race records," those early African American sound recordings which helped signal the cultural presence of the Harlem Renaissance or the New Negro movement, Bert Williams was one of the first Negro performers captured by the so-called talking machine. In the period before Harlem's vogue, his was the only black recorded voice regularly and consistently available, and his hits included classic American popular songs like 1901's "Good Morning, Carrie," his signature song "Nobody," and dozens of others which spanned the transition from "coon" songs to "race records," from ragtime and the blues to vaudeville and Broadway show tunes. He and his partner George Walker so popularized the African American dance the cakewalk—a popular cultural phenomenon in 1890s America— that many attributed it to them. They even took it to England as a part of the command performance of their 1901 show *In Dahomey* and taught it to King Edward VII. Reflecting his enormous popularity, in 1916 Bert Williams began to appear in two-reel comedy films, the most notable of which was *A Natural Born Gambler*; however, two years earlier he had starred in *Darktown Jubilee*, one of the first movies to use an African American in blackface rather than the traditional use of a white actor in blackface—and this a year before D. W. Griffith's *Birth of a Nation*, with its dependence on white blackface minstrelsy in its extremely negative depiction of African Americans in the American South.

So in making the controversial and viciously opposed move to the Ziegfeld Follies, Bert Williams became the first black artist to star with white performers in a major musical production. In response to those many who threatened to leave, Florenz Ziegfeld said simply, "Go if you want to. I can replace every one of you, except the man you want me to fire."[1] However, it must be stressed that before he joined the Follies Williams had already been the most famous performer in the specific world of black popular theater, coming to fame with the Williams and Walker show, which was the largest, most ornate, and best-known black musical theater troupe of its time. In a time of segregation and lynching in America and during what would prove to be the twilight of Europe's formal imperial power, Williams, along with his partners George and Ada Overton Walker, achieved the seemingly impossible. They created, owned, designed, and maintained a massive and elaborate international touring organization that rested on the comic performance of the always tragic, always masked Bert Williams.

Beyond these and so many other highlights from a remarkable career— one made even more so by how quickly it has been forgotten or neglected— Bert Williams's legacy and influence can be found in radically disparate sites. It is there, for example, in the art and writing of the Harlem Renaissance as well as in the life of Ernest Hemingway, who considered him a personal hero; it precedes and makes possible the work of Al Jolson, Eddie Cantor, and W. C. Fields, while simultaneously authorizing the work of Booker T. Washington, Paul Laurence Dunbar, Claude McKay, and Louis Armstrong. Williams achieved all of this and so much more while performing always in blackface, occupying always the shambling and shambolic icon of explicit racism called the "darky." As a black performer who worked within the now universally despised yet still resonant space of blackface minstrelsy, he left a legacy as fraught as it was complex, as troubling then as it is productive now for a reevaluation of contemporary thinking about that crucial period of American and transatlantic modernism. The complex modes of memory and forgetting at work in American and African American literary, cultural, and performance histories impel me to assert that Bert Williams is of greater importance than hitherto acknowledged. His centrality inheres in the reason for his absence: his use and appropriation of blackface minstrelsy itself. Hence a careful consideration of the life, performance, and legacy of Bert Williams as a black minstrel reveals not only a rich and problematic set of perspectives on what is known about modernism but a fresh understanding of how the mechanism of his forgetting has in fact been constitutive of how that period has been canonized.

But none of his celebrity, significance, or fully acknowledged pioneer status could shield him from the weight of opprobrium that was heaped upon him *and* his famous personae as he became more and more successful in a historical moment of both rapid technological transformation and rapid ideological transition. Very few of Bert Williams's political, cultural, and social achievements—which literally set the ground for the emergent Harlem Renaissance—remained in focus as the more radical historicizing of that rising generation found itself empowered by its ability to write its own history and recast its antecedents as distinct from minstrelsy. Those black artists, performers, and even political figures who paced and followed him ranged from James Weldon Johnson to Booker T. Washington, from W. E. B. Du Bois to Claude McKay, from Marcus Garvey to Alain Locke and to a panoply of less-known performers of stage and song throughout the African diaspora. They all felt newly empowered by their need to define their own ideological parameters and articulate themselves into history in ways distinct from the previous generation as well as distinct from the racism that had brought them to these shores.

This empowerment and the self-consciousness that produced it were acknowledged by these and other figures as largely owing to the successes of Bert Williams on the eve of the more aggressively militant politics of assimilation and separation that followed World War I. Ironically, the broader historicizing tendencies of the Harlem Renaissance probably achieved its access into history not via a strict remembering of him but of his mask; not via a recuperation of his intricate masquerade, but partly via a traumatic and sometimes active forgetting of it. Many who followed would repress the anxiety of this masquerade, one of their primary influences, and work to excise those elements of his personae that threatened to unravel the very paradigms they were seeking to establish in their various paths to racial equality. A scant few years after his death, Bert Williams would become a casualty of these cross-currents of history, nearly lost in the vicissitudes of a black American modernist movement struggling for its own historical legitimation while simultaneously struggling against its own historical erasure. Although Williams battled against traces of this will to forget and erase him during his career, a handful of years after his death his name and his art were not linked to success, achievement, and the politics of integration; nor were they celebrated for Williams's influence on the broader world of American popular culture, the cultural institutions he left in his wake, and the other modernisms that depended on his minstrelsy. Instead his name became inextricably linked to the demonic history of possession, caricature, slavery, and dehumanization embodied by the form he in fact reinvented and appropriated to subversive effect: blackface minstrelsy.

Since the fact of a black performer in blackface is more complex than it seems, there is need for a serious study of Bert Williams's life, times, meanings, and techniques. There is also need for a fresh interpretation of his use of blackface and the possibilities enabled by the cross-cultural engagement that is masquerade. This is particularly the case in returning to a cultural climate where masks, masquerade, and cultural border crossings became dominant signifiers of the modernist historical moment. Examples of this range from Picasso's fateful encounter with African masks to Josephine Baker's grand success performing an "authentic" African savagery to even W. E. B. Du Bois's epochal The Souls of Black Folk and its dependence on the trope of "doubling" as a form of cross-cultural masquerade. Despite the ostensibly simple reasons for Bert Williams's dismissal in an era in which race pride, racial identity, and "blackness" were being wrested from the racist discourses of slavery, Jim Crow, and colonialism, his very performance of race via minstrelsy was itself a politicized rejection of those very discourses. After all, he was not simply a black man in blackface, crudely representing—as some would argue—the insidious violence of colonial mimicry as the racist stereotype becomes internalized and commodified by those most harmed by it. Nor

was he a more authentic representation of that racist stereotype, guaranteeing its truth in his supreme ability at mimicking his essential Negro self. Bert
Williams appropriated from whites the very right to perform and symbolically possess "the Negro." In addition he claimed the right to command the
symbolic arena of the Broadway stage, a space of enormous importance and
power in the years before cinema and sound recording became dominant
sites of cultural and political representation for a nascent American imperial
sprawl. Specifically, he was a black man who came to fame masquerading as
a white racist caricature of a "black man" which ultimately mocked and
erased that primary caricature.

However, if all of this weren't enough, there was yet another layer beneath,
beyond, and beside all these implications, a layer which is the primary source
of this project's extended interpretation of Bert Williams, his life, and his
personae. Despite his success and acknowledgment as a pioneer African
American performer and artist, Williams was actually born in Nassau, the
British West Indies, now known as the Bahamas. He was born in 1874, and
his family finally relocated to the United States around 1885 and settled in
Riverside, California, an inauspicious site for one who would so transform
the landscape of American popular culture, music, and cultural politics. Bert
Williams was in actuality a West Indian immigrant, self-consciously performing not as a "black man" but as the white racist representation of an *African
American*, which he may have phenotypically resembled, but which—as he
emphasized—was also culturally other to him. This cross-cultural, intra-
racial masquerade constituted a form of dialogue at a time when tensions
between the multiple and distinct black groups in New York City were often
seething despite various attempts at pan-African solidarity.

The process by which Bert Williams learned to both be and play an African
American is not only a unique narrative of black modernism; it is in fact an
experience of assimilation unique to non-American blacks. The poetics of
this specific form of assimilation and of Williams's black-on-black masquerade is also crucial to the legacy of Caribbean immigration and its own distinct
experience of modernism in a cultural realm dominated by African American
writing, cultural sensibilities, and political concerns. It is dramatized most
powerfully in a work like Claude McKay's *Home to Harlem* and in the work of
other Caribbean moderns like Eric Walrond, Richard B. Moore, Eula Spence,
Marcus Garvey, and African American writers such as Rudolf Fisher. But years
before McKay occupied the vanguard of Harlem modernism, Bert Williams
had so mastered the multiple projections and inflections of race as repre-

sented by minstrelsy and vaudeville that he was able to hint at a modernism perhaps unrepresentable until now.

So despite his elision from so much of the work from or pertaining to that period, as well as the discomfort he generated toward the end of his life, these gestures of masquerade, black-on-black minstrelsy, and intra-racial passing are as important to Harlem modernism as to the transnational discourses of pan-Africanism. One can go as far as to argue that they partly make those latter discourses and movements possible. After all, this layered masquerade enables an interpretation of Bert Williams's minstrelsy; one in which through his performance he can lay claim to authority over the representations of African Americans before the Harlem Renaissance and then to erase and revise those representations in such a way as to empower and encourage an emergent nationalism rooted in the then radical and seemingly unimaginable politics of assimilation. Also, it should be read as a corrective to the growing nationalistic chauvinism of an African American cultural politics that, despite its resistance and marginalization, veered too often toward an exceptionalism that severely limited the transnational borders of race and culture.

But before further specifying the cross-cultural poetics and intra-racial politics of Bert Williams's performance *as* a West Indian immigrant, it must not be forgotten that during this period the notion of minstrelsy and its discourses of authenticity were so formalized and institutionalized that the very notion that a black performer could *outperform* a white performer in a white form such as minstrelsy was unimaginable. Yes, the idea that *a Negro could play a Negro better than a white man* was both ludicrous and heretical. Add to this the fact that Bert Williams and George Walker knew that "the Negro" being performed and constructed via white blackface minstrelsy was an explicitly racist and politically unnatural fiction and so they engaged the form primarily to erase that fiction *from within*. This they did by leaping to fame after naming themselves, ironically, controversially, and provocatively, "The Two Real Coons." They went even further with their critique of racialized notions of authenticity by directly engaging in print, in recordings, and onstage the various contemporary discourses of race which clustered around identitarian questions such as the "natural" qualities of "the Negro," repatriation to the African continent, or the various articulations of "Negro soul" that would achieve validation and poetic realization in W. E. B. Du Bois's 1903 *The Souls of Black Folk*.

Certainly all of this would be enough to guarantee Bert Williams immortality, though one can perhaps understand how easily this delicate tightrope of representation could be misread, as it so often was, and how it could so easily be dismissed and erased because of the growing rejection of minstrelsy itself. This was after all a climate where something as atavistic as minstrelsy needed to be rejected in toto so as to clear the way for a more self-motivated if not more "authentic" cultural politics that would increasingly focus on "representation" as a primary site of anti-racist engagement. Yet much of the ambivalence or antipathy toward Bert Williams and a specifically black minstrelsy has not changed even in today's intellectual and cultural climate. Despite a thriving industry of research, theorizing, and commentary on white minstrelsy and the complex discourses of race, gender, and performativity, the presence and possibilities of blacks in blackface are generally undocumented. In fact, black minstrelsy is most often dismissed as either pathological or an unfortunate and pitiable sideline in the transition from a more passive political era into a much more self-assertive and militant one. This too helps obscure Bert Williams even further behind the mask that he could not escape.

Only in rare cases is the presence of blacks in the contemporary minstrelsy industry fully engaged, but never as central to a study of literary and cultural modernism and the various political movements and tendencies that constituted it. In his time and slightly beyond it, Bert Williams's presence and his use of blackface were not ignored and were in fact at the center of the burgeoning modernist discourses of assimilation, separatism, race-militancy, and internationalism that all came together in the question and concern as to how the "Negro" should be represented. In this context, the concern for representation explicitly and simultaneously signified both the realm of the political and the more aesthetic realm of performance and depiction. It was minstrelsy, specifically the black minstrelsy of Bert Williams, that kept those two realms of meaning and their various implications tense and alive and generative.

In an era where racial identity and representation was being recast and reclaimed, where the African American social world was fervently trying to define itself while struggling against the racist climate of the first century of freedom, Bert Williams—the man behind the mask—existed on the cultural margins. As a West Indian immigrant, he and his family arrived in America years before the first major wave of West Indian immigration that made such a powerful impact on the cultural and political complexity of the Harlem movement. Williams was new to the dialect of African American language and culture. His "blackness" was as distinct as it was destabilizing to the binary racial structure of America in which "black" implicitly meant African American and in a renaissance which was increasingly centered on the local politics and vernacular poetics of first-world blacks in America. Although it was founded on an increasingly diasporic sense of black identity as signified by its various pan-Africanisms, this Harlem movement was produced and threatened by a set of internal cultural tensions as the black immigrants from abroad struggled to find their way alongside those more culturally dominant immigrants from the American South.

Struggling alongside the political need to humanize and ennoble "the Negro" (often meaning the African American) was a more difficult to perceive politics of intra-racial cross-culturality at work beneath the black minstrel mask. Adding even more to this complexity is the fact that as the Williams and Walker shows grew in influence and independence, they began to feature the representation of non-American blacks and set them in exotic cultural spaces—particularly in Africa and in the Caribbean. This stress on black-on-black cross-culturality slightly predates W. E. B. Du Bois's institutionalizing of the pan-African conferences and was first featured by Williams and Walker a year after the Trinidadian barrister H. Sylvester Williams convened the first pan-African conference in 1900. It was also at work years before the presence of the Marcus Garvey movement in Harlem, with its explicitly populist pan-African separatism. Years before this now-canonized moment of a transnationally circulating black cultural modernism, it was Bert Williams and George Walker who dragged minstrelsy from the plantation and Jim Crow topos where it stagnated and forced it to speak to the also emergent black counterglobalization that was pan-Africanism. This was accomplished not only by that aforementioned impersonation of continental Africans and other Caribbean peoples; it also made the symbolic space of "Africa" function in the black popular imagination without the previous associations of backwardness, benighted ignorance, primitiveness, and superstition.

Via the work and life and iconic meanings of Bert Williams, this form of passing was dramatized, problematized, and fetishized in the context of a reclaimed and explicitly nationalist and proto-pan-Africanist minstrelsy. For this comedic performer, blackface masquerade was as much a means of negotiating relationships between and among diaspora blacks in Harlem as it was an attempt to erase the internationally projected racist fiction of the

"stage Negro" (or "darky") from within the conventions of popular performance, from behind a mask produced and maintained by competitive projections and denials of black subjectivity. With these insights in mind, this study
establishes that Williams's minstrelsy maps out yet another pan-Africanist
sensibility, one which runs alongside both Garvey's and Du Bois's but which
differs from them both in its attention to the tensions, differences, and
incommensurabilities beneath the skin of racial typology and the dominant
attempts of both racists and black nationalists to articulate a politics of cross-
cultural similarity rooted in a biological essentialism. This latter is something
that would have and does have a deleterious effect on non–African American
blacks, who often find their cultural distinctiveness and their differential
colonial histories and racial orientations marginalized and erased by the
African American zeal to articulate a race-based solidarity in their own specific terms and according to their own cultural priorities.

In a climate of radical cross-cultural encounters and exchange where blacks
from the Caribbean, the African continent, the American South, and Latin
America found themselves face to face in a transnational migrant zone—a
global crossroads—like New York, Bert Williams's minstrel masking was a
realigning of race in this Afro-cosmopolitan context. Yet inevitably Harlem's
renaissance and the historicizing that it struggled to establish were dominated
by African Americans despite the signal presence of highly visible, audible,
and prominent West Indians like McKay and the writer Eric Walrond, political
leaders and radicals such as Grace Campbell, Hubert Harrison, Richard B.
Moore, W. A. Domingo, and the two Amy Garveys (both Ashwood and
Jacques); also notable were the Puerto Rican bibliophile Arturo Schomburg,
Trinidadian calypsonians like Sam Manning and Wilmoth Houdini, and the
legendary Caspar Holstein, "bolito King" and don of the numbers game who
funded more than a few of Harlem's literary prizes and events. So many of
these crucial figures have been accorded canonical status as "black" when in
fact that categorization was—as demonstrated by the work and life of Bert
Williams—one of many immigrant performance modes and also often a
codeword for the diasporic reach of an African American exceptionalism.
However, embedded in the universalizing racial assumptions of this renaissance is a silencing of a history of black cultural distinctiveness which functioned beneath and against its own skin and was often lost by the binary
construction of race in which it was delimited.

Bert Williams forces us to reexamine the complexion and restore the
dialectal complexities of a black modernism in Harlem. For example, a ca-

nonically "black" and modernist writer like Claude McKay must be read alongside the work of Bert Williams. Indeed, the final chapter of this book is devoted to Claude McKay, particularly his 1928 *Home to Harlem*, famed as the first black bestseller and still one of the most controversial and misread books in the African American literary canon. This text is an homage to Bert Williams by way of McKay's own attempt at a literary black-on-black passing through vernacular masquerade and black blackface minstrelsy. Marcus Garvey too must be read in the context of Bert Williams, since so much of his use of symbols, icons, costumes, and Africentric iconography was made possible by the proto-pan-African spectacles of the Williams and Walker shows as well as the Caribbean carnival complex. These and those many other black immigrants who shaped the ideological contours of a discrepant modernism in Harlem must be traced back to the impact, the influence, and the ultimate forgetting of Bert Williams.

McKay, Garvey, Eric Walrond, and many other minor characters are at the heart of a black modernism rooted in cross-cultural, intra-racial encounters, not the least of which featured the necessary performance of an African American identity in a cultural context where Caribbean specificity was explicitly marginalized, at times violently opposed, and often burlesqued. But what links them all beyond their Caribbean roots is precisely what links them to other blacks whose roots were American: the fact that as black modernists they all depended on some form of black-on-black masquerade in order to produce said modernism and employ it as a strategic method of consolidating as well as questioning group solidarity. For example, the pioneering work of the choreographer and proto-pan-African feminist Ada Overton Walker is here considered for its attempt to reconstruct the image and notion of black femininity in terms of the dominant white discourse of womanhood alongside both the emergent pan-Africanism of the pre-Garvey period and the African American bourgeois exceptionalism that was the primary assumption behind her diasporic performance. This was accomplished years before Josephine Baker's rise to prominence on the stages of Paris and New York, where she would come to fame by way of her own performance of a kitsch-African primitivity. And though Ada Overton Walker's performance was narrated in tandem with the biases and assumptions of an African American bourgeoisie, it was achieved in a play that explicitly mocks those biases, assumptions, and pretensions. In complex performances, she managed to unveil a layer of protofeminist assertion within and against the sexual orthodoxies of both white expectations of black "womanhood" and pan-Africanism itself.

Also considered in this study is the bizarre and long-forgotten work of the legendary huckster Bata Kindai Ibn LoBagola, who made a fascinating career of racial masquerade and cross-cultural fraud on both sides of the Atlantic. Building on the early career of Bert Williams before he began "blacking up," LoBagola erased the borders between ethnography and popular entertainment by means of his black-on-black minstrelsy in the era of colonial expositions and world fairs. But in the endless, pointless, convenient, and strategic search for origins, it is Bert Williams who preceded both Garvey and McKay as well as Josephine Baker and Ibn LoBagola. He will lay the groundwork not just for the West Indian cultural and political presence but for an American legacy of intra-racial cross-cultural discourse that is increasingly in need of a far more sophisticated hearing than that allowed by American racial binaries and the mere mask that black often signifies.

The six chapters into which this text is divided explore the contexts and implications of black-on-black minstrelsy from the historical to the theoretical, from popular culture and stage performance to the African American literary and cultural tradition. Though Bert Williams's story is the convenient fulcrum and opportunity for narrative shape and extended interpretation, the ultimate concern is in fact the intricate patterns of cross-culturality at work within the assumptions of racial solidarity and behind all attempts to fix race into a bi-chromatic schema in the context of an American imperialism that was as dependent on domestic racism as it was on the legacy of European colonialism. The presence of West Indian immigrants during the period under consideration signified not only the traces of a crumbling or restructuring British imperialism in the midst of American modernism. In their interactions with the African American social world, these immigrants signified the tense moment as one empire succeeded another and multiple legacies of racial domination and cultural dispersal were made to confront and catalyze each other by way of the discrepancies and dissonances attendant to their differential histories.

Strangely—and perhaps unbelievably—enough, blackface minstrelsy came to serve a productive function in this context despite its seemingly overwhelming burden of racism and its actual and epistemological violence to those it claimed to represent. This, of course, made it easily susceptible to nationalist erasure.

The first chapter of this book places Bert Willliams's journey to and behind blackface in the context of African American modernism, as a precursor to the complex fictions and gestures of masking that marked the subsequent generation. His own reluctant acceptance of that form of masquerade—that form of racial travesty that he could appropriate *as* masquerade, *as* dissimulating performance—did emerge in relationship to the growing hostility of the African American social world to that particular form of popular culture. His minstrelsy also emerged in relationship to a growing and increasingly vocal set of tensions between that particular social world and the West Indian immigrants who had also come to claim Harlem as a crucial site in their own migrant ethno-scape.

Chapter 2 explores the implications of the intra-racial, cross-cultural positioning of Williams's mask for its attempt to mediate those growing tensions. Here Bert Williams's foundational influence on the politics and artistic production of black modernism is discussed and his performance as a West Indian mimicking an African American (or, more precisely, as an African American stereotype which he hoped to both ennoble and differentiate from himself via that comic mimicry) is argued to signify not only a nationalist reclamation of a black "soul" obscured by white minstrelsy but also a critique of a black modernism that was hardening its own racial borders and becoming intolerant of its own margins through an often parochial language of "soul" or racial identity. His signal influence on the language of black modernism from Booker T. Washington to Paul Laurence Dunbar, from Jessie Fauset to Ralph Ellison and even W. E. B. Du Bois, is here made explicit and the theoretical implications of his denaturing performance of black identity introduced.

Chapter 3 gives those theoretical implications much more attention, detail, and focus. Drawing on and critiquing both Henry Louis Gates's discourse of "signifyin(g)" as articulated in *The Signifying Monkey* and Houston Baker's invaluable *Modernism and the Harlem Renaissance*, I argue that Bert Williams's mask occupies the semantic spaces in between the two differentially black cultural groups that occupy a modernist Harlem. Within his masking, competing signifying traditions are staged and synthesized and the Black Atlantic world is made to witness a minstrelsy that had long left the plantation topos and long been alien to its own name and performance conventions. Through shows like *In Dahomey* and *In Abyssinia*, for example, the Williams and Walker shows began to explore and construct a pan-African worldview through a comic masquerade that, despite its travesty, introduced a much more respectful and accessible vision of Africa to a black popular audience. It was, at the very least, an Africa without trauma, without shame, one which could function as either a kind of utopia or an antidote to the vacuum of forgetting introduced by the slave trade. Moreover, this use of Africa was deployed to simultaneously critique and parody a few other less savory qualities of pan-Africanism: the latent African American imperial desire that helped produce the intra-racial tragedy of Liberia; the "empire envy" that undergirded Marcus Garvey's Universal Negro Improvement Association (UNIA); and the prescient sense of much assimilation as being driven not just by a desire for racial equality but by class conflict and by the globalizing of an American politics that maintained its integrity by masking itself as African American—in blackface as it were.

Chapter 4 then takes a brief but necessary detour, tracing the impact and influence of Bert Williams and black minstrelsy in the black diaspora itself, from the exotic "Dahomey" to the "actual" Africa and to the Caribbean where it had some influence on the arts, culture, and politics of Trinidadian carnival as well as on colonial Jamaica. It is its influence on carnival that functions as the most important link in this transnational poetics and politics of minstrel masquerade—particularly through the folk form of calypso that shared smaller but equally significant cultural space with jazz in modernist New York in this period. The primary concern here is not to argue against the falseness or artifice of these black impersonations of other blacks or to simply read them as more authentic representations of what white racist fantasy had established as historical truth. Nor is it to reduce the complexity of blackface masquerade to a mere performance of self-hate or of the internalization of a negative self-image. Instead the chapter charts an emergent diaspora sensibility that was in fact dependent on artifice, impersonation, and fraud and which then laid the foundations for both pan-Africanism and a contemporary Black Atlantic discourse for which pan-Africanism is its political unconscious. To make these issues much clearer and to root them in primary material, chapter 5 reconstructs in detail the moment and the context of the show that made Williams and Walker much more famous and influential than they could have ever imagined: In Dahomey.

The final chapter brings to the center of this project the work of Claude McKay, most notably his controversial debut novel Home to Harlem, which has not been fully explored for its multiple layers of cross-cultural, intra-racial signifying. His use of both jazz-age poetics and calypso with and against each other has been all too often misread or unread. Home to Harlem and McKay's work in general must be situated in the broader context of Caribbean vernacular culture in Harlem, particularly via its dependence on the transnational form of vernacular signifying that is calypso music. Home to Harlem is explicitly dependent on the myth, the icon, and the politics of masquerade established by Bert Williams as well as a carnival poetics that can be traced beyond the work of Mikhail Bakhtin and to the Caribbean itself. It features techniques of Caribbean signifying operative *within* African American signifying; techniques in which one vernacular tradition is playfully and seriously deployed against the other, as theorized in chapter 3.

It is after all impossible to discuss the cultural form of calypso without engaging the larger historical and theoretical context of carnival. The carnival complex had already established its cultural links to New York by the flourishing of the renaissance, partly as a result of the signal influence of Bert Williams, as well as that of those in the West Indian community and in the Caribbean itself who appropriated his mask in order to construct a face. This was a face that was black, but "other" to the dominant African American cultural presence. Chapter 6 demonstrates that Claude McKay's work exists not in dual locations as contemporary critics argue but in multiple, competing locations, in and around the mask of black minstrelsy, in and around an African American vernacular that McKay performed much in the way that Bert Williams performed the "stage Negro" or the "darky." As a West Indian writer vocal about his fetishized and relentless displacement, McKay made his always tense relationship to African Americans as much the concern of his fiction as was his commitment to racial solidarity.

It bears pointing out that in critiquing a sub-hegemonic "African American" community or social world, this project does not reduce it to an undifferentiated singularity. This is clear by the amount of attention given to analyzing the complexities and differences among the many African Americans Bert Williams worked with and the many more who supported and critiqued his career. Many were themselves aware of the intra-racial, cross-cultural tensions of their historical moment and of the prejudices that each subject group both fought against and maintained. It is worth emphasizing again and again that the stress on differences and tensions is a stress on the productivity of cross-cultural intra-racial encounters that is silenced by the false face of nationalist solidarity. It is also a necessary critique of the forms of power and cultural dominance that remain unchallenged because they lie entrenched in their own marginalization and are often unwilling or unable to recognize their own complicity with dominance resulting from their prioritizing of that marginalization as representative of all others. That 1901's *In Dahomey* was rooted in this seemingly contemporary cultural concern or insight makes it all the more remarkable as a modernist exploration of black-on-black cross-culturality years before the Harlem Renaissance. After all, it is the silence around these differences that has wrought great historical harm and resentment and has reduced so much contemporary black cultural criticism to the empty performance of a broken and fragmented mask nostalgic for a totality—a stable flesh behind itself—that could never and should never be.

And just as these arguments do not intend to generalize and reduce the African American social world, neither do they intend to establish an equally limiting and inaccurate "West Indian" community or identity at work in modernist Harlem or in contemporary America. This would be a significant problem since so many distinct island groups came to and passed through the global crossroads that was and is Harlem, USA. However, the fact that Bert Williams's impact *as* a West Indian was enough to help produce and signal a notable and generalized West Indian cultural presence will address the micro-micropolitics of the West Indian community itself. This concern is explored here in part by way of McKay's obsession with black micropolitics alongside the divisive ethnocentrisms of both Garvey and Du Bois. But since Williams never actually performed as a "West Indian"—only once, which is the primary concern of the first chapter—but performed as an "African American," his significance within the Caribbean and African American community was always generalized if not universalized. Given this constant performance of black otherness, his iconic "West Indian-ness" has never been charted. This book is devoted to unmasking this performance primarily to reshape the transnational cultural context within which it functioned and the cross-cultural discursive space it constructed.

In critiquing the subhegemonic cultural and ideological power of African American history and politics, the reader should not lose sight of the signal influence of African American history, culture, and politics on Bert Williams, pan-Africanism, and Caribbean culture. This would be a gross misreading of this project, one perhaps invited by its willingness to critique and identify the often painful processes by which African American self-assertion has the secondary effect of marginalizing and subsuming multiple black othernesses and their often conflictual microhistories. These othernesses have often gotten lost in the seemingly overwhelming and justifiably influential context of the African American social world and its epic struggle for recognition against a recalcitrant and reluctant American racism. But overall, I hope this project will have some impact on the discourses of black cross-culturality which still depend overmuch on a romantic nationalism that often only differs from a racist essentialism by an ironic inflection.

This project aims at a return to race and the construction of community via a circuitous exploration of masking and performance, inauthenticity, cross-cultural mimicry, and self-parody. These are gestures and performances which emerged with and simultaneously subverted the dominant discourses of authenticity which raged on both sides of a racial divide that was never actually two-sided and perhaps never ever quite as divided as it thought or thinks itself to be. And these discourses rage on as the numbers of non-American "black" immigrants continue to swell and redefine American culture in the skin of limited forms of racial classification. However inescapable these modes of classification and definition may be, they must not be allowed to simplify the truly radical energies of intra-racial difference and micropolitical dissent and dissonance; hence the need for a serious consideration of the work of Bert Williams and the Williams and Walker shows, the many black performances of "African" identity at work in the climate of modernism, and a specific Caribbean American poetics at work within and against African American exceptionalism.

These intra-racial cultural differences and tensions are being increasingly confronted not only in the academy but more pressingly on the transnational street level of diaspora imaginings. They are particularly relevant in America as the numbers of non-American blacks—Caribbean, West and East African, Afro-Latin, and many others—swell to a point where intra-racial cross-cultural competition, misunderstanding, and various tensions are beginning to overshadow the rich legacies of creative contact and political interaction. It is in these multiple sites and discourses that the cultural assumptions and historical authority of African American literature and theory, culture, and politics are being challenged in order to be redefined, reinvented, and opened. This is absolutely necessary in order to make sense of and space for new African diaspora subjects, *new* black Americans who arrive to question that authority alongside new dispensations of racial or cultural power. In questioning that authority, they transform it and its applicability to a world that can no longer be contained, explained, or lived in by way of a bichromatic model of difference; after all, that bichromatism ultimately privileges its two primary elements: the white and the African American, locked in a struggle for mutual recognition which can blind them to the changing landscape of their premises. And in transforming this model, these newly "black" subjects imagine and establish a context wherein American cultural assumptions no longer function as the standard or where conventional American models of racial "oppression," "resistance," or "identity" function as categorical.

CHAPTER 1 Black Minstrel, Black Modernism

By the time Bert Williams appeared in the Ziegfeld Follies of 1915, his career as a performer had taken him from carnivals in California—performing in Santa Cruz, Monterey, Salinas, and other coastal towns—to medicine shows and fairs across the country. Inevitably this led to the vaudeville circuit where he and his partner George Walker headlined for years, becoming major celebrities in a time when celebrity was as rare as it was dangerous for blacks. Although his career continued successfully after the Follies, it was in New York that he made history as the first Negro actor to appear as a regular in a Broadway spectacle.

The Funniest Man We Never Saw, the Saddest Man We Never Knew

Not that there wasn't great opposition; to use Williams's own words, a "tremendous storm in a teacup."[1] The cast itself threatened to boycott the Follies and there were major protests over the idea of a Negro star on the Broadway stage, especially one receiving top billing. Opposition and organized protest came from judges, the police, the media, and, in 1919, the fledgling Actors Equity Association in which Williams could not gain membership. And as the tide of nationalism grew in the years before the Harlem Renaissance, African American critics and journalists also attacked Williams, though he had long been a beloved performer in an African American social world still unaware of how crucial it would be to America's popular culture. He did not assert racial pride loudly enough, they argued. His success was not a sign of assimilation but a comic denial of its possibility. Some even went as far as to argue that he was being "used" by the Follies, offended more by his move to Broadway than the vestigial presence of burnt cork.[2]

According to James Weldon Johnson, Bert Williams "defected" to the Follies in 1910, thereby helping to end the development of a distinct Negro theater.[3] This description of Williams's signing with Florenz Ziegfeld as a "defection" is worth a moment of consideration. It comes from a man known for his narrative of racial passing, The Autobiography of an Ex-Colored Man, which helped signal a Harlem Renaissance that would define itself partly by repressing the image of the minstrel yet simultaneously engage the poetics of masking. But what makes his language interesting is that it reveals that a "distinct Negro theater" in fact depended on blackface minstrelsy. In 1930's Black Manhattan, Weldon Johnson is aware of the difference between "black musicals" which featured African Americans on the stage but rarely in the audience and a Negro musical theater that featured African Americans on-stage, in the audience, and behind the scenes. Hovering over both these uses of race in American popular performance was the still potent memory of a black theater that involved no "black" people at all, just white men in blackface, occupying the mask of black maleness and femaleness as well as the multiple ethnic identities that minstrel theater depended on. So despite the criticism in Weldon Johnson's choice of words, Williams's movement to the Follies was in fact crucial for both the expansion of possibilities for black performers in America and the assimilation/integration that dominated early-twentieth-century black cultural politics, which both Williams and Weldon Johnson firmly supported.

However, this was the epistemological thicket that Bert Williams struggled through, a context where his individual success was beginning to be read as a sign of cultural and political failure; a mise-en-scène in which the space between mask and flesh was being erased by the exigencies of an emergent radicalism. His obituary in the black socialist paper The Messenger sums up how he would eventually be read by the rising generation. Williams, it read, rendered a disservice to black people. . . . He played in theaters that either barred or Jim-Crowed Negroes—a policy born of the conception that all men of color are inherently inferior to white men—and by a strange irony of fate, Bert Williams was himself a facile instrument of this insidious cult. His fun-making, of course, was what they wanted, the lowest form of intellection. They delight in visualizing a race of court-jesters.[4]

There is no allowance here for the subtleties of his performance and its possibilities for multiple readings; indeed, the very idea that any subtlety could exist behind this kind of masking would have struck the writer as being inconceivable, as it still seems to many for whom the blackface trickster lurks behind or nips at the heels of any black public expression or comic perfor-mance. The obituary reads the mask without its complexity and strictly regis-ters its function in a bichromatic set of racial relationships: men of color—that is, African American men—vis-à-vis white men. It forgets that before joining the Ziegfeld Follies Williams had been a star in the Negro musical theater, as Weldon Johnson documents in *Black Manhattan*. The obituary also goes out of its way to imagine a history in which African Americans them-selves did not engage and consume minstrel theater from complex and un-orthodox subject positions.

What is perhaps more crucial is that, by reading Bert Williams in relation simply to "white men" or a white audience, his intra-racial and cross-cultural performance is excised from American cultural memory, as is the very space of the "intra-racial" and of cross-culturality. After all, minstrelsy was bigger and broader than its immediate American context and traveled farther even than the limits of the nascent American imperial sprawl and its attendant dis-courses of race. Its meanings were relentlessly reappropriated and inflected by cultural groups external to the black/white dialectic that so defined American cultural politics, as was the case with Williams's performance. In the obituary from *The Messenger*, the many other forms of cultural difference within and behind his unruly mask are silenced by the prioritizing of African American/white relationships in the movement toward full assimilation and the re-criminations that mark that movement. The varieties of protest, resistance, and political expression *enabled* by his use of the mask are likewise unimagined and heartily disallowed. Typically, the obituary also assumes that the contest of race is an exclusively male one, suggesting that blackface minstrelsy was simply a ritual of interracial masculinism for being primarily conducted by males; this despite the gender cross-dressing that was also a part of its form.

But the primary reason this repression of black minstrelsy was necessary is this: Esu-Elegbara—the West African trickster figure and the messenger to the gods conjured by Henry Louis Gates in *The Signifying Monkey*—does in fact have two faces. In a subsequent chapter, much will be made of this figure as a sign of an intra-racial, transatlantic continuum of signifying—and the minstrel, at least in Bert Williams's appropriation of that figure, is also a product of this continuum. In an era where both white racism and black resistance were erected with phallic tropes of masculinist authenticity and the organic fetish that is "soul," once removed from the binary stage, the promiscuous figure of the black minstrel threatens both positions. This figure denatures the hierarchy of black and white, which assumes that such a performance could only be pulled off by white men behind the mask who emphasize the racial dialectic. But by ironizing and reclaiming the previously white artifice that was the racist fiction of the "darky" or the "coon," the once absolute space between black and white was whittled down by the presence of a black minstrelsy. Would this were enough. This lamp-blackened child of Esu would then go further, revealing the layers of artifice and performance involved in the resistant political fiction called black "soul" in an era of rising nationalism that had little space in its ranks for irony, difference, or profound self-questionings.

In his time with the Follies Bert Williams was a cross-cultural pioneer; but as Ethan Mordden reminds us in *Broadway Babies*, "Ziegfeld did not make Williams a star; he already was one."[5] Because of his presence in the suddenly integrated cast, the Follies no longer toured southern towns. Yet despite the organized opposition of the forces of law and social order, Williams was fully acknowledged by the press and by the audience as the featured performer. Some members of the same revue have themselves become legend while Bert Williams's name has almost disappeared after generations of nationalist erasure. He was the most famous black performer of his time, a veritable global superstar, and was rumored to make more money than the American president. He would later be cited as an influence by as quintessentially American a writer as Ernest Hemingway, who idolized him; and he so impressed George Bernard Shaw that Shaw thought to cast him in one of his plays. At his funeral, Irving Berlin was among the luminaries who were his pallbearers.

Performers in the revue who now have a prominent place in American theater and film history include Ed Wynn, Fanny Brice, and W. C. Fields, who famously called Williams "the funniest man I ever saw, and the saddest man I ever knew." A year after Williams joined the cast, Will Rogers arrived and was followed by the comedian Eddie Cantor, with whom Bert Williams would perform minstrel skits that had attained classic status by this time. Both of them would perform in blackface as end-men Tambo and Bones, singing Irving Berlin's "I Want to See a Minstrel Show" while surrounded by the "Follies Pickaninnies."[6] The image of both the Negro and the Jew sharing a stage in burnt cork is an image of modernist American popular culture that still awaits consideration and analysis. The sadness that W. C. Fields identifies in Williams offers a glimpse of the performer behind his mask of comic melancholy. It is the sadness of the black performer held by racialized performance conventions; the tragic sadness of black skin trapped underneath a black mask held firmly in place by racism and the complex symbolic value of race in fin de siècle American popular culture.

For Williams, as one of the most visible personalities of Black Harlem on the eve of its renaissance, the tragic weight of his comic performance was no doubt produced by the racist implications of minstrelsy that he could critique and momentarily transcend but never escape. But considering Williams's own intellectual and political concerns and commitments, the sadness must also have been associated with the political assumptions of an African American nationalism, for which assimilation was its goal, and a separatist Garveyite nationalism which would be established in Harlem two years later with the founding of the UNIA in 1917. As a self-professed "race man," a celebrity, and an omnivorous reader of African and African American history, Williams was decidedly aware of these dual tendencies in black cultural politics as well as the changing meanings of the minstrel mask. Yet as someone personally aware of the distinct histories of and rising tensions between African Americans and West Indians in Harlem, he knew that the meanings of masking could be made more flexible in order to address these tensions and histories even if one could not ever fully escape the mask itself.

To see Williams, as a minstrel performer, as a harbinger of American and transatlantic modernism, it must be noted that the tradition of minstrelsy itself spans the centuries and underwent changes in its technological apparatus. It marks the transition from southern plantation to vaudeville to Broadway and then, in a gesture that signals its lasting effect on both modernism and postmodernism, to motion pictures. Even though it was not as impressive as his recording career, Williams's identity as one of the earliest black stars of the still new medium of film was of great significance. Returning to those early years before the official birth of a New Negro sensibility, Bert Williams made the epochal stage show *Shuffle Along* possible by integrating Broadway and by his tireless efforts to maintain and develop black musical theater in New York. In fact, the orchestra from the Shuffle Along company performed at his funeral in 1922. So despite the repressed memory of subsequent generations, it is safe to say that the modernism of the Harlem Renaissance would not have been the same without Williams. But in the endless visions, versions, and revisions of Harlem's New Negro Renaissance, Bert Williams is—if remembered at all—rendered as a side-note.

As stated at the beginning of this chapter, Bert Williams's performance during the 1915 season will prove significant in identifying a specifically black modernist sensibility subtly but significantly different from the one that dominates American and African American literary and cultural history. By listening for the voice he employs on one particular night during one particular performance, it is possible to explore the multiple black immigrant communities in early-twentieth-century New York City—their inflections and silences and the city's various "black" vernaculars that shared geographic and often cultural space. By a fully historicized hearing of this heretofore inaudible voice, the modernism of Bert Williams's mask can be sounded as paradigmatic and argued as central. But before exploring the necessarily anticlimactic moment of his voice's unmasking, it is crucial to contextualize the very politics of the minstrel mask itself as appropriated by its best-known wearer up until that moment.

To fully situate this 1915 performance in the changing politics of modernism, immigration, and minstrelsy: it was one where the slippage between mask and flesh, originary place and vernacular mimicry, was exposed before being quickly recuperated and repressed by a cultural climate unready for what it suggested. That it occurred in 1915 is notable—the year in which Booker T. Washington died and D. W. Griffith released his infamous Birth of a Nation, with its well-known use of racist minstrel stereotypes in his representations of free blacks as a threat to national integrity. But by then minstrelsy had become as much a product of subversion as it was of repression. Even Griffith's dependence on minstrel stereotypes and images could be read as a subversion of an earlier tradition, in which minstrelsy was used to contain a threat and render it benign through comic representation and nostalgic evocations of a safely and permanently preindustrial space that could and would only exist in memory. In Birth of a Nation the plantation stereotypes become malevolent and threatening as comedic farce becomes surreal chaos and as the Negro stereotype transforms from smiling darky into an expressionistic sign of white national trauma.

No one performer took the complexities and contradictions of subversion as far as Williams, who represented that fragile yet crucial tradition of black minstrelsy that explicitly attempted to appropriate and transform the already troublingly complex white tradition. At the time of his performance on Broadway, the meanings of minstrelsy were more fragmented than ever before, as much so as the black community itself. It was now possible to imagine one use of the mask deployed against another, though the politics of the African American social world seemed intent on erasing the mask in favor of the fiction of something more "authentic" which lay occluded behind it; something foundational, some essential "soul." In addition to these tensions, there were more personal and particular reasons for the sadness that Williams carried with him on that stage and in that moment. Clearly he still strongly felt the loss of his celebrated partner, who died in 1911. George Walker had been the straight man, Zip Coon to Bert Williams's Jim Crow. As such he had provided the anchor for the complex navigations around self, language, identity, and national self-consciousness coded in Williams's performance since the two men met in San Francisco in 1893.

Friendships with white performers were very difficult, and Williams suddenly became a solo act, leaving behind the huge and complex machinery of the Williams and Walker spectacles. Despite his star status, he could not eat or socialize with his peers or even stay in the same hotels. He once said that what made discrimination so bad was that he could always still hear the audience's applause thundering in his ears. Yes, Bert Williams finally made history by integrating Broadway and appropriating minstrelsy. But he did it at the price of the masquerade, wearing a mask he hated but was never allowed to remove onstage. Moreover, it is arguable that his great international success on Broadway, in film, and in recordings helped keep the dying form of minstrelsy alive far longer than it would have survived had he never lifted it beyond its roots in sideshow spectacle and made it, for a time, legitimate art.

It is true that Ada Overton Walker, the last member of his celebrated team, had died just months before the 1915 performance season. Wife of Williams's partner George Walker, Ada Overton Walker was one of this century's most important and neglected black choreographers and dancers. In a history of black dance and theater performance that draws explicitly from African American vernacular culture, minstrelsy, and the activist primitivism that would characterize the Harlem Renaissance, her contribution cannot be overstated. What is being called activist primitivism here is something akin to what I will soon describe as nationalist minstrelsy. In it, the primitivist representation of the Negro is deployed against its racist intent—one mask (black) versus another, despite various and often rival claims to authenticity. The performance troupe was officially known as "Williams and Walker," named after the two male leads; but Ada Overton Walker had been acknowledged by the two men as well as by the public as a part of its creative core and was as famous as either of them. Indeed, after George Walker's death, Bert Williams and Ada Overton Walker were encouraged to continue as "Williams and Walker." During her husband's illness and after his death from paresis, Ada Overton Walker allowed the successful Williams and Walker shows to briefly continue by impersonating her husband—wearing his costumes and performing his signature song "Bon Bon Buddy." In a performance tradition in which gender-impersonation was paralleled by and often deployed in tandem with racial impersonation, this move to perform her husbands' persona must stand for something in the evolution of the contemporary discourses of drag, performance, race, gender, and minstrelsy.

More will be said about Ada Overton Walker and her contributions in chapter 5. Her struggles with the gender politics of the minstrel and vaudeville tradition were undertaken alongside a struggle with and within the so-called cult of domesticity that characterized early-twentieth-century African American protofeminism. In her work with the Williams and Walker troupe, Ada Overton Walker would resist the dominant constructions of black women's sexuality as "savage" by deploying that "cult of domesticity," or "cult of True Womanhood." However, as I will argue, she accomplished this resistance through a countercolonial gesture which assimilated a diaspora of black female differences into the gendered mask of a privileged African American subjectivity. Despite its affirmative political work, its explicit pan-African gestures, and its subtle fragmentation of race by gender, her performance ultimately functioned to consolidate intra-racial differences under the sign—the mask—of an African American exceptionalism.

So first George Walker died, then Ada Overton Walker, whose death effectively ended the troupe. More than likely Bert Williams's sadness that season was primarily rooted in this immediate sense of loss. To compound matters, in his move to the Ziegfeld Follies he lost a much more integrated audience for his comic inflections and dialect games. He suddenly found himself no longer a surrogate for a black audience who assumed the humanity behind the mask but now exclusively a victim of a gaze skeptical of that humanity and which needed to be convinced of it. In short, the semantic field shifted and the line between the ironic and the literal threatened to evaporate as he approached closer and closer to the light of megastardom.

Yet, to further historicize the 1915 performance, there was a deeper sadness behind his phenomenal success, one that went back to the moment in the 1890s when he "just for a lark" blackened his face with burnt cork, only to be shocked when his performance suddenly struck a chord.[7] Before this definitive performance he had refused to wear blackface in order to escape a stereotype that he always thought humiliating. Looking back in 1918 on that primal scene of black masquerade, he wrote: "Nobody was more surprised than me when it went like a house on fire. Then I began to find myself."[8] One is reminded here of the old axiom in Trinidadian carnival: when you play "mas'" (masquerade) you play yourself. But despite the traces of existential angst and de-individuation which would forever color the mask, he describes this discovery—in which the mask seems to choose him despite his own resistance to it—as a strategy: "It was not until I was able to see myself as another person that my sense of humor developed."[9] What is to be noted here is how Williams describes the very process of masking as one in which the self is not banished, obfuscated, or erased; instead it is multiplied, and its self-consciousness rendered prismatic. The sadness beneath his humor would later become tragic as the weight of the mask grew in direct proportion to the scale of his success and as the many faces he balanced were all reduced to one dour visage. Eventually the self he played by masking became less and less a strategic double domesticated and controlled by the displacement required by performance. Comic melancholy eventually gave way to the insidious violence of mimicry, as the persona became the kind of malevolent deity who consumes one who dared to host and summon it. In some ways this is a familiar if not clichéd story: the performer losing his or her identity in the role; the mask attaining an authenticity in performance that the "real face" either never had or can no longer compete with; or the iron mask being welded shut by the oppressive power of popular misapprehension and dominant misrepresentations. It is a familiar story in that it evokes a fairly conventional set of narratives from and about the stage and from and about modern subjectivity.

What makes this story unfamiliar is the intricate history of modern black-on-black border crossings that occur behind the mask and constitute Williams's inflection of it. For what is being argued through Bert Williams is that the space between black skin and black mask is more than the space of Du Boisian "double-consciousness," modernist "fragmentation," or post-modern performativity. It is certainly far more than even the noble attempt to humanize a dehumanizing signifier. Not only does his use of blackface mediate cultural and political relationships in black and white; it ultimately re-veals the black diaspora as an intersubjective and micropolitical process. The minstrel mask mediates and silently complicates the institutionalized dy-namics of black and white through a form of intra-racial and cross-cultural signifying. This practice occurs within an African American social world struggling to construct itself in the face of more than racism and the assault on its self-consciousness and political positions. The minstrel mask as worn by this minstrel—a West Indian minstrel at that, an immigrant "coon"—is also forced to mediate the relationships between the sub-hegemonic African American community and the immigrant presence of radical black cultural differences.

Black Soul, White Artifact:
Black Minstrelsy on the Eve of Renaissance

As a harbinger of Harlem's modernism, Bert Williams's influence was even greater and more practical than his increasingly controversial legacy, which was haunted primarily by his symbolic value and perhaps secondarily by his cultural patrimony. The flat on 53rd Street in New York that he and George Walker rented became the primary site of a small renaissance of their own. In Walker's words:

> The first move was to hire a flat in Fifty-third street, furnish it, and throw our doors open to all colored men who possessed theatrical and musical ability and ambition. The Williams and Walker flat soon became the head-quarters of all the artistic young men of our race who were stage struck. Among those who frequented our home were: Messrs. Will Marion Cook, Harry T. Burleigh, Bob Cole and Billy Johnson, J. A. Shipp, the late Will Accoo, a man of much musical ability, and many others whose names are well known in the professional world. We also entertained the late Paul Lawrence Dunbar, the Negro poet, who wrote lyrics for us. By having these men around us we had an opportunity to study the musical and theatrical ability of the most talented members of our race. At that stage of the develop-ment of Williams and Walker, we saw that the colored performer would have to get away from the ragtime limitations of the "darky" and we decided to make the break, so as to save ourselves and others.[10]

This collective was a think tank of sorts, devoted to liberating the entire tradition of African American performance and literature by making the break from minstrelsy in the language of minstrelsy: that is, as a proto-renaissance, it was primarily founded on the desire to transcend the minstrel tradition of representation not by rejecting it but by engaging it. Named in the passage quoted above, however, are many who would become trapped by it and many who are often merely remembered for being trapped by it. Paul Laurence Dunbar is the most notable among them, author of the classic statement of African American split subjectivity "We Wear the Mask" and central collaborator, along with Will Marion Cook, on the Williams and Walker stage shows.

Williams's and Walker's flat would soon become home to the black cultural and benevolent association called the "Frogs" whose mission was to promote "education of blacks about the race's achievements" and which provided "a social group for discussing these achievements."[11] Their initial purpose was to establish an archival collection of literary, historical, social, and political materials for a theatrical library in a clubhouse that was built later at 111 West 132nd Street. In light of the celebrity of Williams and Walker, the Frogs' annual Frolic Ball was a major social affair for New York blacks. James Reese Europe served as its orchestra director in 1913, only six years before he and his band, after introducing jazz to Europe, would lead the honored black 369th Infantry Regiment in the now-famous postwar victory parade that many cite as a crucial moment in the coming to consciousness of a New Negro sensibility.[12] In fact, just before being ordered to report for training, the 369th were feted by a parade through the streets of Harlem; though waylaid by an unfortunate mistake (his horse had ideas of its own), Bert Williams had been invited to be the grand marshal.

Thus, years before the coteries of Harlem and on the eve of a modernism of movements and collectives, Williams and Walker begin the century with the founding of an organization devoted to racial uplift through culture and performance and minstrelsy. They had even planned at some point in their career to build what they hoped to call the "Williams and Walker International and Interracial Ethiopian Theatre in New York City."[13] Adding to this interest in culture and cultural politics was Williams's commitment to an explicitly Booker T. Washington-esque strategy of economic and civic empowerment. With other successful black professionals he cofounded the Equity Congress in 1911, an organization devoted to economic and political issues facing the Harlem community. They succeeded in obtaining New York's first black National Guard regiment. They also encouraged patronage of African American and West Indian businesses and even financed many lawsuits against restrictive covenants. From the Equity Congress grew the United Civic League, which would later help blacks obtain political office.[14]

In order to accomplish these achievements Williams had first to violently wrest minstrelsy from whites, which he did through the bold and ironic gesture of advertising himself and George Walker as "Two Real Coons." However, it is important to note that the struggle for "realness" or authenticity in a minstrel's performance existed within the tradition of white minstrelsy itself. As the pugnacious Nick Tosches documents in his challenging and utterly fascinating book on minstrelsy, Where Dead Voices Gather, white minstrels competed and were prized for their ability to perform as "natural nigger singers" or even were celebrated as "natural born nigger singers." In this case racial authenticity was utterly independent of race and utterly dependent on performance. Tosches offers us a helpful neologism to name this particular collusion of cross-racial fascination, racism, and the obsession with mimetic fidelity: "negrisimilitude."[15] The minstrel performer Emmett Miller—the subject of Tosches's book—was so highly rated for his authenticity that he was known by the honorific title "Nigger Miller" even when offstage. For black performers to perform the realness of the fictional "coon" was a direct political contestation that occurred in the realm of American racial fantasy. This gesture was an act of reclamation that links black minstrelsy to the emergent black nationalisms in turn-of-the-century America.

Certainly minstrelsy was the only national space allowed black theater performers and, in many cases, writers, dancers, singers, and musicians up until and beyond the "jazz age." Tosches makes a persuasive case for minstrelsy as not a distortion of African American and American popular music but instead its culturally prismatic root. As he notes, it is arguable that without the Mississippi-based Rabbit Foot Minstrels there would not have been a Harlem Renaissance. This troupe brought to the world Ma Rainey, Alberta Hunter, Ida Cox, Louis Jordan, and Skip James. Without the "coon song"—the earliest recorded African American song form—would "race records" have been possible? For Williams and Walker, inhabiting the "coon" mask was explicitly an act of political retrieval, which made assimilation possible through performance, through blackface. In George Walker's words, "As the 'Two Real Coons' we made our first hit in New York while playing at Koster and Bial's. Long before our run terminated we discovered an important fact, viz.: the one hope of the colored performer must be in making a radical departure from the old 'darky' style of singing and dancing. So we set ourselves the task of thinking along new lines."[16] As "natural black performer[s]" they unmasked the stereotype in its own language—a classic example of what Houston Baker would call the "mastery of form."[17]

Like all such discursive products, their naturalness was highly studied and meticulously performed. Williams studied pantomime in Europe under the great Pietro, who taught him that "the entire aim and object of art is to achieve naturalness."[18] The contradiction implicit in the notion of performing the natural was so unproblematically accepted as fact that one critic, after seeing the premiere of *In Dahomey*, could write this of Bert Williams: "Nature has endowed him with a comic mask."[19] One wonders if this contradiction was naturalized simply because of the long-standing equation between race and nature in the Western imagination; in other words, because the "Negro" had some privileged connection to "nature," its mimicry did not subvert or trouble the discourse of nature with the fact of artifice—it only emphasized it. In her biography of the comedian, Ann Charters writes that he was in no way "naturally" suited to perform "The Negro":

> From the beginning, Bert Williams selected his theatrical personality with reluctance and deliberate detachment. He possessed none of the traits of the stage caricature popular in his time—neither the exaggerated Southern dialect nor the eccentric behavior that constituted the public's image of the tamed but only imperfectly Americanized African savage. . . .
>
> But after a valiant attempt to go his own way as a singer, Williams took on the conventional stage role because it seemed that this was the only way he could ever leave the cabarets. At first, in the early years of his study and analysis of the Negro comic character, he had to acquire the basic elements of his role. Setting out to become a minstrel man, he struggled with the "stage Negro" language, which he said, "to me was just as much a foreign dialect as that of the Italian."[20]

What stands out in this passage is the emphasized distance between Bert Williams and "the stage Negro," which was merely a convention of performance as well as a means to advance his career. Clearly, it was also a necessary step for the advancement of blacks on the American stage and toward the center of American popular culture. Despite the assumption that as a member of his race he would have particular access to the vernacular and to its habits, gestures, and innate sensibilities, the "stage Negro" stands alongside "Italian" as equidistant from Williams, owing in part to the fictive nature of the "stage Negro" but also to his struggles to master the culturally distinct African American vernacular—not to naturalize it (or be naturalized into it), but to perfectly mimic it. The distance here can be described as partly ironic, partly strategic, and partly a function of aesthetic curiosity: it was an artistic challenge for him to occupy the racial stereotype and bring to it his research and analysis of the "Negro comic character." It would also be a political challenge to inhabit the skin or claim the tongue of the dominant minority in Harlem.

To historicize the politics of black dialect usage: it would have been a complex issue at that time because it was rooted in that white fascination with the African American vernacular as a departure from the rational structures of Standard English as well as a sign of American folk authenticity. Again, black dialect was also literally a foreign language for Williams since his cultural origins were nowhere near the literal or mythic American South. On many levels, then, occupying the persona of the "darky" was hard work for both these black minstrels because they were motivated by something other than the need to exploit racist projections and maintain minstrelsy's status quo and the bichromatic socioeconomic order that it balanced and justified. Perhaps it was even more difficult for them than for white performers. For one thing, they had to learn something that did not already exist unproblematically in their imaginations as it did in the imaginations of the whites who wore the mask—the "darky" itself. Also, as black men motivated by the almost Victorian sensibilities of bourgeois assimilationism, they were denied the pleasures of that total abandonment to the libido that gave minstrelsy its ludic ritual value. For them "the Negro" simply did not mean the "id." If anything, as represented by the "darky," it was a negative image of the white superego that relentlessly sought entry into the black psyche; a demon to be exorcised. Minstrelsy for them had to function within the discourse of racial uplift which, of course, by the time of the Harlem Renaissance had uncritically positioned the minstrel as a figure of the ignoble past. But by this very gesture—by naming their fear—the minstrel was then empowered, as an image of the movement's own political undoing. As a representation of the undoing of its self-image, that fiercely guarded self-image would then have to be severely and continually policed, purged from the "soul" as well as from the tongue.

Bert Williams would go even further in distancing himself from the "stage Negro" while still wearing blackface. In doing this he would begin to betray more of his own originary black difference, which was itself a product of the emergent sprawl of the American empire as well as the micropolitical fissures within the early-twentieth-century African American community. In an interview for the *Age* in 1908, Williams's relationship to the "Negro" becomes murkier and his national self-consciousness less clear than they would otherwise appear in a black performer:

> The American Negro is a natural minstrel. He is the one in whom humor is native, often unconscious, but nevertheless keen and laugh-compelling. He dances from the cradle stage almost, for his feet have been educated prenatally, it would seem. He usually has a voice, and there is not much necessity for schools of voice culture to temper with a natural voice. There is soul in the Negro music: There is simplicity and an entire lack of artificiality.[21]

Obviously the racial stereotypes of white minstrelsy are here maintained and the emphasis on performance as a denaturing strategy is gone. This essentializing and emphasizing of "the American Negro" would prove crucial to Bert Williams's own micropolitics of difference as manifest in and mediated by the blackface mask and became common in West Indian American discourses of differentiation during the Harlem Renaissance and beyond. In the quoted passage, Williams anticipates Zora Neale Hurston's assertion in "Characteristics of Negro Expression," which would appear in Nancy Cunard's *Negro: An Anthology* in 1934: "The Negro's universal mimicry is not so much a thing in itself as an evidence of something that permeates his entire self. And that thing is drama."[22] So Willliams is not the only black modern to make such statements, though he may have been one of the first to do so explicitly in the context of minstrelsy and to actually speak of blackface in such sophisticated ways. It should be remembered that the very stress here on naturalizing minstrelsy must be kept in line with the political attempt to claim a self-motivated racial representation. In keeping with his time and his generation, his emphasis on Negro music as the repository of a black "soul" also echoes and validates itself through W. E. B. Du Bois's *The Souls of Black Folk*. This great text, published a mere five years before the interview quoted above, would also argue that black "soul" via black music was innately organic and external to the forces of industrialization and mechanization that were redefining the early-twentieth-century landscape.

However, Bert Williams's techniques of theorizing and distancing himself from the mask he wore and was never allowed to remove onstage did not make the job of "darky" any easier. Irony could only lessen the blow, not evade it. Perhaps the greatest difficulty came from having to stick so closely to the norms of the racist tradition in order to get work, while at the same time projecting a modern black subjectivity which made specific political demands—but not in a too loud or too unrecognizable voice. It soon became clear that despite their politics and their complex navigations around burnt cork, the characters Williams and Walker created could still only be described as "darkies" and "coons" since the only language available to describe these novel creations was the language of the tradition they were deconstructing. Theirs was in fact a unique and legitimate form of musical theater, as most commentators would recognize and most black audiences would appreciate. But it was the presence of Williams's blackface mask that anchored the performance for the white audience. In the Williams and Walker stage shows, he was the only one left onstage who wore it. George Walker did not, Ada Overton Walker did not, nor did the supporting cast. If one is lucky enough to see Williams's 1916 film *A Natural Born Gambler*, one is surprised to notice that he is the only one wearing the mask onscreen, though the entire cast—but for one or two "real" whites—is black. He is the only minstrel left, the last "darky"; other black performers could appear onstage and onscreen utterly unmasked though never quite "natural."

This point is absolutely crucial—not only for the title of this book but for the analysis of the Williams and Walker stage shows which will come later in it. Because of the aesthetic and political safety associated with the symbol of the mask, Williams's and Walker's performances were allowed to function *as* minstrelsy despite the very obvious and very radical formal departures they brought to the stage. It is as if Williams and Walker were able to sneak a legitimate and innovative black musical theater into popular culture underneath Williams's mask, complete with complex, original, and progressive (for the most part and for their time) depictions of African American men and women. As James Weldon Johnson writes in *Black Manhattan*, in this period "minstrelsy flourished and it was developed and elaborated to such a degree that it became less and less an imitation of Negro plantation life, and towards the end of the last century it provided the most gorgeous stage spectacle to be seen in the United States."[23] These creations were themselves products of a racialized ethnographic gaze, but one that looked as much at the white viewer as it did the "stage Negro"; or rather, it looked at what the white viewer saw, perfected it, and rendered it alien to its very name. In the words of George Walker:

> Black-faced white comedians used to make themselves look as ridiculous as they could when portraying a "darky" character. In their "make-up" they always had tremendously big red lips, and their costumes were frightfully exaggerated. The one fatal result of this to the colored performers was that

they imitated the white performers in their make-up as "darkies." Nothing seemed more absurd than to see a colored man making himself ridiculous in order to portray himself.[24]

Williams and Walker begin evolving their technique by studying the fictive "stage Negro" and by then looking at the black mask as itself a sign of whiteness.

Walker is here anticipating Ralph Ellison, who, in his influential 1958 *Partisan Review* essay "Change the Joke and Slip the Yoke," cautioned against confusing the black signifier with its problematic sociocultural referent: "the role with which they are identified is not, despite its 'blackness,' Negro American."[25] It is important to note that Ellison emphasizes this distinction despite his own redefinition of the minstrel as an avatar of the trickster. The "darky" was merely a white performance convention, rich in what Michael Rogin calls "surplus symbolic value" and produced by the white cultural power "to make African Americans represent something beside themselves."[26] Although he would sympathize with Rogin's politics, George Walker would subtly disagree; he would no doubt claim—were he a poststructuralist, of course—that in Williams's and Walker's stage performance, that which they portrayed refused the white ritual mask by presenting a reconstructed "Negro American" whose naturalness was a product of deep study, whose "soul" could be authentically replicated through a system of gestures, sounds, signs, and dialects all motivated by assimilationist nationalism. George Walker, however, is like Ralph Ellison in that his black modern/ist gaze sees the representation as having nothing to do with "the Negro" at all. For him, the minstrel mask is an exaggeration of whiteness: his words quoted above clearly show how white comedians made *themselves*—not African Americans—look ridiculous. The "darky" is metonymic, not metaphoric, despite Rogin's possibly unintentional use of the word "beside," which suggests contiguity. It was a doppelganger, but one which haunted whiteness, not blackness.

Walker says of Williams: "My partner, Mr. Williams, is the first man that I know of our race to attempt to delineate a 'darky' in a perfectly natural way."[27] Not surprisingly, what governs both Williams's and Walker's politics are those nineteenth-century biocultural notions of race that dominated turn-of-the-century American thought: race and group identity as fixed in biology and immutable in blood. However, his acknowledgment of Bert Williams's ability to play "the Negro" better than it was being played suggests that "the Negro" was more a site of contested performance traditions than it was a biocultural category. In one of the many angry letters he wrote to newspapers to protest racism (he was always the more vociferous one of the pair), Walker describes how their investment in "the natural" distinguishes their minstrelsy from racism: "Williams and Walker seek to make people happy by giving them a clean-cut show, composed of and acted entirely by members of the African race. We seek to be natural."[28] Without exploring too deeply the class biases embedded in the term "clean-cut," the "natural" here must be seen as a very specific political fiction. It is that same commodity that motivates the aesthetic and political struggle of the Harlem Renaissance as well as its legacy to global black cultural politics. Alain Locke in *The New Negro* would also distinguish his generation from the past by their having achieved "the courage of being natural."[29] In essence, "the natural" is homologous to W. E. B. Du Bois's notion of black "soul." This fiction had to be claimed in performance quite simply because it was already being constructed in the performance of post-reconstruction and modernist whites whose "stage Negro" retarded the steady evolution of what will be called the "New Negro." Walker's "natural," which predates the claims of the Renaissance generation, is, however, itself undercut by his own admission that it must be delineated and performed and that it is in fact a quest, a career. By Williams's own admission, "the American Negro" was a pursuit that took him years to achieve—though he never became, could never or ever wanted to be, one.

These performers achieved the natural by doing much more than simply reversing the specularity of the white viewer and claiming a position as primary spectators in the drama of parodic self-invention. Certainly they parodied the parody and deployed mask against mask; but they simultaneously maintained the quest for an emergent and authentic black "soul" through minstrel performance. One is reminded here of Fanon's words in *Black Skin, White Masks*: "what is often called the black soul is a white man's artifact."[30] A close reading of this suggests not just that the "black soul" is an invention of the omnipresent "white gaze." It suggests that the presumed space behind the mask (the "soul") is itself a mask (an "artifact"). To look behind the mask leads one to what C. L. R. James, in his writing on Trinidadian carnival in the 1920s, called "mimic warfare."[31] In this context, "mimic warfare" is identical to the trope of "plural masking" evoked by the Guyanese theorist and writer Wilson Harris.[32] With Bert Williams we are witness to an endless profusion of masks which make possible two ways of reading minstrel masquerade: (a) masking as itself a mask for discursive, political, and cultural moves rendered invisible by the act of this restless and eminently visible masquerade; and (b) performativity itself as being rendered profoundly anti-utopian by the mask-on-mask violence of the endless layering of mimicry, irony, and appro-priation that this ritual generates and entails but cannot resolve despite its relentless and seductive gestures of revelation.

A Camouflage of Self Evaporation: Unmasking Nobody

As previously noted, to appear in Florenz Ziegfeld's follies, Williams had to leave both all-black and integrated shows to become a self-conscious pioneer in the world of Broadway theater. In his words: "I reached the conclusion last spring that I could best represent my race by doing pioneer work. It was far better to have joined a large white show than to have starred in a colored show, considering conditions."[33] What allowed him to cross that color line, in fact the agreement made between early-twentieth-century American spec-tacle and race, was the blackface mask. To enter on the white stage as a black performer required that he wear the minstrel mask as if hyperbolically to signify his difference as other while simultaneously comforting the audience with the warm, familiar, unthreatening meanings of minstrelsy. So where Eddie Cantor's mask was worn to emphasize that he was not a Negro, Bert Williams's was worn to emphasize that he emphatically was one—and in so doing he maintained an epistemological balance, a social contract.

Given that traditional minstrelsy was based on the absence of actual Ne-groes, the mask signified what Wilson Harris calls the "absent body" of the represented.[34] Bert Williams's presence onstage was thus rendered through a hyperbolic absence, and his performance danced in and around that "zone of non-being" that Fanon locates behind the mask that is overdetermined black flesh.[35] It is no mere coincidence that Bert Williams's most well known song, first performed in 1905, was the great paean to self-negation "Nobody." A smash hit upon its first performance, it came to haunt him as much as did his persona:

> Before I got through with "Nobody," I could have wished that both the author of the words and the assembler of the tune had been strangled or drowned or talked to death. For seven whole years, I had to sing it. Month after month, I tried to drop it and sing something new, but I could get nothing to replace it, and the audiences seemed to want nothing else. Every comedian at some point in his life learns to curse the particular stunt of his that was most popular. "Nobody" was a particularly hard song to replace.[36]

It is painfully ironic how he was trapped by his own strategic erasure—the performance of a self-erasure trapped by the American logic of race. This particular logic is one in which race is necessarily visible, so impelled by a scopic drive that his West Indian disappearance could only be read as an African American presence, or the fiction of it. In fact, Williams's entire oeuvre was based on a constant erasure of the black subject through the hyperbolic presence of blackface.

But instead of lingering too much on the tragic implications of such a performance of active invisibility or disappearance, we should keep in mind the possibilities of camouflage when theorized from within a Caribbean theoretical lineage that stretches from C. L. R. James to Wilson Harris to Frantz Fanon, Edouard Glissant, and Claude McKay and the tropes and topoi of calypso and carnival, which were alive and well in the midst of Harlem's renaissance and blared within and alongside the age of jazz. As George Lamming puts it in his great work The Pleasures of Exile: "There is a camouflage of inflation. . . . And there is a camouflage of self evaporation, which results in the role of Thing, excluded, devoid of language. The first can be easily detected; but the second contains an incalculable secret whose meaning stays absent until time and its own needs order an emergence."[37] Bert Williams's camouflage would become so successful, his diversion so like complicity that it would mutate over time into a new kind of skin. Generations of black writers and performers too threatened and wounded by the very evocation of minstrelsy would thus continue to read and hear the mask inside out. It is to that "emergence" that one must turn to unmask that "incalculable secret" which in turn unravels the assumptions upon which conventional histories and racial truths are based. It is in the space of "nobody," the "role of Thing, excluded, devoid of language," that one must turn to sound out the historical and cultural impact that Williams's absence so loudly signifies.

As a doubly black "Nobody," Bert Williams was much more than simply a black presence. Although based in anti-black racism and segregation, black-face was made to speak to a larger economy of difference in turn-of-the-century America. As Eric Lott and Ann Douglas have observed, the minstrel stage was the site of all manner of racial and ethnic impersonations, and the site of all manner of sexual cross-dressing and drag. Along with many other scholars and critics, they read minstrelsy as an American popular form that subsumed all forms of racial, sexual, and socioeconomic difference into the black mask and depended on "theft and parody" in order to work its essential cultural and political alchemy. This historical scenario should not be analyzed merely for how structures of oppression operate via performance and negative stereotyping. "Theft and parody" also must be identified as forms of mimicry and masking which are primary responses to cross-cultural contact in a context of wildly unbalanced power relationships. In *Terrible Honesty*, Douglas describes the performance aesthetics of black minstrelsy with the term "double doubling."[38] I will return later to this term, as it suggests something beyond a simple mathematical equation: after all, in the context of layered representations—not contiguous ones—to double a double is to do what exactly? Douglas's use of the term "double mimicry" will also serve well in an exploration of Bert Williams and his specific relationship to an African American modernism.[39] This is because multiple doubling is where Bert Williams would excel, performing the limits of Du Boisian double-consciousness in the midst of a form already defined by "theft and parody."

For black performers to engage this ritual theater of difference in which no "real" blacks, no "real" women, no real "Irish," or no "real" anything were traditionally present is to complicate and challenge the ritual itself, which did serve to naturalize racism and sanctify Jim Crow while laying a foundation for an American popular culture in which pleasure could be derived explicitly from these political imbalances. These "double doublings" may have denatured social identities in performance, but they simultaneously maintained a social and symbolic hierarchy with African Americans at the bottom and so many "others" increasingly arranged in relationship to them. As if to underscore minstrelsy's larger signifying possibilities, what marked the Williams and Walker vaudeville shows was their engagement with so many of the different ethnic, political, and international concerns in early-twentieth-century America. Vaudeville shows were already the site of socially sanctioned ethnic humor and reinforced any number of racial, sexual, and socioeconomic stereotypes as new immigrants poured over the borders of the fledgling American empire and encountered a variety of seemingly incommensurable "others." In the Williams and Walker shows, minstrelsy both reinforced and critiqued multiple forms of difference. For example, in *The Policy Players* (1899) Williams impersonated the "Ex-President" of Haiti a full sixteen years before the official U.S. occupation of that island in 1915. It is worth noting also that this performance predates Eugene O'Neill's *The Emperor Jones* by slightly more than a decade. It is further worth noting that O'Neill's theme of intra-racial, cross-cultural hierarchy and a tragicomic colonialist desire embedded in African American nationalism occurs in *In Dahomey* three years later, also preceding *The Emperor Jones*, which was made fully iconic through the performance of Paul Robeson. But although *The Policy Players* was hardly subversive or conventionally political by any stretch of the imagination, it did help the performers stretch burnt cork beyond the confines of the plantation topos and helped them incorporate a global set of references in which race, colonialism, and the Caribbean were juggled in tandem with race, the South, and Jim Crow.

In 1906's *Abyssinia*, about a group of African Americans traveling to Ethiopia, Ada Overton Walker and her troupe of dancers impersonated "Falasha" and "Amhara maids."[40] This performance helped establish a tradition of black-on-black representation that would give rise to the activist primitivism of Harlem's renaissance, from the poetry of Langston Hughes and Claude McKay to the work of Josephine Baker and Duke Ellington. It would also prove influential for pan-Africanism itself in that it featured African Americans and African Americans *as* Africans against an international and transhistorical backdrop. *Abyssinia* was, of course, one of the many attempts to replicate the phenomenal success of *In Dahomey*, which featured and was based on the impersonation of continental Africans. These and other performances were the first large-scale public spectacles constructed, produced, and performed by African Americans in which their own myths, fantasies, memories, and misconceptions of "Africa" were staged. And as the Williams and Walker shows grew larger, more elaborate, and more powerful, the troupe began to explore all kinds of impersonations and addressed various topics through minstrel parody. For example, during its American tour, *In Dahomey* included two songs referring to the then-recent American takeover of the Philippines: "A Dream of the Philippines" and "Dear Luzon," the latter reported to have been performed by "Filipino Misses and Chorus."[41] In 1909's *Mr. Lode of Kaol*—another fantasy set in "exotic lands"—the performers Brown and Navarro performed "a Spanish dance" while Chinese impersonator Tom Brown performed the awkwardly titled novelty tune "Chink Chink Chinaman" credited to Bert Williams himself.[42] It is worth noting that before he had ever donned the burnt-cork mask and learned to portray the "stage Negro," in 1893 Bert Williams worked in California impersonating Hawaiians.[43]

Thus minstrelsy went beyond the black and white binary by exploring "racial cross-dressing" in its function as a popular theater which addressed a society clumsily and violently engaging its own cultural complexity. The Williams and Walker shows went further than any, actually specializing in inter- and intra-ethnic cross-dressing, continually stretching Williams's minstrel mask to address cultural experiences and signifying possibilities that minstrelsy hadn't previously—or since—accounted for. Yet they were working within and against a tradition of masquerade that was never a stable dialectic. It was never a static or binary set of oppositions between black and white, rich and poor as is usually argued. Michael Rogin's *Blackface, White Noise* helpfully goes beyond those binaries and asserts the presence of a third component in the battle for the minstrel mask: Jewish immigrants for whom minstrelsy was a strategy of projection used to achieve social whiteness while distancing themselves from the extreme otherness of the African American. Rogin cites Williams as the greatest of those black performers who denatured the mask and attempted to sever the essential connection between the signifier and signified: "Williams masqueraded as a minstrel black, and one need only listen to him sing his signature song, 'Nobody,' to hear him turn self-denigrating irony against the viewer."[44]

Much more will follow on the relationship between Rogin's Jewish immigrants and the migratory politics of Bert Williams's mask and his wandering vernacular, which also took refuge in the tongue of another. But most interesting here is Rogin's perhaps unintentional though productive recourse to "meta-signifying": Bert Williams didn't portray a "black" but a "minstrel black," which is to say that he portrayed a portrayal, or more accurately, a portrayer. With all this in mind, it should be clear that minstrelsy as masquerade was never simply a ritual defamation of "the Negro," especially since masquerade enables both envy and disgust, love and hate, admiration and disdain. Its defamation of "the Negro" was in fact a part of a larger and more intricate ritual of power and difference, mimesis and alterity where otherness was always multiple and masks were always, in Wilson Harris's words, "plural." It is therefore essential that the active participation of black minstrels be aligned within the history of blackface minstrelsy as constitutive of its ritual, its history, and its counterhistory. After all, to switch identities and to perform the other—or the other's version of "the other" in the case of Bert Williams—was not just to play with mimicry and destabilize the "real" by performance. It was also to suggest that both sides of the social dialectic could occupy the same space and be intimate with each other. Both could share and play and struggle with each other's absent bodies within the shared space of racist fantasy. And in this sphere of mimicry and countermimicry, the active presence of black blackface performers is constitutive of the racial and ultimately sexual politics of this back and forth—especially since "real" black and white women were generally absent from "classic" minstrelsy yet were often conjured up, impersonated, "possessed" by the ritual.

Bert Williams's use of blackface engaged issues of gender and sexuality in a more specific way, however, once he entered onto the vaudeville stage. His contract stipulated "that at no time would he be on stage with any of the female members of the company," as if their restricting him to comic roles wasn't distance enough from the threat of black male sexuality and as if the tension between the masked and the unmasked suggested too much about the layers of artifice required by both gender and race.[45] Or, returning to the point made earlier about Eddie Cantor and Williams, perhaps what grounded both uses of the mask and enabled their stage presence was the fact that they were both male behind the masquerade. Perhaps the complex maneuverings of race and gender would have been too great if a black minstrel male and a white woman occupied the same semantic field. What makes this even more interesting is that, according to Ann Douglas, it was Williams's own idea to put this stipulation into the contract.[46] It is easy to imagine the practical reasons for this. Even before Williams joined the Follies, both Williams and George Walker were often threatened by racist whites. During the Tenderloin race riots at the turn of the century that helped force many blacks to migrate to Harlem, white mobs ran through the streets screaming, "Let's get Williams and Walker."[47] Given this and the fact that Williams well knew that the tension between race and sex in America often translated into violence, it was no doubt a decision well made.

But it is more suggestive. Here the integrity of one form of difference already in performance was threatened by the presence of the other. Eric Lott addresses this symbolic miscegenation coded in the black mask:

> The black mask offered a way to play with collective fears of a degraded and threatening—and male—Other while at the same time maintaining some symbolic control over them. Yet the intensified American fears of succumbing to a racialized image of Otherness were everywhere operative in minstrelsy, continually exceeding the controls and accounting, paradoxically, for the minstrel show's power, insofar as its "blackness" was unceasingly fascinating to performers and audiences alike. This combined fear of and fascination with the black male cast a strange dread of miscegenation over the minstrel show, but evidently did not preclude a continual return to minstrel miming.[48]

For white performers the black mask allowed them to represent and mock the other by conflating and collapsing all forms of difference—race, gender, and certainly class—into the black mask. In this highly charged context, burnt cork functioned as not only a representation of "the Negro" but, as noted earlier, a primary site in America's privileged racial binary around which all other "others" would be aligned, thereby enshrining and privileging both elements of that binary—the white and the African American. But despite this, traditional blackface is about difference within its reductive binary, not about its elision or its denial; it is about performance not as simplistic subversion but as complex recuperation. In this regard this form of masquerade functioned very much like the Caribbean carnival complex where a ritualized destabilization is as necessary a ritual of resistance as it is a necessary ritual of power. Eric Lott suggests just this in *Love and Theft*:

> At every turn blackface minstrelsy has seemed a form in which transgression and containment coexisted, in which improbably threatening or startlingly sympathetic racial meanings were simultaneously produced and dissolved. Neither the social relations on which blackface delineations depended, the delineations themselves, their commercial setting, nor their ideological effects were monolithic or simply hegemonic.[49]

To see minstrelsy in the light of this "top-down" discursive maneuvering also argues against the utopian spirit of much contemporary discourses of performativity by showing how the West transforms and maintains its dominance, through—not against—difference(s) and how the blurring of sociobiological and sexual categories may serve power rather than disrupt its flow. It is perhaps this insight that inspires Marjorie Garber to assert something akin to what Judith Butler has also said about the necessarily subversive politics of drag: "Far from undercutting the power of the ruling elite, male cross-dressing rituals here seem often to serve as confirmations and expressions of it."[50]

In *Afro-Creole*, Richard Burton asks a similar question of the comic-burlesque mask as a sign of Afro-Caribbean resistance. This question—"does the Quashie mask finally usurp the personality of the slave who adopts it and take over the very core of the self?"—helps force a simultaneous reading of three distinct but interrelated discourses: African American minstrelsy, the Caribbean carnival poetics, and gender/race performativity.[51] Reading through the lens of the Caribbean and the never-ending tension between resistance and acquiescence (both of which often depend on irony), one is spared answering this question because one is no longer able to posit a "core self" despite the racist essentialism of Williams's time as well as the corresponding black cultural nationalism which felt the need to articulate a more accurate "soul" in response to that racism. Bert Williams—Nobody—is a convenient historical site in the confluence of all these discourses given the assumption of a "core self" or "black soul" shared by all of them and given his consistent problematizing of such an entity by layers and layers of erasure.

Certainly by the time of Bert Williams's black-on-black minstrelsy on Broadway, by the time of his very public act of disappearing behind his hypervisibility, minstrelsy had undergone a series of transformations. It had been reclaimed by nonwhite performers, though few of them had the kind of self-conscious politics of the Williams and Walker stage shows. Williams and Walker, it must be stressed, worked within the assumptions of assimilation-ist nationalism. They had the sanction of political figures like Booker T. Washington and W. E. B. Du Bois, and initially the wider black community for whom their success as independent Negroes was enough to reduce the lingering traces of minstrelsy to merely vestigial aches. Their transforma-tions of the form of minstrelsy would be repressed or evoked as a sign of racial trauma by subsequent generations of black culture producers in the United States; from the Harlem Renaissance up to the contemporary mo-ment, as, for example, in Spike Lee's deeply troubled film *Bamboozled* (2001), which features multiple images of Bert Williams as well as some of his most well-known costumes.

For these generations the very mask was too shameful to even quibble about its various and intricate semantic or signifying possibilities or to even dare connect to Du Boisian double-consciousness or assimilation. It was too traumatic a sign to even mention in the context of both of these latter con-cepts; after all, to do so would be to suggest that these notions were mere performances. Also, the politics of disappearance or "self evaporation" would be unthinkable for a culture already too used to silencing as well as cultural and political invisibility; nor could it be claimed or acknowledged by an African American cultural politics that had already begun to fetishize vocality, voice, and sound as the primary if not dominant technique of resistance. Understandably, the repression of Bert Williams was an effect of the trauma done to African American culture by the legacy of minstrelsy; yet it was that trauma that motivated him to continue throughout his illustrious career de-spite his deep wish to be taken seriously as an actor and to be able to perform without blackface. Jessie Fauset's celebration of Williams in *The New Negro* anthology and Langston Hughes's well-known affection for the comedian (and his blood relationship to George Walker) could not save his reputa-tion, however. Despite Booker T. Washington's admiration and respect, and

W. E. B. Du Bois's acknowledgment that Williams helped give "the world a peculiar and characteristic kind of stage humor and comedy," in the eyes of subsequent generations he'd come too close to the thing they feared and was in their remembering of him indistinguishable from the hated mask.[52]

As if to identify Williams's legacy and defend it from the rising criticism and rejection of the newer generations of black audiences and critics, the Caribbean writer Eric Walrond wrote this of him months after his funeral:

> Bert Williams bore the brunt of ridicule—of ridicule from the Negro press—and fought his noble fight. Today the results are just coming to light. The demand for Negro shows on Broadway is taking a number of Negro girls and men out of kitchens and pool rooms and janitor service.
>
> Bert Williams' tree—to him one of gall—is already beginning to bear fruit, and there is no telling how long the harvest will last.[53]

Written for Garvey's *Negro World*, the passage comes from an article entitled "Bert Williams Foundation Organized to Perpetuate Ideals of Celebrated Actor."[54] It is no surprise that Garvey's paper would take a distinctly different view of the comedian from the one provided by the socialist *Messenger* in the passage quoted earlier in this chapter in which Williams is castigated for rendering "a disservice to black people." Both organs were deeply antagonistic toward each other, with the latter being very much a part of the rabid "Garvey Must Go" campaign that Du Bois would lead from his pulpit at the *Crisis*. For many of Harlem's West Indians this campaign was identified for its not so subtle anti–West Indianism. Even the not so subtle and often himself rabid Harold Cruse could see this in 1967's *Crisis of the Negro Intellectual*: "An anti–West Indian bias was implicit in some of the relentless editorial assaults in [A. Phillip] Randolf's *Messenger* against the Garvey movement, as part of the 'Garvey Must Go!' campaign carried on by the American leadership."[55]

This enormous cloud of historical controversy is what makes Williams's performance during the 1915 Ziegfeld Follies season so interesting and what forces Bert Williams's emergence into contemporary conversations about postcolonial hybridity, diaspora, pan-Africanism, and postmodern theories of "performance." That it was the West Indian writer Eric Walrond and a primarily West Indian organ like the *Negro World* which attempted to reclaim Williams from the mask is significant, considering the growing tensions between African Americans and West Indians in New York that were evident by the time of Williams's death. That Walrond would hear in Williams's many voices the prophetic "harvest" of a cultural renaissance is also significant since this renaissance will ultimately establish a dominant African American global exceptionalism despite feeding from multiple sources in the African diaspora and despite establishing its potent pan-African gestures. Because it was on one particular night that the voice beneath the voice, the dialect beneath the dialect, the face beneath the mask revealed itself not as the "true" sound of Bert Williams but as the infinitely deferred and transnationally displaced sound of a black modernism that could not be contained on the Broadway stage or even in Harlem or even in North America.

In a critically well-received skit written by Gene Buck, Williams played a bellboy/switchboard attendant in an Upper West Side Manhattan apartment building, handling and confusing the phone calls of the residents. In her biography of Williams Ann Charters writes that in this sketch he "completely transcended the blackface caricature."[56] *Variety*, the *New York Times*, and the *New York World* all gave Williams high marks for his portrayal of Thomas the beleaguered bellboy, one of the roles in which he so stretched the conventions of minstrelsy that only the mask remained to remind the audience of the performance's roots in cross-racial caricature. Although it is always problematic to trace complex historical transformations back to singular incidents or dates, this performance can arbitrarily function as a myth of origins for a modernism coterminous with the Euro-American modernism that often uses "jazz" as its signifier and rarely admits that "race" is its true signified; it is a myth also of a specifically black modernism born out of intra-racial yet crosscultural contact despite being silenced as "Negro" or "black" by the American and African American discourses that could brook very little fragmentation behind that mask.

On that stage, on that night in 1915, Bert Williams for the first and only time in his stage career "used his native West Indian accent on the stage."[57] This was an accent which had always been repressed in order to achieve "authentic" blackface minstrelsy since the "authentic Negro" spoke specifically and exclusively in the African American vernacular. And though neglected by the audience and the critics of his time, in a modernism of multiple and multiply black masking, this emergent voice revealed just how much the mask he wore and the dialect he spoke were produced by a minstrelsy of a higher order. His minstrelsy was at least a double minstrelsy and featured a black West Indian immigrant transcending the racist characterizations of the white minstrel tradition by way of his remarkable invention and performance of an African American voice and persona. Bert Williams was black, but his mask was African American. Through the voice and personae of the African

American, he struggled to enact a distinct West Indian presence in an African American cultural climate which may have celebrated a mythical "Africa" and embraced the poetics of black migration, but which was often uneasy with the historical presence of black otherness in its discourses and in its neighborhoods. And in a social world where West Indians often scorned African Americans and made cultural appeals to their British colonial patrimony in rejection of their sudden minority status in America, Bert Williams served to equate these distinct histories by occupying and dignifying the skin and sound of the African American other.

The presence of his "real" voice was unremarkable, though, precisely because he was so good at mimicry, at cultural cross-dressing, and at speaking the master's voice in addition to the voices of the master's varied subjects. Bert Williams was the one who was multiple, yet who stayed within the range of race because there was nowhere else to go. In Deleuze's and Guattari's words, as a subject of American racial history and of modern black border-crossings, he "accedes to a higher unity of ambivalence and overdetermination . . . Only thus does the one become part of the multiple: by always being subtracted from it. Subtract the unique from the multiplicity being constituted; write n to the $n-1$."[58] Unlike the endless assertions of presence and cultural noise that mark the Garvey movement, the NAACP, and the generation of the New Negro, Bert Williams was actively and strategically silent in the din of multiple overdeterminations. He became and occupied "Nobody." But in doing so, his absence was not invisibility. The weight of the tragicomic mask was the weight of multiplicity, what Wilson Harris would call a "tragic centrality" which features and dramatizes "a capacity for plural forms of profound identity."[59]

CHAPTER 2 Migrations of a Mask

Black skin, black mask: the space behind the mask was occupied by another mask; and this in a time when the politics of flesh seemed not arbitrary but immutable. And since the color of this flesh rendered its cultural distinctiveness invisible within the bichromatic context of American race relations as maintained by minstrelsy, only the sound of his English—a dialect for once unmasked—could sound something entirely else. Even Booker T. Washington was aware of Bert Williams's ancestry. In one of his essays on the famed minstrel, he writes:

> Bert Williams was born at New Providence, Nassau, in the British Bahama Islands, and is now thirty-five years of age. His grand-father was a white man, the Danish and Spanish Consul for the Bahama Islands, who married a quadroon. His grandfather, who owned a number of small ships, made considerable money during the Civil War, which he lost later in investments in the United States. When he was two years old, Frederick Williams, Mr. Williams's father, came to New York. Here he learned the trade of papier-mache maker, and this brought him into connection with the New York theatres. Thus Bert Williams got his first acquaintance with the theatre when he was a boy.[1]

A brief correction: although Bert Williams first arrived in the United States at the age of two, his family stayed there only a short time and returned to the Caribbean for about ten years. Washington knew that Bert Williams was not an African American, as did everyone else; but considering the governing racial logic of the time, he could not fragment the space behind Williams's mask sufficiently to contemplate the radical multiplicity of Williams's performance. This governing logic was one that informed both racism and Black Nationalism, effecting an inability to fully question "race" via "culture" and to fully explore the impact of immigration on the political body and fragmented desires of "the Negro." Although Locke would proclaim in *The New Negro* that "the answer" to the question posed by Harlem modernism lay "in the migrating peasant," he was also unable to think through the questions and challenges that radical, global black immigration would present to blacks themselves, particularly in America, particularly in New York.[2]

The Secret History of a Known Incommensurability

To Washington's eyes, Bert Williams was the ultimate icon of the politics of accommodation:

> Bert Williams is a tremendous asset of the Negro race. He is an asset because he has succeeded in actually doing something, and, because he has succeeded, the fact of his success helps the Negro many times more than he could help the Negro by merely contenting himself to whine and complain about racial difficulties and racial discriminations. The fact is that the American people are ready to honor and to reward any man who does something that is worth while, no matter whether he is black or white, and Bert Williams's career is simply another illustration of that fact.[3]

The irony of this icon's accommodationism being manifest through both a performance and a persona was no doubt lost on Booker T. Washington. Considering his politics, in fact, any breaking apart of the counter-hegemonic category of "Negro" would probably have resulted in a hyperfetishizing of racial and cultural differences which would have been anathema to his accommodationism, as it would also be to Locke's assimilationism. It would have threatened these political strategies because of the untidy, unwieldy, and seemingly uncontrollable differences within the race that were already beginning to threaten the stability of black leadership in the early twentieth century as well as the very notion that a "black leadership" was even possible or necessary. So for Washington to acknowledge the cultural difference of Bert Williams while simultaneously asserting the preeminence of "the Negro Race" was to accommodate the dominant racial logic of the time, which required intra-racial, cross-cultural differences to be minimized. Washington's celebration of Williams as a political asset arose from this need to minimize racial difference and cultural otherness. In this regard, he no doubt could see burnt cork as a force of resistance through its own exemplary containment of those differences, through Bert Williams's rendering of a transcendental "Negro" via a silencing of a Caribbean distinctiveness. However, it is that silencing that ultimately reveals how much of this "Negro" was a sign of African American cultural priority.

As noted earlier, Williams had steadily been attacked by militant African American critics for his lack of assertiveness concerning his racial pride. For them his silence was just that—silence at a time when volume was needed, particularly for someone who so captured the ear of the white other. More militant West Indians no doubt felt the same. However, despite the ironies at work in Washington's reading of Bert Williams, one needn't think that Washington was fooled by Bert Williams, since Williams's politics were in fact far less militant and aggressive than those of many other West Indians and were not radically out of step with the wizard of Tuskegee's. In Williams's own words: "Since I have been with the Follies of 1910, I am more and more convinced that each member of the race must take it upon himself to solve the Negro question. I believe that the Negro is bound to get on top eventually, but it will be by pursuing a conservative policy."[4] Another crucial element in this context is the sometimes extreme self-policing of the immigrant, the common reluctance to draw too much attention to oneself in an alien culture and in an alienating social context. Ann Charters argues that this conservatism, Williams's seeming quietism and his refusal to publicly throw his support behind the movements led by Booker T. Washington and W. E. B. Du Bois, was due in part to "a feeling of alienation as a West Indian."[5]

Contrasting with Washington's view of Bert Williams is the view of the great blues singer Alberta Hunter in her autobiography. Describing her first meeting with the then immensely famous Bert Williams, this queen of the African American vernacular wrote: "He didn't pay any attention to me. I wasn't even alive. He was a West Indian. They're full of baloney, a lot of them. Thought they were better than God made little apples. Forgive me for saying it, because so many of my friends are West Indians and I love 'em so. But they've always been big shots."[6]

Despite his celebrity Bert Williams was not immune to the tensions between the African American community in Harlem and the West Indian migrants who made up a sizeable and culturally significant portion of the black
population. Unlike Booker T. Washington, Alberta Hunter fractures the category of "Negro" by identifying a competitive sense of cultural difference on
the level of micropolitics. For others, the space between the performer and
the role was sutured by the overarching logic of race and the assumption of
cultural commonality. But what is perhaps less clear here is not only how
much of that space between was perceived as cultural but how the mastery of
that other culture—one that merely looks like your own—was achievable
through a control of its vernacular and through a wearing of its skin, so to
speak, or a hiding behind the dominant definitions of that skin. When not
onstage, Bert Williams spoke with a strong West Indian accent. It is a well-
known fact of American Caribbean life that immigrants often resist cultural
(as opposed to economic) assimilation by exaggerating their dialect. This
exaggeration was a technique employed to make public and evident the not so
obvious differences between them and the dominant African American community and in many cases contained within it no small amount of disdain and
resentment.

In her biography of Bert Williams, Ann Charters writes, "Like many Negroes from the British West Indies, the Williamses felt somewhat superior to
their American neighbors, and although his father's job lacked much social
prestige, Bert was raised to be conscious of the family's past distinction."[7]
She also tells us that his "West Indian origin had given him a sense of
superiority to the American Negro background that remained with him all his
life."[8] Charters goes on to describe his life as a celebrity in Harlem:

> Although Williams had lived in America since he was ten years old, his
> strong identification with his West Indian birthplace meant that he never felt
> completely comfortable with his neighbors in Harlem, and he was denied
> companionship and support from people of his own race. He hired a West
> Indian chauffeur to take him to the theater, insisting that cafes lowering the
> color bar to serve him, must also serve his driver. Williams was in a constant
> state of exile: from the white culture, from which he was barred because he
> was a Negro; and from his Harlem neighbors and theatrical acquaintances,
> because he remained at heart a West Indian.[9]

The resistance to both Americanization and Afro-Americanization is reflected in the fact that even though he had emigrated from the Bahamas in the

mid-to-late 1880s, he did not become a naturalized citizen until 1918 and had maintained—like most West Indians during this time—his British colonial citizenship. Williams died in 1922, a year particularly significant for the West Indian presence in Harlem. It was the official moment of the Harlem Renaissance, the year Marcus Garvey was jailed for mail fraud and the year Claude McKay's *Harlem Shadows* was published; it was also the height of the anti–West Indian fervor that struck black Harlem during the months before the Garvey indictment, which came soon after his fateful meeting with the Ku Klux Klan. But since his career spans the period of the greatest Caribbean migration to the United States, from the last decades of the nineteenth century to and just beyond the period of the Harlem Renaissance, Bert Williams's persona dramatizes the tensions at work in the migrant black West Indian psyche upon transatlantic landfall. Rather than simply functioning as a convenient sign for a heuristic and excessively materialist "Black Atlantic" discursive framework, he allows an interrogation of the micropolitical and psychosocial impact of these post- and neocolonial black migratory patterns, the shifting patterns of identity, affiliation, and differentiation.

In the passage quoted above, Charters makes a helpful slip in that fissure between race and culture that defines a transnational black modernism. Although she dramatically overstates Williams's relationship to black Harlem when she writes that he had no companionship and support from "people of his own race" she clearly means "African Americans," not West Indians. This passage accurately describes the fissures between race and culture and the contradictions and complexities of Bert Williams's politics and his performance; it also evidences the complexities in how white Americans read West Indians vis-à-vis African Americans. But despite the sense of cultural superiority that many West Indian immigrants were notorious for, he still challenged the color line by extending his celebrity to include others like George Walker, Ada Overton Walker, and many other African American performers. Although Williams was a minority within a minority, the American logic of race may not have reduced all difference to sameness in his view, but it allowed for a sense of political if not cultural similarity. Arrogant or not, supercilious or not, Williams was in the parlance of his time a "race man." What Charters describes as "a constant state of exile," though, is what will concern us now that the African American mask is off and all others fully engaged. This must be read not as simply another romanticization of the transcendental homelessness that defined so much modernist art and which has become the most tiresome cliché of postcolonial literature and thought.

For the early-twentieth-century Caribbean community, increasingly mobile in their back and forth movements and increasingly grounded in Harlem as well as in multiple sites, "exile" was mediated by the mobility of their discourses of authenticity.

Charters's phrase evokes Deleuze and Guattari, who champion that vertiginous state of being "a nomad and an immigrant and a gypsy in relation to one's own language."[10] It is this state that inspires Williams's "own patois, his own third world, his own desert."[11] It also precipitates his own disappearance, which, like the invisibility of Ellison's Invisible Man, does not quite signify erasure and remains a palpable absence: a signifying vortex of multiple meanings, languages, dialects, and masks. What the inestimable Wilson Harris says of the Invisible Man, driven underground in part by the loud sound of West Indian Garveyites, one can now say of Bert Williams: his invisibility is "a fissure in the womb of space, a ripple upon uniform premises, a complex metaphor of the imaginative descent of masquerading stone or solid body into a psychical pool on which concentric circles and horizons appear."[12] This state speaks not only to Bert Williams but to the position of West Indians during the New Negro movement and more broadly to the position of global black difference within a dominant African American discursive and cultural context. With Bert Williams and his mask as the acknowledged focal point for an "imaginative descent," it is now possible to explore the multiplicity of shadows cast by the glare of a dominant whiteness.

To return to Booker T. Washington's interpretation of Bert Williams against the backdrop of black cross-culturality, and also to Wilson Harris's notion of "invisibility" and George Lamming's "camouflage of self-evaporation": the tragicomic mask still remains between Washington and Williams. What does this do to the politics of accommodation or assimilation if performance and masking are what mediate it or make it possible? Also, what kind of black modernism is this, and assimilation into which social or racial context—the white American or the African American? The next section of this chapter will explore these issues in more detail via a closer reading of Booker T. Washington's use of Bert Williams's mask alongside the emergence of African American modernism; and the tensions of "double assimilation" will be fully discussed in the following chapter. But in the passage quoted earlier, Washington collapses the mask into the face, celebrating the performance as the performer, and reads the mask inside out, as all too many would. For him the actions of Bert Williams's persona are indistinguishable from Bert Williams himself: "Bert Williams has done more for the race than I have. He has smiled his way into people's hearts. I have been obliged to fight my way."[13] And Williams's use of dialect and the minstrel tradition is not parodic or multilayered in this hearing—nor is it self-hating and regressive. It is no more and no less than a refusal to "whine and complain." The comedian's incredible success was proof of America's progress from racism toward a true meritocracy, and minstrelsy—black minstrelsy—could be a sign of that movement.

However, by the time of Williams's death, the editor of the *New York Herald* wondered whether Williams's gift for mimicry was in fact *so* good that everyone, black or white, West Indian or African American, was bamboozled. This writer doubted that the majority of Williams's audience even "realized that his work was a conscious artifice."[14] As if to prevent this misinterpretation, the editor of *The American Magazine*, which published Williams's fine essay "The Comic Side of Trouble," prefaced the essay with what seems to be a caution against such a hearing of this minstrelsy. In describing Williams's comic technique, the editor wrote that Williams "deliberately makes himself appear unfortunate in order to make you laugh at him."[15] One wonders if this cautionary description was deemed necessary because Williams was already being read incorrectly, as he would be, tragically, by the younger African American moderns for whom the trickster figure was helpful only if it was explicit and aimed in one way—in the white direction (as if tricksters could ever "belong" to a side despite their emerging from specific cultural contexts).

Jessie Fauset was the only young black modern to begin to explore the complexity of Bert Williams's iconicity in ways that built on yet departed from Booker T. Washington's essays. In an essay on the Caribbean performer, published in *The Crisis* in the year of Williams's death, she adds a great deal to our understanding of his cross-cultural, intra-racial performance as a sign of another modernism within the skin of Negro newness. The essay is interestingly titled "The Symbolism of Bert Williams" and argues that, for reasons of his complex gift of mimicry and masquerade, to the African American audience "he was the racial type itself. That is why he is symbolic."[16] That the essentialist language of racial types exists alongside the de-essentializing language of symbolic performance may not have seemed contradictory to Fauset, as it did to Washington; however, it allows a contemporary reading to imagine a modernist discourse of racial authenticity that is explicitly performative but simultaneously rooted in the collective assumptions and fears of a given community and its linguistic and cultural practices. Fauset's essay "The

Gift of Laughter" goes far in thinking about what vistas lay behind the comic mask and how much distance was covered by Williams's vernacular expression as well as his function as a "symbol" for the early-twentieth-century African American and West Indian communities. This essay is a vital early attempt to theorize Bert Williams's cross-culturality and penchant for plural masking in the context of black modernism. It therefore must be quoted at length:

> Natively he possessed the art of mimicry; intuitively he realized that his first path to the stage must lie along the old recognized lines of "funny man." He was, as few of us recall, a Jamaican by birth; the ways of the American Negro were utterly alien to him and did not come spontaneously; he set himself therefore to obtaining a knowledge of them. For choice he selected, perhaps by way of contrast, the melancholy out-of-luck Negro, shiftless, doleful, "easy"; the kind that tempts the world to lay its hand none too lightly upon him. The pursuit took him years, but at length he was able to portray for us not only that "typical Negro" which the white world thinks is universal but also the special types of given districts and localities with their own peculiar foibles of walk and speech and jargon. He went to London and studied under Pietro, greatest pantomimist of his day, until finally he, too, became a recognized master in the field of comic art.
>
>   But does anyone who realizes that the foibles of the American Negro were painstakingly acquired by this artist, doubt not that Williams might just as well have portrayed the Irishman, the Jew, the Englishman abroad, the Scotchman or any other of the vividly etched types which for one reason or another lend themselves so readily to caricature? Can anyone presume to say that a man who traveled north, east, south and west and even abroad in order to acquire accent and jargon, aspect and characteristic of a people to which he was bound by ties of blood but from whom he was natively separated by training and tradition, would not have been able to portray with equal effectiveness what, for lack of a better term, we must call universal roles?[17]

In "The Symbolism of Bert Williams" she further elaborates on his gift for mimicry and its relationship to the African American "other":

> Without the slightest knowledge of the dialect of the American Negro, he set to work to acquire it. He watched, he listened, he visited various Negro districts North and South, he studied phonetics. He could make his listener distinguish between variations of different localities. He affected, his admirers will remember, a shambling, shuffling gait which at intervals in his

act would change into a grotesque sliding and gliding—the essence of awkward naturalness. But awkward or graceful, it was not natural to him, but simply the evolution of a walk and dance which he had worked out by long and patient observation of Negro prototypes.[18]

Before delving fully into Fauset's extraordinarily rich and nuanced reading of Williams's minstrelsy, another layer must be peeled away. In attempting to reveal Williams's own pre-American performative transformations, a fellow Caribbean modernist in New York, J. A. Rogers, multiplies Williams's penchant for cross-cultural pantomime and vernacular mimicry by locating a mask behind the mask behind the mask:

> Bert had developed a particular interest in the mannerisms of a certain type of peasant while in Antigua. He later shifted his attention to a similar type of African American—the humble, shiftless, slouch Negro who could neither read nor write but who had a certain hard, and not altogether inaccurate, philosophy of life. He would study this type patiently and rejoyce whenever he discovered a new twist of dialect or expression . . . From this Bert would go on to develop an act into what became his trademark character—"Mr. Nobody" (Charlie Chapman [sic] would later develop a white character who was similar), and the accompaning [sic] song he composed, "nobody," became his signature work.[19]

His signature was "Nobody." His persona was Mr. Nobody. His performance was erasure, not invisibility. Despite misplacing Williams's island origins, as Fauset does, Rogers routes the performer's mimicry through an already performative sensibility in relationship to his cultural origins: the Caribbean peasant becomes the ground zero of his mimicry. In other words, before he performed "the Negro" or performed a Hawaiian, as he did in the lean years before meeting George Walker, even before In Dahomey, he was performing a "native" folk identity. This of course places Williams early in those emergent conversations about "the folk" in African American modernism and the cross-class ventriloquism of the vernacular that would be at the heart of the poetics of the New Negro movement. This is the context in which the younger artists of the black middle class began to represent themselves and the race through dialect and by way of a romanticized authenticity of an increasingly less-rural black poor—a gesture as much against the elitism of their elders as it was a more aggressive critique of white racism.

Williams's own father would trace this gift for mimicry even further back to his talented son's formative years in the Caribbean:

Bert never stood out as a shining light at school. He studied just enough so that he passed and his reports were good, but I am inclined to think that all the joy he ever got out of studying came from his own observations. Indeed he seemed delighted with each new achievement in mimicry and he developed this gift to a degree while only a child. He brought to light and emphasized the idiosyncrasies of every native man, bird and beast, including all the barnyard gentry.

We punished him for this at first, but soon discovered that punishment was of no use. I am mighty glad now, that that spark was there and that it developed in spite of us older folk who were so slow to understand and appreciate it.[20]

Perhaps the only performance of his career that was even more self-referential than this was the one described by the playwright Channing Pollack in *Harvest of My Years*, his autobiography: "One evening, seeking amusement, a dozen of us went to a burlesque theatre in the Bowery where Bert Williams appeared on the stage as an amateur giving an imitation of Bert Williams—and was a complete flop."[21] At the risk of overly psychoanalyzing Williams, it is worth wondering if his "innate" sense of performance and mimicry arose in part from his mixed racial heritage. This is worth contemplating if his sense of "otherness" in relationship to his own people even there in the Caribbean and in the American Caribbean community had anything to do with his interest in "passing" as the even darker black other—even if that darker black other was the persona he created.

To return to Fauset's reading of Bert Williams: it is indebted to the logic of blood despite her awareness of the foundational influence of "training and tradition." As is to be expected for the time, blood will ultimately win out over culture and history in her analysis. But what is stunning is how aware she is of the fact that Bert Williams performed both what he was (racially black, according to contemporary logic) and what he was simultaneously not (a working-class, illiterate African American). Only once did he apparently perform something even vaguely Caribbean—and that was in the 1915 performance that here serves as a convenient "break" which allows for a re-historicizing of American and African American modernism. Considering how the white racism of early-twentieth-century America often proffered more favorable treatment to foreign blacks than to home-grown African Americans, perhaps that is why so many saw in this particular performance a final "transcendence" of the Negro stereotype. Rather than transcendence, it was more accurately a displacement of one form of black for another, one form of dialect for another. Again, in Williams's own words: "I took to studying the dialect of the American Negro, which to me was just as much a foreign dialect as that of the Italian."[22] In this moment, Bert Williams escaped one mask by revealing another, and in that act of false revelation he accomplished two things: he dramatized an emergent poetics and politics of black cross-culturality (West Indians vis-à-vis African Americans) and, in this stress on masking and unmasking which only emphasizes the logic of authenticity, he diverted attention from the fact that cultural power emerged less in the act of revelation than in the inexorable process of masking.

Mimicry and minstrelsy are deployed cross-culturally in Fauset's essays, though not in a specific attempt to render the cultural and historical diversity of the African dispersal or the micropolitics of diasporic encounters. Instead it is her concern to construct "universal roles," which is a gesture that asserts a transnational racial solidarity while at the same time maintaining the assumption of African American exceptionalism that undergirds the politics of assimilation. This sense of the iconic and universal significance of Williams's persona brings Fauset back in line with Booker T. Washington, Alain Locke, and W. E. B. Du Bois, for whom "the Negro," despite global sprawl and the overwhelming presence of the Garvey movement, was ultimately representable as an African American. As we will see in chapter 5, it is a tragic irony that the resistance to the racism of an American global hegemony also borrows from the rhetoric of the universal and consolidates its own discursive power through the positioning of its marginalization as the site of racial allegory and the privileged site of historical resistance.

In other words, the "universal" status of "the Negro" or the "stage Negro" enabled the specifics of the African American context to masquerade as fully diasporic, as globally representative in ways that were ironically supported by the cultural power of the United States. And despite the fact that Garvey was seen to represent an internal cultural threat which partly motivated the Americocentric parochialism of the coteries of Locke and Du Bois, he too made claims on the "universal": after all, his organization was the Universal Negro Improvement Association (and African Communities League). His description of himself as the "Provisional President of Africa" along with the various titles he bestowed—such as "Duke of the Niger," "Lord of Uganda," and so forth—should be read as a competing universalism meant to wrest discursive control from the largely African American and painfully middle-class New Negroes who came to define the Harlem movement. I will argue later that Garvey's penchant for vainglorious masquerade, elaborate costuming, and the carnivalesque had more than a little to do with the Williams and Walker shows, particularly In Dahomey. However, these black modernist discussions of Bert Williams's stage persona open up the contradictions and complexities at the heart of an emergent African American nationalism that bore some ever-uneasy relationship with the growing imperial sprawl of the American empire.

Strangely enough, even media organs like the New York Herald were aware of some of these tensions between race and culture, language and dialect behind and made manifest through Williams's mask. An editorial reflects this:

> Bert Williams amused a generation of playgoers who looked on him as an exponent of the native humor of the American Negro, yet he was born in the West Indies and brought up in San Francisco, so that he was little under the influences which are supposed to create the dialect and the mode of thought of the southern darky. But he set out to win his way as a Negro entertainer and was so successful, that he became in the last twenty years, the most popular Negro comedian the stage has known.
>
> Williams acquired the ability to indicate the simplicity, the indolence, the credulity of the Negro, which are important elements in his stage success.[23]

Bert Williams's secret was an open one yet incommensurable in its maintenance of the doubled tensions between being West Indian but the foremost "exponent" of the humor and sensibilities of African American "natives"; between his genius as a mimic and a performer, and the fact that this genius was best manifest in his portrayal of "the southern darky," a fiction accepted—even by the writer of this editorial—as real. One wonders if that is because the writer saw Bert Williams as black yet a West Indian who presumably existed external to the dynamics of race in America and was thus able to maintain the reality of the "southern darky" without the contradiction that the very act of performance implies. By accepting that this racist fiction was authentic, the writer could see it as specific to African Americans, not to Bert Williams. This way self-conscious artifice of the minstrel would not contradict the assumption of the biocultural reality of the "darky" beneath the mask. As will be explored much later, Williams's performance could be read for its ability to highlight intra-racial distinctions via cross-cultural mimicry; however, in this case, such a reading is being used to emphasize certain domestic pathologies and the unique flavor of a racism directed at African Americans via the conduit of an immigrant group often rendered nonpathological by white America: a black model minority, as it were.

Again, Bert Williams's performance of cross-culturality was known but was incommensurable. His cultural distinctiveness was identified, yet its implications remained invisible, primarily for reasons of his seemingly accurate and effortless portrayal of "the Stage Negro," the "darky," and "the African American," which was precisely how "the Negro" was being defined at that moment in history—either by the staged stereotype or by resistant alternatives to the stereotype. To be "Negro" was to be an "African American" because that was maintained as a corrective to the equally assertive horror of the racist "darky" that seemed to mock all black pretensions to high seriousness and political equality. And for the foremost "exponent" of the "darky" to not be African American, well, that was no doubt a fascinating political and cultural scenario, particularly since it was through his doubly black mask that a revived African American dialect poetics was being proffered. As Alain Locke so boldly declares in his manifesto, the New Negro bore "the consciousness of acting as the advance-guard of the African peoples in their contact with Twentieth Century civilization."[24] These strident tones were meant to orient the "Negro" not only politically but around the cultural priorities and racial assumptions of African American politics. Du Bois, of course, goes much further with this assumption in keeping with the exceptionalism that marked generations of black racial discourse before The Souls of Black Folk. His manifesto also features this same consciousness and historical trajectory, one in which the "souls" of all "Black" folk are ultimately claimed and represented by the African American folk. In it Du Bois famously writes:

> One ever feels his twoness—an American, a Negro; two souls, two thoughts, two unreconciled strivings; two warring ideals in one dark body, whose dogged strength alone keeps it from being torn asunder.
>
> The history of the American Negro is the history of this strife—this longing to attain self-conscious manhood, to merge his double self into a better and truer self. In this merging he wishes neither of the older selves to be lost. He would not Africanize America, for America has too much to teach the world and Africa. He would not bleach his Negro soul in a flood of white Americanism, for he knows that Negro blood has a message for the world. He simply wishes to make it possible for a man to be both a Negro and an American, without being cursed and spit upon by his fellows, without having the doors of Opportunity closed roughly in his face.[25]

Du Bois is a crucial link between the nineteenth and the twentieth centuries in terms of the categories employed to comprehend and classify human group affiliation. He is at the cusp of the nineteenth century and its obsession with "blood" as both fact and metaphor of social organization. He is also well into the mythical and psychological fetishes of twentieth-century nationalisms. Both these categories are blurred where the Negro is concerned, perhaps because "he" is new on the historical stage and fully located in the American grain as a novel creation cursed or blessed by landfall. So despite its clearly diasporic and transcultural significance, double-consciousness is here articulated as the condition of the American Negro. Race certainly forces wider, transnational connections; but it is the American Negro who is the "seventh son" and who is gifted/cursed with the kind of consciousness that marks him as modern and well suited for a self-assumed role in the vanguard of black struggle.

As almost a riposte to the ethnocultural assumptions behind these discourses of "soul," Claude McKay, in his autobiography *A Long Way from Home*, claims that of all black diaspora communities and cultures it was precisely the American Negro who had no soul: "The American Negro group is the most advanced in the world. It possesses unique advantages for development and expansion and for assuming the world leadership of the Negro race. But it sadly lacks a group soul."[26] Clearly the black modernist debate around "soul" was a sign of not just cultural authenticity but ultimately transnational political authority. The final chapter of this book will have much more to say about McKay's relationship to African American exceptionalism, minstrelsy, and Bert Williams. But to fully situate McKay's critique in a longer tradition of cross-cultural, intra-racial, and even transnational concerns over the assumption of African American cultural and political priority, it is worth noting that in 1911 the West African nationalist and writer J. E. Casely Hayford asserted, in his magnificent treatise *Ethiopia Unbound*: "The work of men like Booker T. Washington and W. E. Burghart Du Bois is exclusive and provincial."[27] His reading of Du Bois's famous lines quoted above is also one that takes umbrage at the explicit nature of this attempt at rendering Africa and its own cultural contexts, traditions, and classificatory systems secondary, tertiary, or even backward. Upon finishing Du Bois's famous section, Casely Hayford writes of a racialized soul divided: "Poor Ethiopia! How sorely hath the iron of oppression entered into the very soul of thy erring children!"[28] Double-consciousness, in *Ethiopia Unbound*, is described as a form of false consciousness produced by that landfall: "It is apparent that Mr. Du Bois writes from an American standpoint, surrounded by an American atmosphere. And, of course, it is not his fault, for he knows no other."[29]

In light of these debates and criticisms of "the Negro" and ultimately of "soul" (that which presumably lies behind the mask), Gerald Early asks a very pertinent set of questions: "Would it not have been more accurate, certainly more mythologically compelling, in the opening sentence for Du Bois to have used the word 'African' instead of 'Negro'? And is there a difference between 'the Negro' and 'the American Negro'? In short, how does consciousness relate to ethnicity and race?"[30] Rather than answering them, double-consciousness exacerbates them by providing a sense of modern Negro consciousness as ultimately wavering between two modern, Western constructs—Negro and American, not African American and African; in part, this was Casely Hayford's insight. This reading of The Souls of Black Folk contests Paul Gilroy's idea that the text "was the first place where a diasporic, global perspective on the politics of racism and its overcoming interrupted the smooth flow of African-American exceptionalisms."[31] Granted, the global perspective is there, but it does not interrupt the cultural elitism of this vision of diaspora. If anything, the global gesture is used to privilege the African American experience of landfall and "the Negro" as the felix culpa of colonialism and slavery. Claude McKay's above-quoted statement on "soul" seems to have been produced by a slight suspicion that the Du Boisian discourse only maintained and confirmed the flow of African American exceptionalism at the expense of black immigrants who in his view were much more cohesive.

As with Du Bois's discourse of "soul," Locke's own descriptions carry with them a claim to the iconic, in which to be an African American was to symbolically represent if not speak for the entire diaspora despite the actual presence of West Indians and West Africans in the streets of Harlem. This, however, was an act of political masking akin to the use of African motifs and images throughout the New Negro to authorize the reconstructed authenticity of a new kind of blackness. Less charitably—or less romantically—one can read the use of the myth of blood kinship as also a method of symbolically appropriating "Africa" in a naked attempt to compete with the white moderns who were doing just that during the modernist period; by upending white exoticism with an African American exoticism that could authorize itself by blood and cultural retentions, a black modernism could flourish. It is this kind of black-on-black masking, this activist and opportunistic primitivism, that would ultimately manifest a complex discourse of political and historical representation, fantasy, and cross-cultural competition. In other words, it turned the theater of Williams and Walker into cultural politics.

"The pulse of the Negro world has begun to beat in Harlem," claims

Locke, perhaps slyly alluding to Garvey's very popular *Negro World* news-paper.[32] This organ of the UNIA should have reminded him that the pulse may have been beating in Harlem, but the veins were each distinct and rhizomatically connected to multiple sites of cultural origin; and the blood they contained was also as contentious as the West Indian Garvey whom Locke dismisses a mere page later by describing his influence as "a transient, if spectacular phenomenon."[33] A faulty description if there ever was one. It was clearly an attempt to wish this other strand of competing blackness out of existence, much like the Du Bois–fueled "Garvey Must Go" campaign with its pronounced anti–West Indian bias. As it happened, a year after the death of Bert Williams, Du Bois established a curious connection between Garvey and Williams. In one of his editorials deploying the phrase "Garvey Must Go"—the one in which he infamously describes Garvey as "a little, fat black man, ugly, but with intelligent eyes and big head"—he describes a UNIA meeting or ceremony like this: "A casual observer might have mistaken it for the dress-rehearsal of a new comic opera, and looked instinctively for Bert Williams."[34]

Acquiring Authenticity: Dialect Poetics and Black Masquerade

"At the turn of the century" writes Allen Woll, "a modern minstrel appeared on the musical stage. He wore shabby clothes, ankle-length pants, oversized shoes, an old top-hat, and a heavy layer of burnt cork on his face."[35] This description of Bert Williams as a modern minstrel suggests that his black-on-black minstrelsy was a break from the tradition itself, much like the aggressive assertion of a "New" Negro identity was meant to separate itself from something older and much less liberating. Unsurprisingly, the "old" Negro was often imaged as a minstrel figure, particularly in texts like the *New Negro* anthology. In it, Alain Locke wrote, "The days of 'aunties,' 'uncles' and 'mammies' are equally gone. Uncle Tom and Sambo have passed on, and even the 'Colonel' and 'George' play barnstorm roles from which they escape with relief when the public spotlight is off. The popular melodrama has about played itself out, and it is time to scrap the fictions, garret the bogeys and settle down to a realistic facing of facts."[36] Although minstrelsy is here figured as a sign of the past along with its dialect, Locke's dependence on the binary of performance and the "realistic," the mask and an authentic space beneath it, allows room for a specific form of minstrelsy that is not only "modern" but, according to Houston Baker, modernist as well. This is evidenced by Locke's dependence on theatrical metaphors, on the "popular melodrama" of conventional race relations and the image of both "George" and "the Colonel" removing the mask "with relief when the public spotlight is off."

This gesture of generational unmasking is consistent with the general description of the emergent New Negro psyche; for example, Locke's description of the Old Negro as "more of a myth than a man," and the modern refusal of a "protective social mimicry forced upon him by the adverse circumstances of dependence" which is shattered by the "new psychology."[37] "Similarly the mind of the Negro seems suddenly to have slipped from under the tyranny of social intimidation and to be shaking off the psychology of imitation and implied inferiority. By shedding the old chrysalis of the Negro problem we are achieving something like a spiritual emancipation."[38] Not only is this a triumphalist unmasking and a political refusal of dominant representations; it is a liberation from mimicry itself, protective or otherwise. But "George" and "the Colonel" in fact represent a primary strategic masking, a performance of "the Negro" in the spotlight of the white American gaze as well as in something that figures often too little in debates about this time period: the middle-class African American nationalist gaze. Both these gazes were fixated on the minstrel for very different reasons and in very different ways, but it is the assimilationist-nationalism that is at work in Locke's poetics and politics. This politics sees racial emergence and the "new psychology" as key to integration and equality and sees "the natural" as the assimilable and mimicry as the problem. But in a close reading of the above passage the minstrel serves a more central function than one would think based on Locke's overtly dismissive language. There is the vague suggestion that even before the New Negro's heyday a strategic and "protective" use of the mask was in fact possible—this despite the widespread fear and loathing of minstrelsy among younger black moderns. This is the case since Locke admits that George and the Colonel were wearing masks in the first place. There is also here the perhaps even more important fact that the very language of racial transformation, generational transcendence, and renascence depends on the very language of masking and unmasking. So where Locke and the contributors to The New Negro would define themselves in a more general opposition to the minstrel tradition, the binary between "minstrelsy" and "the natural" features an implicit dependence on an antecedent black blackface performance at the root of this modernist refusal.

For the generation of the Harlem Renaissance, however, the space between mask and flesh was too precarious for diversion and too historically overdetermined by whites for self-conscious irony in an age more militant than ours. The minstrel figure becomes for them the fixed sign of a slave past and a slavery symbolically linked to dialect as well as symbolic caricature. Its ambivalence and ambiguity were lost or erased by the need to consolidate and control representations of "the Negro." Bert Williams, who had once been respected for his attempts to dignify the stereotype and who had claimed it from the depths of epistemic violence, became a sign of the "old Negro" when it is his use of the "old Negro" that helped move it from the plantation, to the city and even—as in In Dahomey, Bandana Land, Mr. Lode of Kaol, and Abyssinia—out into the increasingly polluted and profane space of the black diaspora and into the popular pan-African imagination. But in order to express the "new psychology" of the Negro and to achieve "full racial utterance" once the Harlem movement officially began, the minstrel tradition and its deleterious effect on black poetics and black representations had to be transcended, not theorized.[39] This transcendence was wedded to an emergent literature and practice of writing that was seen as the key to discarding the tropes and topoi of minstrelsy and as the primary site of a new kind of black expression; one that was self-motivated, self-constructed, and could be witnessed in a language that was suddenly freed from dialect masking. In short, to be black and modern according to Locke was to have "shaken . . . free from the minstrel tradition and the fowling-nets of dialect."[40]

The desire to move from dialect existed as a firm political stance despite the presence of dialect in many of the poems in Weldon Johnson's The Book of American Negro Poetry and in The New Negro anthology itself. Dialect works are present even in Nancy Cunard's 1934 Negro: An Anthology and would come to mark an intergenerational battlefield once younger black moderns like Langston Hughes and Zora Neale Hurston began to deploy it. Of course, it had been an even more conflictual but necessary field of play for earlier Caribbean moderns like Bert Williams himself, and the specificity of this West Indian appropriation and engagement with the African American vernacular would characterize the work of Eric Walrond and Claude McKay. For these black, transnational moderns the question of "dialect" was itself mediated by their own Caribbean Englishes that had to be displaced onto and often masked within the increasingly canonized and commodified African American vernacular. But years before Harlem's vogue, the African American retreat from dialect signaled the strong desire of Weldon Johnson's generation to define a black modern voice not mired in the overdeterminations of the white ear.

They sought a voice, which "sounded" differently than the auditory fiction or white racism and which was able to sound—as Houston Baker suggests—African American modernism in an annunciatory and distinct way. It was a shift determined by the extreme limitations placed upon the black poetic voice by the signifiers of plantation slavery and the desire on the part of white urban America to keep, symbolically at least, the Negro at "home" in the premodern South and as close to slavery as possible. Of this Weldon Johnson writes:

> Negro dialect is at present a medium that is not capable of giving expression to the varied conditions of Negro life in America, and much less is it capable of giving the fullest interpretation of Negro character and psychology. This is no indictment against the dialect as dialect, but against the mold of convention in which Negro dialect in the United States has been set.[41]

Ten years later in his preface to the revised edition of *Black Manhattan*, Weldon Johnson sealed the connection between black speech and premodernist African American poetry. Like Locke and so many others, he identified the true culprit who stole the Negro's voice: "Today even the reader is conscious that almost all poetry in the conventionalized dialect is either based upon the minstrel traditions of Negro life, traditions that had but slight relation—often no relation at all—to actual Negro life."[42] Du Bois in *The Souls of Black Folk* will also celebrate "the loss of the old-time Negro" who through the image of the minstrel poses a problem for African American cultural and political advancement.[43] Dialect poets, then, were not just influenced by the poetics of minstrelsy but were themselves minstrels, speaking the voice of the "Negro" as constructed by racist whites. As Paul Laurence Dunbar complained to Weldon Johnson, "I've got to write dialect poetry; it's the only way I can get them to listen to me."[44] Dunbar here is not just a minstrel but a *black* minstrel like Bert Williams, for whom the black mask was the only way he could get "them" to look at and listen to him.

Yet decades before Locke's *New Negro* anthology and Weldon Johnson's *Book of American Negro Poetry*, Bert Williams had already redefined the possibilities of dialect. He functions as a necessary link between the generation of the dialect poet Paul Laurence Dunbar and the generation of Langston Hughes, Zora Neale Hurston, and Claude McKay, who all used dialect in a distinctly modern/ist context. In *The New Negro*, Jessie Fauset is sympathetic to Williams's legacy, though she is careful to mark some distance between that which he performed and that which was seen by the white audience: "at length he was able to portray for us not only that 'typical Negro' which the white world thinks is universal but also the special types of given districts and localities with their own peculiar foibles of walk and speech and jargon."[45] Given that Paul Laurence Dunbar was one of the primary lyricists for the Williams and Walker extravaganzas, it is absolutely necessary to draw the multiply masked voice of Bert Williams into the literary conversations around the African American dialect that mark the transition from "old Negro" to "New Negro" and perhaps even resituate the "origins" of a black modernism in his take on the American minstrel tradition. Even James Weldon Johnson would identify Dunbar's very use of the African American dialect as significant despite his opposition to its legacy and its contemporary usage. In his preface to the first edition of *The Book of American Negro Poetry*, he writes: "Of course, Negro dialect poetry was written before Dunbar wrote, most of it by white writers; but the fact stands out that Dunbar was the first to use it as a medium for the true interpretation of Negro character and psychology."[46] However, the very same or more could be said of Bert Williams, who employed and inspired Dunbar.

In 1897 Paul Laurence Dunbar made his claim on a black vernacular modernism in his *Lyrics of Lowly Life*, which features the classic poem "We Wear the Mask." But given the presence of Bert Williams, there is much more to this poem than has heretofore been said. At the time when he was the most celebrated modern African American poet, Dunbar was simultaneously working on minstrel operettas like the successful *Clorindy: Or the Origin of the Cakewalk* that premiered in 1898. This show starred the black blackface minstrel Ernest Hogan, who subtly reversed the pathology that blackface exaggerated by billing himself as "the Great Unbleached American."[47] Four years before he worked with Bert Williams and George Walker, the poet whose generation wore a soul-killing "mask that grins and lies," whose disguise was the "debt we pay to human guile," was already struggling with and exploring mimicry for some tortured poetics of racial genesis. He was also in quintessentially American form commodifying that struggle, that exploration. Houston Baker, however, argues that because Dunbar doesn't seem to acknowledge that his subject position is a product of white not black guile, the poet "plays the masking game without an awareness of its status as a game."[48] But Dunbar's presence in the minstrel market suggests a greater self-consciousness of both the traps and the liberating possibilities in the complex game of black masking—via the tongue, the pen, or on the stage. Dunbar's work as vernacular poet and lyricist for black minstrel shows sets the stage for *In Dahomey* and the rise of Bert Williams as an icon of the breaks in/from standardized representation achieved through a strategic use of blackface mimicry. In the final line of "We Wear the Mask" Dunbar repeats the phrase with an ironic and triumphalist exclamation point. This suggests that there was more to his use of minstrelsy than simple lamentation or protest, that there was perhaps more room behind the mask than visible to the naked eye or to the untuned ear.

Dunbar's poem echoes and parallels Du Bois's use of "double-consciousness" or the "veil" in "Of Our Spiritual Strivings," which appeared in the *Atlantic Monthly* in 1897: the same year as Dunbar's *Lyrics of Lowly Life*. This essay would be reprinted unchanged as the first essay in 1903's *The Souls of Black Folk*. Despite his aversion to minstrelsy, Du Bois's essay arguably depends on it as a metaphor for the renascent "soul": "It is a peculiar sensation, this double-consciousness, this sense of always looking at one's self through the eyes of others, of measuring one's soul by the tape of a world that looks on in amused contempt and pity."[49] Du Bois stages a cross-cultural encounter here that is structured by the racist white gaze but is given its emotional charge by the assumption that what that gaze is constructing is much less than the "truer self" which is being split into double by the epistemic violence of that very gaze.[50] Since what this white gaze is seeing is a fiction, this doubling features a split between a black mask produced by racist fantasy and an allegedly more authentic identity other to it or displaced by it, one that cannot be seen by the viewer. Neither can this allegedly "truer self" be properly seen by the subject of that gaze, since the black subject can only see "through the eyes of others," through the eyes of a white audience, one might say. This is a "witnessing" also of those white others, who themselves are being seen by the black subject as they watch, construct, and police that subject. Here the viewing black self knows precisely what the others are seeing and understands what motivates that "amused contempt and pity"; and it is a shared intimacy because both black and white subjects share this experience of "looking at" the black subject, albeit from radically different positions. And in Du Bois's aesthetics both black and white subjects share the fiction of "the Negro," though the former acknowledges it as such and the latter does not.

However, because of the black awareness—or presumption—of what lies behind the constructions of the white gaze, the black viewing self knows also what the others cannot see, what the mask hides. This is the gift/curse of double-consciousness and the core of both Du Bois's African American exceptionalism and his pan-Africanism. This scenario recalls also Bert Williams's own notion that "it was not until I was able to see myself as another person that my sense of humor developed." He would in fact base his humor on this very peculiar sensation. With Williams in mind, what is not obvious in this very performative context is how much the specularity of Du Bois's double-consciousness is dependent not just on minstrelsy but on a specifically black minstrelsy. Again, Du Bois's theorizing is one in which the black subject knows exactly what is being seen by the white gaze and recognizes it as being untrue, as less than "authentic," as a black mask. But though they may share the psychovisual experience of looking at "the Negro," the intimacy of shared knowledge cannot exist between the black spectator and the performer behind the mask if that performer is white. Obviously, the "self" here is "the Negro" gazing back at itself through the eyes of an audience torn between contempt and pity, but still clearly amused. Although dependent on minstrelsy, a *white* minstrel could not fit into this paradigm of specularity and masking called "double consciousness"; he would not be pitied or laughed at or mocked due to a shared acceptance of the buffoonery characteristic of the "real" identity beneath the mask.

In its very reversal of specularity, the black face behind the mask in Du Bois's scenario also differs from the bichromatic specularity of conventional minstrelsy in which whites watch and judge and create blacks. It is marked by a *prismatic* specularity in which the black subject looks at the white audience, refusing the static and passive position of traditional racial, visual, and political dynamics. This black subject watches the white audience looking not at an "authentic" black "soul" but at an ambivalent fiction that is rooted in white projections—hence the peculiarity of the sensation. However, because the "self" here in Du Bois's description is in fact truly black beneath the misreading and the racist projections that mask "him," this is nothing less than a vision of black minstrelsy: of a black subject trapped beneath the black mask constructed by generations of white racist representations of the black subject.

This form of specularity that can be located in double-consciousness is very close to what the anthropologist Michael Taussig calls a "Nervous System" in which "the interpreting self is itself grafted into the object of study. The self enters into the alter against which the self is defined and sustained."[51] Du Bois provides us with a reading of the colonial other as interpreting self, the black as primary subject though adrift in a system of meaning-making that is a painful simulacrum. It should be obvious at this point how very intimate

Bert Williams's work is with this, though the doubling operative in his claiming of interpretive spectatorship via an appropriation of both the "coon" and its "realness" is located simultaneously inside and outside American racial dynamics. But Du Bois provides a scenario in which black self-apprehension is not only perpetually displaced by the gaze of others but can only be acknowledged by grafting one's own interpretive schema onto that of the dominant, white other. Bert Williams's black minstrelsy was a form based on just this practice.

In the Land of Masking Jokers:
Performing Assimilation, Hiding in the Light

In the attempt to periodize a specifically African American modernism where masking, minstrelsy, and renascent self-consciousness are linked, both Du Bois's and Dunbar's work in 1897 have proven to be epochal. But in *Modernism and the Harlem Renaissance*, Houston Baker isolates 1895 as the year for his origin myth of a black modernism. The *New Negro* anthology would itself choose this year as the beginning of the Harlem Renaissance and bring together the two performers necessary for Baker's theorizing of minstrelsy, which is clearly indebted to Du Boisian double-consciousness: "The Negro renascence dates from about 1895 when two men, Paul Laurence Dunbar and Booker T. Washington, began to attract the world's attention."[52] In the anthology, William Stanley Brathwaite emphasized that as a figure of the "modern," Dunbar "expressed a folk temperament, but not a race soul. Dunbar was the end of a regime, and not the beginning of a tradition, as so many careless critics, both white and colored, seem to think."[53]

Rather than selecting Dunbar "as the quintessential herald of modernism in black expressive culture," as is often done, Baker selects the very specific date of September 15, 1895.[54] The year functions "as the commencement of African American modernism."[55] This is the date of Booker T. Washington's Atlanta Exposition address in which "Washington changed the minstrel joke by stepping inside the white world's nonsense syllables with oratorical mastery."[56] It must be emphasized that this commencement features a "stepping inside" or behind the "white world's" black mask much in the way that George Walker would see white minstrelsy as a performance mode in which whites were ultimately making themselves look ridiculous. Baker convincingly argues that Washington's speech was a performance in which the "sounds of the minstrel mask" were employed in a navigation of the threadbare line between resistance and compromise, between the reconstruction of a black self and the encapsulating forces of dehumanization that also employed the language of mimicry:

> A liberating manipulation of masks and a revolutionary renaming are not features commonly ascribed to the efforts of Booker T. Washington. Yet the narrator's clear awareness of the importance of such strategies appears at the very opening of *Up from Slavery*. What causes one to bracket (in an almost phenomenological manner) such liberating strategies is the way the narrator keeps culturally specific information hushed to a low register beneath his clamorous workings of the minstrel tradition.[57]

What is not clear is whether Baker is aware that Booker T. Washington held Bert Williams in awe after seeing him in New York during the 1907-9 run of *Bandana Land* and was moved to even write and publish those aforementioned essays in praise of him. One in the *Atlantic Monthly* of 1910 concludes with Washington proclaiming that, owing in part to his minstrel strategies of assimilation, "Bert Williams is a tremendous asset of the Negro race."[58] Baker does, however, connect the accommodationism—or the performance of accommodation—in Washington's vocal sounds to the tradition of black blackface minstrelsy of which Bert Williams was the virtuoso voice:

> Like Billy Kersands stretching the minstrel face to a successful black excess, or Bert Williams and George Walker converting nonsense sounds and awkwardly demeaning minstrel steps into pure kinesthetics and masterful black artistry, so Washington takes up types and tones of nonsense to earn a national reputation and its corollary benefits for the Afro-American masses.[59]

It is that "successful black excess" that demands an inclusion of Bert Williams into the histories of transatlantic modernism, situated in its complex and ever-shifting center. This form of excess builds on Jessie Fauset's description of Bert Williams's skill at performing not just a nonexistent "universal" Negro stereotype but local, specific, and international forms of vernacular blacknesses—in his penchant for black differences. Unlike Garvey and Du Bois, he made use of that black excess to make a strategy of self-evaporation—of hiding in plain sight—through plural masking rather than one of the assertive presence that characterizes the various political factions of the New Negro movement.

Significantly, the period delimited by Baker's gesture of inauguration is also the period in which Bert Williams began to find and lose his voice through blackface. It was 1895 when he wore the mask for the first time comfortably, having been in his first minstrel show "so gripped by stage fright that he never gave himself a chance to feel comfortable with black-face."[60] By 1898, after a few years on the carnival circuit, things changed. In his own words:

> I was all for parodies in those days. I would get hold of popular songbooks and write parodies on anything. They must have been pretty sad. At any rate, they never got me anything but experience. Then, one day at Moore's Won-derland in Detroit, just for a lark I blacked my face . . . Nobody was more surprised than I when it went like a house on fire. Then I began to find myself.[61]

1898 is also the year in which Williams and George Walker headed off to Chicago and then to New York where they began appearing in vaudeville shows like The Gold Bug by Victor Herbert, the well-known composer of Babes in Toyland. After settling in New York, Williams soon met the two men who would help make him and Walker famous: Will Marion Cook, one of the most important composers and cultural figures in the history of early African American musical theater, and, of course, Paul Laurence Dunbar. Dunbar may have been the "end of a regime" in his use of dialect just as Bert Williams may have been as a minstrel. Both of them felt trapped by the conventions of minstrelsy that had gained them great recognition, and, by dint of being trapped by those very conventions, both of them felt rejected by the subse-quent generations of African American literature and performance.

For Baker, it is the reclaiming of the black mask from the white min-strel tradition by a black performer that is the central move in a specific modernism:

> That mask is a space of habitation not only for repressed spirits of sexuality, ludic play, id satisfaction, castration anxiety, and a mirror stage of develop-ment, but also for that deep-seated denial of the indisputable humanity of inhabitants of and descendants from the continent of Africa. And it is, first and foremost, the mastery of the minstrel mask by blacks that constitutes a primary move in Afro-American discursive modernism.[62]

It is important to make a simple but necessary distinction that Baker does not make: not all black minstrels were motivated by the politics of Wil-liams and Walker and very few of them had as elaborate mechanisms of irony and reflection as the stars of In Dahomey. Certainly this caveat does not dis-miss Baker's greater point about the very claim on blackface itself regardless of motive. It is important to identify Williams's and Walker's own self-conscious attempts to erase the mask from behind it, since so many would forget this in the years after Williams's death. Williams and Walker would also erase that mask by stretching its meanings into dramatic spaces where too many different forms of "difference" existed and where no one mask could contain or represent what the audience expected. But despite being a product of yet another generation haunted by the minstrel mask, Baker touches on something that must be isolated and identified: the possibility that a white commitment to the play as the thing itself—to a one-to-one correspondence between signifier and signified, mask and face—could be exploited by blacks fully aware of the joke and empowered by that awareness.

Of course this last point is also a generational claim, one that the generation of Harlem's renaissance couldn't articulate in language, though it is there in practice and in the many uses of masking, passing, and veiling that characterize their poetics. They were too committed to the biocultural concept of "soul," which they assumed as the stability behind the mask and which was now renascent after having suffered too many years behind various imposed and imputed masks. Baker connects the minstrel to the trickster, a connection worth a good deal of consideration, knowing how both icons/strategies function in various black diaspora traditions. To bring these figures together cannot be done casually, though Baker is correct in doing so. However, he does not contend with the fact that the trickster figure cannot be claimed by any ideology or any emergent nationalism despite its foundation in a specific racial folklore or tradition of resistance. How can a trickster be on any political side? In short, Bert Williams's minstrel persona is as much a friend of "soul" as he is an enemy of it, as much a critic of white racism and supremacy as he bedevils the politics of assimilation and undoes the assumption of a "soul" behind the mask.

And here is Fanon once again from Black Skin, White Masks: "what is often called the black man's soul is a white man's artifact."[63] With all due respect to a thinker who was well aware of the "pitfalls of national" or nationalist consciousness, what is called black soul is also a reactionary black reconstruction: a doubled and darkened copy of that artifact. Keeping this in mind, with the coming to voice of an African American modernist sensibility it becomes clear that the "black man's soul" is claimed also within the "race" as cultural capital. Claimed and reclaimed from those who construct it externally, it thus becomes the most contested commodity within the diaspora itself. Yet these various attempts to identify, represent, and commodify "soul"—from Du Bois to Alain Locke to Berry Gordy—and the constant rejections of its "false" representations, only emphasize how dependent it is on the masks that represent it. Because it is attuned to the signifying traditions of the entire African dispersal, this modernism features a polyphony of masks—not the essentialist dream of pure flesh that motivates it. The minstrel figure as trickster threatens to undo all attempts to construct and maintain a consistent and foundationalist sense of "soul" by keeping masks perpetually alive and perpetually in motion.

But Houston Baker's point is worth underscoring: despite its dependence on Du Boisian aesthetics, an African American modernism does not emerge from the removal of the "false" face of white projections and the revelation of an intact subjectivity. To use a postcolonial cliché, this is not a modernism of plenitude revealed (despite the essentialist assumptions of the time) but one more closely related to that great modernist cliché: fragmentation. It is a modernism that emerges from the black mastery of white fantasy and the dissolution of that fantasy through that mastery. As a "primary move" this gesture is important to that moment when Bert Williams through language removes his mask onstage and articulates a voice which has a significant presence in American thought but very little history other than by being either interpellated as African American or marked as supplementally "other" to it. Although Baker's "sounding" of an African American modernism begins with the revealing of a mask through the wearing of another, Bert Williams's voice echoes far wider than that nation signified (and whittled down) by Baker's patently Americocentric analysis. It is a voice that also cannot be contained by Du Bois's double-consciousness, itself a condition of masking and unmasking, of veiling and unveiling, and certainly of speaking in (someone else's) tongue.

As Nathan Huggins points out, "Language—a symbol of civilization and social class—was another cloak of travesty for the stage Negro."[64] As an opportunity to articulate the hidden, forbidden, or taboo aspects and aspirations of an increasingly urban and industrial white America—to simultaneously criticize and celebrate the famed Protestant work ethic—minstrelsy required that the performer speak through dialect but more specifically speak it through the Negro's mouth. There was in fact a great fascination with the "stage Negro's" lips. By means of and exaggerated stage conventions, performers attempted to create the "illusion of cavernous mouths."[65] The Negro stereotype's reputation for its insatiable appetite—for food, for sex, for song—contributed to this fascination: "Blackface, whatever desire lay buried in the form, assaulted the people through whose mouths it claimed to speak."[66] With only a passing nod to what this suggests about capitalism, consumption, desire, and post-reconstruction-era fears about "the Negro's" coming to political "voice," suffice it to say that language was as much the space of "racial cross-dressing" as was the burnt-cork mask. The minstrel's penchant for malapropisms and his comical attempts to achieve language came in an era in which linguistic standardization was, as Michael North argues in *The Dialect of Modernism*, the key to a troubled American identity.[67] Linguistic standardization also guaranteed that that identity would be as racially and economically uninflected as possible. In this context, minstrelsy was the primary spectacle of linguistic and cultural differentiation as well as a threat to standardization and modernization with all its implications for massification. This was also the case globally, as Standard English became the marker of status, citizenship, and representation (in all senses of the word) throughout a colonial world shifting in its balance from Great Britain to the United States. Linguistic standardization allowed for "race," color, and class to shift, reverse, and often exchange positions in places like Jamaica, Trinidad, and other islands in the Caribbean where the relationship between social position, complexion, and dialect was perhaps more fraught than in the binary racial economy of North America.

As would later Caribbean moderns like Claude McKay, Eric Walrond, and the less well known playwright Eulalie Spence, Bert Williams took dialect much further than caricature because he had access to multiple black dialects. His performance also went beyond merely recuperating Standard English through the parodic negation of black folk speech. In his mouth, black dialect was the ground of self-conscious (versus "natural") parody and mimicry. It featured a high level of linguistic play that caused Booker T. Washington to write this of Williams's gift for language:

> As I have said, if I were a dramatic critic I might give some sound reasons for liking Bert Williams, but I suppose the best reason I can give for liking his quaint songs and humorous saying is that he puts into this form some of the quality and philosophy of the Negro race. In fact, it seems to me that Bert Williams has done for one side of the Negro life and character just what the old plantation Negroes did for another—given expression and put into a form which everyone can understand and appreciate something of the inner life and peculiar genius, if I may say so, of the Negro.[68]

Like most theater critics, Washington saw the dignity expressed not beneath but through the masquerade and recognized in Bert Williams's performance of dialect that great black modernist fetish/commodity: the "peculiar genius" of the race or Du Bois's "soul." On the surface it would seem that Bert Williams represented the "race" in accordance with Washington's own political views: "Bert Williams is a tremendous asset of the Negro race. . . . The fact is that the American people are ready to honor and to reward any man who does something that is worthwhile, no matter whether he is black or white, and Bert Williams's career is simply another illustration of that fact."[69] Rather than seeing the continued humiliation of African American people in the minstrel grotesquerie and rather than seeing the black face beneath the black mask as a sign of the greatest form of internalized racism and ritual self-immolation, the author of Up from Slavery saw "the quality and philosophy of the Negro race." For Washington, this could only mean one thing: his interpretation of Bert Williams's stage persona finds in it that accommodationism that Du Bois will describe not as modern but as antebellum.

Despite his own fears and hostilities toward the "old plantation Negro" and the ritualized remembering of that icon that was minstrelsy, even Du Bois himself was able to find some value in the specific mask of Bert Williams. Upon the comedian's death, the leader of the Talented Tenth wrote:

> When in the calm afterday of thought and struggle to racial peace we look back to pay tribute to those who helped most, we shall single out for highest praise those who made the world laugh; Bob Cole, Ernest Hogan, George Walker, and above all, Bert Williams.
>
> For this was not mere laughing: it was the smile that hovered above blood and tragedy; the light mask of happiness that hid breaking hearts and bitter souls. This is the top of bravery; the finest thing in service.
>
> May the world long honor the undying fame of Bert Williams as a great comedian, a great Negro, a great man.[70]

Alongside James Weldon Johnson and his brother Rosamund, Bob Cole was the co-writer of songs like the Tin Pan Alley hits "Under the Bamboo Tree" and "The Congo Love Song"; he was also the producer of the first show to have been organized, produced, performed, and written by African Americans—A Trip to Coontown (1898). Ernest Hogan was responsible for the Georgia Minstrels and in his blackface performance was known for his ability to consume watermelons in the most grotesque and extreme ways. He is perhaps most infamous for having written one of the most popular songs of the 1890s, "All Coons Look Alike to Me," a song that introduced the phenomenon of "coon songs" into American theater and popular culture. His song

"Won't You Come Home Bill Bailey" is an American classic. This brief sketch of authors praised for their "service" to the racial struggle alongside Williams and Walker should serve to show just how crucial black minstrel travesty was to even Washington's fiercest opponent. It should now be obvious how much of Du Bois's tribute to Williams and black minstrelsy depends on a notion of double-consciousness. The burnt-cork mask functions as the "veil": the smile hovering "above blood and tragedy," the "mask of happiness" covering or shielding "breaking hearts and bitter souls." Here masking is considered bravery, just as minstrelsy is considered activism.

For Williams, Booker T. Washington's praise was no doubt important. He had always been clear about his desire to "carry the words of Tuskegee Institute to every village and hamlet and into every home, white or black."[71] Washington's essay, however, allows for a creative confusion between Bert Williams and his minstrel persona. He proclaims Williams's humor to be "the real thing" and celebrates the lack of the militancy usually attributed to his darker-skinned partner George Walker:[72]

> During all the years I have known Bert Williams I have never heard him whine or cry about his color, or about any racial discrimination. He has gone right on, in season and out of season, doing his job, perfecting himself in his work, till he has reached the top round in his specialty.[73]

Yet the only encounters with Bert Williams that Washington reports—despite knowing him for years—are from a distance:

> I have noticed him standing about in a barber shop or among a crowd of ordinary colored people, the quietest man in the whole gathering. All the time, however, he was studying and observing, enjoying the characters that he was around and getting material for some of those quaint songs and stories in which he reproduces the natural humor and philosophy of the Negro people.[74]

Even though Bert Williams represents in Washington's view the "inner life" of the Negro that is so much the concern of the writers of the Harlem Renaissance, there is a sense that he is still onstage here, silently witnessing the performance around him, silently performing the "natural humor and philosophy of the Negro people" *for* the Negro people; or to be more precise, he is performing an assimilated African American persona for this particular African American spectator. This description depicts Williams as being as much an outsider as his stage persona: invisible while without blackface, publicly wearing the mask that he wore beneath burnt cork. Despite being fully aware of Bert Williams's cultural difference, in Washington's view the mask here seems to have grown into a new skin as the black immigrant finds himself absorbed into the norms and expectations of a universalized African American self-image.

In reflecting on Williams's humor, Washington read the minstrel mask as both studied and natural, as both performance and pure expression:

> There is nothing second-hand or second-rate about it. His fun seems to flow spontaneously and without effort, as if it came from some deep natural source in the man himself. Besides, there is a quality and flavor about Williams's humor which indicates that it is the natural expression of a thoughtful and observing mind.[75]

Here the stress on "the natural" is meant to argue against the dominant colonial model of mimicry, which establishes repetition as second-order creativity, mimesis as a sign of inferiority. At the same time it is obviously meant to ennoble this act of mimetic performance by removing it from that sphere of "natural" creativity that in a racist cultural logic is also thought to be without intellectual foundation and to exist purely in the realm of instinct. So for Washington the category of "the natural" was—as it was for Williams and Walker themselves—something that existed between essence and performance, something that could encapsulate both however clumsily. Yet the forced and clumsy elasticity of the category of "the natural" in the essay is generated by that very space between Washington and Williams. This is a space indistinguishable from the space between audience and actor—again, Bert Williams is performing for Washington, and is still in makeup despite the absence of burnt cork. This is not simply to suggest that Washington was "fooled" by Bert Williams or that he missed the point of Williams's performance; it is to suggest that there is no sense of Bert Williams existing off-stage, and that may in fact be the point and the tragedy of who Bert Williams was as a West Indian performer in a context defined by the presence and the suffering and the poetics of African Americans. Anyone who read and heard his performance of the African American "Negro" as having anything to do with who or what he naturally was, was being bamboozled by their own desires for a consolidated and transcendental African American image, discourse, and cultural politics. In an article in *Green Book Magazine* Bert Williams responded to Washington's praise. He adds an interesting note further complicating Washington's attempt to essentialize his performance in order to safeguard it from the colonial model of mimicry as second-hand, inferior replication. However flattered he was by Washington, he writes, "I am a successor, not an originator."[76]

All of this maneuvering around Williams and his mask merely reveals something in Washington's own politics, something that Houston Baker forces us to consider: accommodationism is itself a form of performance and, by extension, assimilation requires some form of minstrelsy. Indeed, even other blacks can be fooled by this kaleidoscopic condition of plural masking and relentless racial performances. Certainly Williams fools the subsequent generation of black culture-producers who read the mask but not the complex spaces behind it. As suggested by Baker's portrait of Booker T. Washington himself, some alternative intention exists grinning behind the accommodationist mask. It is this same thing that Locke discovers as he reflects back on "George" and "the Colonel." According to Baker, Washington himself takes on a black minstrel persona in order to speak to power in a subversively forked tongue. Like Williams, he uses the dialect as a strategy of diversion enabled by the double-voicedness of black signifying—saying one thing to mean another, using language as a form of diversion, masquerade. However, what is being said outside of and against a "double voicedness" or a double-consciousness rooted in the bichromatism of American race relationships is another matter entirely.

In "Change the Joke and Slip the Yoke" (1958), Ralph Ellison daringly critiques minstrelsy while simultaneously claiming it as a strategic possibility for a resistant, "bottom-up" American folklore. This essay is important as a generational marker because, as William J. Mahar has written, the 1960s were "a decade that marked the appearance of the first strongly negative appraisals of blackface comedy."[77] For the purposes of this study, Ellison's essay will mark the far limit of the minstrel/modernism continuum as it inches toward an alleged postmodernism. Baker's situating of Booker T. Washington's Atlanta Exposition address can then function alongside Bert Williams's discovery of his tragic genius through blackface as the earlier limits of this necessarily arbitrary origin myth of multiple modernisms.

As evidenced by Williams's obituary in The Messenger discussed earlier, negative appraisals of minstrelsy were hardly a Civil Rights–era product. This is evident in the negative feedback that Williams and Walker often generated from the progressive and radical black press, and also evident in the fact that despite their popularity in the African American social world, black minstrels

fully acknowledged that they were doing something politically and psycholog-
ically dangerous. They were engaging a form and a forum that alienated many
blacks, one which, before the black appropriation of the form, had always
been more than slightly offensive despite its ability to produce complex modes
of pleasure for even those who were the erstwhile subjects of its buffoonery.
But Mahar is correct to draw a generational line between an earlier set of
appraisals that ranged from the positive to the mixed and a later tradition of
thinking which was decidedly negative. He is wrong, though, to place Ellison
squarely in the latter tradition, as Ellison's take on blackface as folklore is
infinitely more complicated than that of his rising generation. As would be
the case for subsequent generations of black and white writers, thinkers,
scholars, and nonscholars, Ellison focuses exclusively on the function of
blackface within a bichromatic and masculinist socioeconomic order and
locates its value in an almost primordial American "ritual of exorcism" where
the black mask "was an inseparable part of the national iconography."[78]

The language of ritual is crucial here. This language links Ellison to the
kind of exploration of Caribbean carnival that characterizes the work of
Caribbean thinkers, most notably Wilson Harris, for whom masking is a
"dialogue" and an "imaginative necessity and strategy that engages word,
mask, dance and space within the cross-cultural mind of our age."[79] It also
precedes the work of Houston Baker, which builds on Ellison in its use of the
language of theater and ritual in the context of emergent yet fluid American
identities. *Modernism and the Harlem Renaissance* also draws on Ellison's seminal essay equating the minstrel and the trickster, though Ellison was more
aware of the political ambiguity and ambivalence of this figure than Baker,
who attempts to corral the trickster for certain liberationist aims. Despite
its national specificity, Ellison's essay does enable a reading of minstrelsy
against a broader postcolonial landscape than the one provided by Baker or
most histories and explorations of minstrelsy that find it hard to go beyond
the plantation of an American context. Ellison provides an interpretation of
blackface masquerade that is well suited to the Williams and Walker shows,
since they did engage issues of colonization and American imperialism while
also juggling the still necessary Jim Crow/plantation stereotypes.

"For the ex-colonials," Ellison writes, "the declaration of an American
identity meant the assumption of a mask, and it imposed not only the disci-
pline of national self-consciousness, it gave Americans an ironic awareness of
the joke that always lies between appearance and reality, between the disconti-
nuity of social tradition and that sense of the past which clings to the mind."[80]
Here minstrelsy functions as a postcolonial American theater which ritualizes

through race and the performance of the black vernacular the tensions of national birth. Even in his critique of the racism of the tradition and its implicit historical and symbolic violence, Ellison accepts it as an indigenous American form rather than rejecting it as simply an aberration. Yet the essay does not claim minstrelsy as African American theater, despite the awareness of a postcolonial context and the presence of black skins under black masks:

> Social changes occurring since the 1930's have made for certain modifica-
> tions . . . but the mask, stylized and iconic, was once required of anyone who
> would act the role—even those Negroes whose natural coloration should, for
> any less ritualistic purposes at least, have made it unnecessary.
>
> Nor does the role, which makes use of Negro idiom, songs, dance mo-
> tifs and word-play, grow out of the Negro American sense of the comic
> (although we too have our comedy of blackness), but out of the white Ameri-
> can's Manichean fascination with the symbolism of blackness and white-
> ness expressed such contradictions as the conflict between the white Ameri-
> can's Judeo-Christian morality, his democratic political ideals and his daily
> conduct—indeed in his general anti-tragic approach to experience.[81]

Again, Ellison is writing a generation after the Harlem Renaissance. His is the generation of Civil Rights assimilationism, which was as threatened by the minstrel mask as were the New Negroes, but its members were perhaps less obsessed with masking themselves with symbols of "Africa" than their immediate children would be: those of the "Black Power" generation. Yet the significance of this passage is in Ellison's definition of minstrel theater as an indigenous form that emerges not from African American culture but from white America's racial fascinations and fears and its ambivalence toward its rhetoric and its sociocultural and economic realities; between its mask and the skin of its possibilities. As such, blackface could become the ripe ground for black appropriation and engagement even for those Negroes who would "act the role" despite the seeming redundancy of their natural coloration.

Bert Williams, though, along with George Walker, had already claimed minstrelsy as an African American form by redefining it as something other to the tradition and to the meanings that Ellison critiques. In an essay entitled "The Negro on Stage" written in 1910, Bert Williams proclaimed:

> Our race has taken root upon this soil; after two hundred years of struggle
> upward, we may be apart here, but not alien. And I firmly believe that we have
> contributed our share to American entertainment. . . .
>
> The one new stage form which has been developed in this country is of

plantation origin; I refer, of course, to minstrelsy. The only music that may
be regarded as typically American music is Negro music.[82]

In reflecting on the preponderance of ethnic caricatures and racist stereotypes on the American stage, he wrote: "My observation has led me to the
theory that when a strange unassimilated element exists in a nation, it almost
immediately finds its way to the stage in comic types, usually caricatures."[83]
These "unassimilated elements" are often no more or less than immigrants,
newly added to the "carnival dialogue" that Wilson Harris argues is a painful
but necessary product of the shock of cross-cultural encounter. The mask,
therefore, functions in relation to America's impending global hegemony
which is a greater concern for the generation of modernism than for the
generation of reconstruction and is a great concern for a performer like Bert
Williams who was intimately aware of America's global reach. Harlem, after
all, was the modern/ist home of immigrants and the new victims and products of American imperialism. Homi Bhabha puts it this way: "If colonialism
takes power in the name of history, it repeatedly exercises its authority
through the figures of farce."[84] Minstrelsy is that "farce," that painful joke at
the center of the impending American sprawl which is produced by the
tensions between the mask of democracy and the denial of it that lays on the
surface of the skin beneath.

However, in Williams's case the "joke" is particularly hard to discern in an
oeuvre defined by a placeless-ness and a melancholia that had more in common with the "transcendental homelessness" of high modernism or the postcolonial malaise of exile that is more common today. Perhaps a more helpful
term in this case is the "ambivalence" that Bhabha locates at the nexus of
colonialism, mimicry, and resistance. This "ambivalence" locates in the colonial stereotype a form of cultural engagement possible through a "bottom up"
parodic repetition, which destabilizes the authority of colonial power. Ellison,
of course, is no stranger to the fetishization of ambivalence as the dominant
sensibility in America's game of race. Despite his insistence on reading minstrel masking as primarily white, Ellison also generalizes the mask in such a
way as to highlight its ambivalence and emphasize how its use is a defining
facet of American history as well as its social and cultural relations:

> Here the "darky" act makes brothers of us all. America is a land of masking
> jokers. We wear the mask for purposes of aggression as well as for defense;
> when we are projecting the future and preserving the past. In short, the
> motives hidden behind the mask are as numerous as the ambiguities the
> mask conceals.[85]

This stressing of ambiguity works against the simplistic reading of blackface as that which would "veil the humanity of Negroes thus reduced to a sign" because of those ambiguous signifying possibilities that had already been mapped and claimed from within by Williams and Walker, but also by Paul Laurence Dunbar, Ada Overton Walker, and others.[86] It is significant that Ellison here points out just how much ambivalence and ambiguity exists behind as well as in front of the strategic mask. In identifying the black mask as an essential part of the national iconography, Ellison finds ambivalence, ambiguity, and mimicry defining a common heritage in which cross-cultural performance is a prerequisite for citizenship.

Bert Williams's burnt-cork mask is an even more complex icon of race and national ambivalence because his use of mimicry bears a distinct, more critical relationship to the emergent national self-consciousness of African Americans than does the masquerade of, say, Eddie Cantor or Al Jolson or even African American minstrels like Ernest Hogan and Billy Kersands. During the early decades of the twentieth century the question of which "nation" or community he "represented" was no doubt increasingly difficult to answer. Was it racist America and the impossible necessity of assimilation? Was it the "Negro race" as constructed by way of Booker T. Washington's accommodationism or one more in line with Du Boisian assimilationism, or even pan-Africanism? Could he have been at home in Garvey's mythical "Africa," or within the dwindling boundaries of the British Empire that so many Caribbean immigrants still clung to despite their years in Yankeedom? Was it one based on the bourgeois assimilationism of the black middle classes, or the urban primitivism of its children which was in no small part inspired by plays like In Dahomey? Despite the movement toward racial consolidation in the African American cultural politics of the time, the diversity of the black community was becoming great enough to constantly threaten that very movement. In this case Bert Williams's presence and persona addressed the unsettled profusion of masks produced by an increasingly fragmented black community as well as a violently racist status quo. And it is clear that this black appropriation of an already ambiguous and ambivalent image of race and nation also addressed specific intra-racial ambiguities and ambivalences and fears. Indeed the black minstrel threatened this consolidation, particularly since it was driven by puritanical, bourgeois values and by the chromatic and social hierarchies of the Talented Tenth, which demanded a kind of cultural, self-policing that would feed and strengthen the ludic chaos of the "darky's" appeal.

CHAPTER 3 Theorizing Black-on-Black Cross-Culturality

Perhaps the best way to frame and conceptualize the intricate position of West Indian immigrants in relationship to the cultural explosion of the Harlem Renaissance is to make use of a phenomenon known to naturalists. This sudden dependence on "the natural" is reminiscent of—and authorized by—Houston Baker's own ironic turn to zoology in *Modernism and the Harlem Renaissance*. One could also find it in Ralph Ellison's famed essay "On Bird, Bird-Watching and Jazz" as he uses the mimicry of both the goldfinch and the mockingbird to explore the translation/transformation of vernacular jazz styles in African American folk culture.[1] Baker's dependence on "nature" is the most ironic not only because it is a turn to biology while attempting to argue for forms of racial performance but also because it is a study of race based primarily on the study of primates. All this while historicizing an intellectual climate dominated by social Darwinists like Herbert Spencer and Edgar Rice Burroughs, famed author of *Tarzan of the Apes* (1914).

Such racist primitivism is parallel to the romantic primitivism and "pseudo-Africanisms" of the radical modernist avant-garde but will find its most monolithic popular expression in a film like *King Kong* in 1933.[2] One could perversely read *King Kong* as American popular culture's response to all forms of New Negro assertion and resistance in the preceding two decades. In it, the hyper-white Faye Wray obviously stands in for a gendered idealization of America. Through her, the hyper-masculinized black ape's political quest for an abstract freedom becomes reduced to a much less abstract ideology of lust for that ideal. Kong's death on the streets of New York elicits sympathy, for, like so many, he was an immigrant, albeit one forcibly brought in chains to the United States, physically different from other beings in his host country, and whose dialect was not only unreadable but bestial. Just before he falls to the base of the Empire State Building, there is an iconic moment. He poses with one arm up to grapple at the airplanes shooting at him; with the other, he clutches at the top of the indomitable skyscraper, a sign of American financial and imperial power. It is a critical moment, because in it he seems to mimic the Statue of Liberty, becoming for a split second the perverse shadow of a freedom denied.

A Tale of Spiders and Monkeys

For Houston Baker to ground his history of racial signifying via the complex history and trope of the ape forces a rehearing of "nature" outside the dominant tradition of racism in which the ape was merely "the Negro" without the mask of civility and without those uppity aspirations to literacy and political enfranchisement. The ape was the Negro unmasked, motivated by lust and desire. He—and the ape always signified the black male—was a danger to social order as well as a sign of forbidden, primal desire. But the ape was the Negro also because he elicited some vague sympathy or perhaps guilt, given his anthropomorphism, his vague and in Freudian terms "uncanny" semblance to humanity, or perhaps simply his accidental mimicry of mankind. Indeed, the scientific notion that apes had a special evolutionary relationship to humans and the fact that they often seemed to make claims on that relationship of similarity by mimicking human behavior are also behind the turn-of-the-century obsession with primates. The various attempts to control and repress the ape are all motivated on some level by a flitter of recognition, a frightful symmetry. Most importantly, Baker's turn to nature forces a hearing of nature not as the stable pole of representation—"the real" or the "organic"—but rather as the primordial site of mimicry, replication, reproduction, and artifice.

Relying upon the work of the zoologist H. B. Cott, Baker identifies two forms of natural mimicry of use to his New Negro sounding. The first is "allaesthetic," which Cott describes thus: "the phenomena fall broadly into three main categories—namely, concealment, disguise, and advertisement; on the functional side, these elusive, deceptive or attractive features are variously concerned with other organisms of the habitat—whether predators or prey, mates or rivals, parents or offspring."[3] Baker defines allaesthetic characteristics as "biological masks—elusive constellations designed to enhance inclusive fitness" and describes as an example the praying mantis "as an insect whose 'allaesthetic' characteristics allow it to master the form of the green stalk so completely that predators—at a distance, and even close at hand—cannot distinguish its edibility."[4] As entomologists would point out, certain spiders also perform in this way; some of these "kleptoparasitic" spiders will go so far as to live in the web of a larger species of spider, moving synchronously unseen with the larger spider in order either to steal its food or to avoid being identified as vulnerable prey. The distinction between predators "at a distance" and predators "close at hand" will take on a more interesting resonance in the context of the West Indian immigrant community's relationship to both the dominant white American society and the African American culture. Also, the term "kleptoparasitic" in its very sound suggests the justification for the anti-immigrant/anti-foreigner discourses that some segments of the African American community participated in during this period—the immigrant as thief and parasite, or as economic threat when resources are threatened within the always present and much larger web of a racist capital.

The second form of mimicry adapted by Baker comes from Colin Groves in his study of gorillas' response to human predation. Rather than strategically disappearing into the landscape as does the praying mantis, the gorilla takes recourse in the world of noise: moving, shaking, leaping, gesticulating, running back and forth over a fixed space, rearing up and back, thumping, and leaping on the ground. Cott calls this form of display "phaneric" and Baker employs it thus: "Rather than concealing or disguising in the manner of the cryptic mask (a colorful mastery of codes), the phaneric mask is meant to advertise. It distinguishes rather than conceals. It secures territorial advantage and heightens a group's survival possibilities."[5] In other words, the phaneric is reminiscent of dialect when deployed for spectacular identitarian purposes. Regrettably, Baker (and perhaps Groves) does not tell us if there are differential gender dynamics involved in phaneric display; from the perspective of human society, such display does seem stereotypically male. This display as described by Groves and creatively appropriated by Baker could be called a kinesthetic masking, where disguise depends on motion, gestures, and performance rather than on a mimetic representation of the image.

Through this discourse of "nature" Baker ultimately reifies the discursive position of the African American majority minority. This is audible in his primary interest in sounding "national" books and "American" possibilities through race despite the presence of non-African American black transnationals like Marcus Garvey, Claude McKay, Bert Williams, and the Nigerian/British pop singer Sade in his text. But overall one can't help but draw a distinction between "allaesthetic" and "phaneric" that sounds like the distinction between assimilation and separation; the former blends and threatens to disappear and the latter distinguishes and insists on distinctiveness. This also sounds like a distinction, very crudely put, between Du Bois and Garvey, each of whom was a performer in his own right. Of course, none of this is to suggest that both sides of this dialectic were discrete and did not share characteristics; clearly Du Bois was no advocate of bleaching the "Negro soul in a flood of white Americanism," just as Garvey's separatism did feature a strong case of white empire envy and a strident mimicry of its methodologies of racial and cultural separatism.[6] And despite the open hostility between the two leaders, the former's sense of assimilation included a stress on black "difference" where the latter's separatism also was rooted in a perhaps more romanticized notion of Africa as the pole of ultimate representative similarity. This African exceptionalism (or "fundamentalism," to signify on Tony Martin's term for Garveyism) did not prevent Garvey from mobilizing the biases of his day in which continental Africans were seen as "backwards" and primitive.[7] In both his and Du Bois's imagination, Africans were in dire need of Western black "missionaries of culture," as Du Bois would have it, to provide a benevolent colonialism to replace that of the white West.[8]

Yet the strategies both used were in a sense divided along allaesthetic and phaneric lines with the middle-class advocates of black assimilation claiming a gradualist approach, blending into the mainstream, while Garveyite nationalism expressed itself in parades, costumes, ceremony, ritual, color, and flash. The latter's dependence on the phaneric is clearly why Du Bois was able to describe Garvey and the UNIA as a little more than a coon show. His physical description of Garvey itself rings with quasi-Darwinist terms: again, "A little, fat black man, ugly, but with intelligent eyes and a big head." Garvey responded to this in the Negro World, making it clear that the description indeed depended on traditional stereotypes of blacks, which likened them to primates. In the not-too-cagily entitled response-essay "W. W. BURGHARDT DU BOIS AS A HATER OF DARK PEOPLE," Du Bois is described as a Negro "misleader" who "Calls His Own Race 'Black and Ugly,' Judging From the White Man's Standard of Beauty."[9] For Garvey this description "is typical of the African" and only strengthened his claim to blood-purity, "nature," and therefore a transnational cultural and political authority.[10]

Du Bois's essay "Back to Africa" also depends more explicitly on the trope of the ape in reference to Garvey's histrionics. It establishes a subtle cultural difference between the "black folk" that Du Bois represents and the puerile performance of this similarly black but culturally othered community which shared its fragile web as well as its problematic claims to blood: "many American Negroes and some others were scandalized by something which they could but regard as simply child's play. It seemed to them sinister, this enthroning of a demagogue, a blatant boaster, who with monkey-shines was deluding the people and taking their hard-earned dollars; and in High Harlem there rose an insistent cry, 'Garvey Must Go!'"[11] In light of Baker's reclamation of apes and primates and despite being clearly dismissive in Du Bois's usage, the term "monkey-shines" can be employed to explore the two signifying traditions at work when discussing West Indian and African American folk-based urban cultures in this period. Monkey-shines is also a description of the trickster function, the behavior of the "signifyin(g) monkey" that Henry Louis Gates will argue as the primary (if not primal) figure of black vernacular language use in a fraught and politically imbalanced context. Yet since cultural if not racial difference is the primary tension at work, what must also be kept in mind is the presence of the kleptoparasitic spider that is an imported (or immigrant) Anansi, another trickster figure here dwelling in a web not of its own creation. Garvey's response to Du Bois's own "monkey-shines" features his own participation in ethnic pseudoscience: because Du Bois celebrated his own hybridity, being "a little Dutch, a little French, and a little Negro," the UNIA article concludes that due to this blood-mixing "the man is a monstrosity."[12]

But the description of Garvey as clown, charlatan, minstrel, or as masquerade artist does not derive simply from Du Bois's rancor : it runs throughout the entire period of his presence upon the Harlem stage. In 1922, the year he published *Harlem Shadows*, Garvey's fellow Jamaican Claude McKay said of Garvey's penchant for phaneric performance: "Garvey's arrest by the Federal authorities after five years of stupendous vaudeville is a fitting climax."[13] And in 1937 the sharp-witted and ever-controversial George Schuyler would reflect back on "the halcyon days of race racketeering, when the Hon. Marcus Garvey rode through Harlem's yokel-banked canyons arrayed like an Oxford don" at the head of his "comic opera movement."[14] In his 1940 *Harlem: Negro Metropolis*, McKay goes so far as to describe Garvey as a carnival showman, a voodoo priest, a magician, and a huckster. In his words, Garvey "bewitched" his audience with "gaudy paraphernalia":[15]

> The movement of Marcus Garvey in Harlem was glorious with romance and riotous, clashing emotions. Like the wise men of the ancient world, this peacock-parading Negro of the New World, hoodooed by the "Negromancy" of Africa, followed a star—a Black Star. A weaver of dreams, he translated into a fantastic pattern of reality the gaudy strands of the vicarious desires of the submerged members of the Negro race.[16]

McKay's tone is ambivalent in this text, shifting between a mockery of Garvey and a deep respect for the man's ability to use the strategies and tools of popular theater toward political empowerment and both antiracist and anti-colonial forms of resistance. In light of McKay's well-known antipathy for what he felt to be the staid, alienated, and effete world of the African American intelligentsia, Garvey's colorful noise was a welcome though doomed explosion. Even the radically unsentimental Schuyler would admit a similar nostalgia: "he furnishes a note of humor and ridiculousness in a world that is worried and blue. And on the other hand his weird and grandiose schemes and pronouncements are as an island of glamour in a sea of practicality."[17]

"Island," versus "a sea," "humor and ridiculousness" versus "practicality," or perhaps pragmatism; this is a curious description of an imported, phaneric explosion amid the rigidly defined context of an African American social world; a crucial series of symbolic connections to deploy against a West Indian Anansi in the larger flow of an American modernism that felt itself divided along bichromatic lines. Indeed, throughout his entire book on the panorama of Harlem, McKay consistently describes the entire Harlem Renaissance period as a "carnival" with Garvey's particular masquerade being just the grandest of many.[18] Although he does not specifically identify the vaudeville stage or minstrelsy per se, Eric Walrond describes the UNIA in a by-then familiar way:

> Garvey creates a fairy dream world. . . . Aping the English royalty, he manu-factures out of black peasants of the lower domestic class dukes and duch-esses, princes and princesses. . . .
>
> All the glamour, all the techniques of delusion, is employed to satisfy the

craving for this other thing which is missing in the lives of these long-repressed peasant folk. Essentially a movement of the black proletariat, Garveyism owes its strength largely to jangling swords and flaming helmets, titles and congeries of gold braid.[19]

For this Caribbean writer whose earliest literary efforts were published in *The Negro World*, all of Garvey's political acts were delivered for "theatrical effect."[20]

Assaults on Garvey's penchant for costuming and public performance were so common, so relentless, that in her *Garvey and Garveyism*, his second wife, Amy Jacques Garvey, felt moved to defend and explain what was being misunderstood:

> Failing serious criticism of Garvey, his flea-like rivals took to calling him "a clown strutting around in gaudy uniforms." The facts are that all the members of the Executive Council of the U.N.I.A. wore academic gowns at special mass meetings and in parade only. The Potentate, and the Provisional President of Africa (Garvey) had uniforms with matching hats; the Potentate's was more elaborate than Garvey's as he was higher in rank. These were full-dress uniforms and only worn in parades, and at the opening of conventions. . . .
>
> The wearing of uniforms and robes of office by Garvey-ites had a deep significance and psychological effect. Had Garvey landed in Africa he would have discarded the uniform and European attire for tribal gowns, to become a part of the masses, and thus impress them, while satisfying his inner longing for Africanization.[21]

That the "inner longing for Africanization" could be sated by wearing the clothes of continental Africans is a curious idea and causes one to wonder what "inner longing" was being served by the often gaudy pomp and circumstance of Garvey's paramilitary and quasi-academic masquerade. A longing for power seems obvious, and Schuyler satirized it in his mid-to-late 1930s tales from the Pittsburgh *Courier* that would be collected as *Black Empire*. However in 1901 Williams and Walker would make this longing the very core of their history-making show *In Dahomey* via a painful satire. In their performance as in Schuyler's pulp fictions—as well as in his 1931 critique of the African American colonization of Liberia, *Slaves Today*—it is revealed as an aspiration so overwhelming that in its expression it cannot help but burlesque the displays of wealth and power typical of great Western nations. In *In Dahomey* as in Schuyler, this "inner longing" quickly transcends the desire for equality and enters a sphere of malevolent mimicry, where the worst of one's oppression become embraced as the sign of one's freedom attained. Yet despite consistently being described as a P. T. Barnum–like huckster or a magician or even a mimic who apes white colonial power, Garvey used the trope of vaudeville and black minstrelsy to ground his own dependence on the pseudoscience of blood. In critiquing the political authority and authenticity of Du Bois and the NAACP, his response-article to Du Bois's "Back to Africa" argues of Du Bois, "Anything that is black, to him, is hideous, is monstrous, and this is why in 1917 he had but the lightest of colored people in his office, when one could hardly tell whether it was a white show or a colored vaudeville he was running at fifth avenue."[22]

In his wonderful essay "Making Noise: Marcus Garvey, Dada, August 1922," the esteemed Garvey scholar Robert Hill (editor of both the Marcus Garvey papers and the pulp fictions of George Schuyler) brings together the connections between phaneric noise, dada aesthetics, Caribbean immigration, cross-cultural display, and militant spectacle. Hill describes Garvey as a man "given to enigmatic twists, dazzling histrionics mixed with constant role-playing."[23] This description of Garvey as "a consummate showman" reads his masquerade politics as a sign of cunning and guile rather than as an example of the country-bumpkin charlatanry that both Du Bois and McKay explicitly intend despite their respect for Garvey's accomplishments.[24] For Hill, Garvey's self-conscious performance, his masking, was a crucial element in his popular pan-Africanism and key to its enduring success. What is perhaps most important about Hill's essay is that he argues that this phaneric display is itself specifically cultural; not "black" but Afro-Caribbean. He reads it as an example of how the carnival complex emerges within the American and African American context much in the way that Bert Williams's minstrelsy represents the collusive presence of carnival masking before and during the Harlem Renaissance:

> The UNIA's parades embodied a powerful element of burlesque, although it has proved difficult for commentators alien to the folk culture of the Caribbean to appreciate them. Participants within the movement were not so handicapped. In the Negro World's description of the opening of the 1921 convention, for example, the writer asserts that he saw "the Potentate riding in his auto looking like an emperor, the Chaplain General looking like a Pope, the President General like a king, the American leader like a cardinal and the International Organizer like a queen." He could have been describing the ensemble of monarchical elements that go to make up West Indian

masquerade, except that here the parade was occurring in the United States and in the service of a social movement.[25]

In 1940, reflecting on the Garvey movement, C. L. R. James would suggest the very same thing about the origins of Garvey's penchant for masquerade: "His array of baronets, etc., with himself as Emperor of Africa was a hangover from his early life in the West Indies."[26] This very insight is available in Du Bois's "Back to Africa," though with much less sympathy for pageantry and unable to deconstruct the cultural and political assumptions of his own NAACP—clearly a "sea of practicality"—via the "comic opera" of the UNIA. What Du Bois mocks as childish spectacle, Hill reads as Bakhtinian subversion rooted in a West Indian cultural context. An awareness of these intra-racial, cross-cultural political differences is present in Du Bois's representation of the "American Negroes" in their encounter with a Garveyite spectacle that threatens their assumptions of racial universality and cultural power. The threat it presents is diminished through laughter—that well-known method of mistranslating critique into travesty, difference into error, signifyin(g) into noise. But the threat here makes evident a context of competing cultural nationalisms and competing traditions of signifying within the same socio-economic space—kleptoparasitism at work.

The threat of internal black cultural otherness can also been seen in how the global dimension of racial struggle functioned in Du Bois's mind at that point in his complex evolution. This was after all a man whose trajectory was long and multifaceted, a man whose turn to Marxism and a more self-critical pan-Africanism was decades away. In this moment, Garvey and his penchant for phaneric spectacle forced a crucial admission from him:

> His reasoning was at first new and inexplicable to Americans because he brought to the United States a new Negro problem. We think of our problem here as the Negro problem, but we know more or less clearly that the problem of the American Negro is very different from the problem of the South African Negro or the problem of the Nigerian Negro or the problem of the South American Negro. We have not hitherto been so clear as to the way in which the problem of the Negro in the United States differs from the problem of the Negro in the West Indies. For a long time we have been told, and we have believed, that the race problem in the West Indies, and particularly in Jamaica, has virtually been settled.[27]

Without spending too much time on the erroneous notion that the Jamaican Negro problem had "virtually been settled" in 1923, the year this essay was published, it is worth returning briefly to Du Bois's essay-report of his 1915 visit to Jamaica. Here he claims that "for the first time in my life I lived beyond the color line—not on one side of it but beyond its end."[28] Despite Jamaica's being poverty-stricken and utterly exploited by Europe and increasingly by America, Du Bois discovers its specific gift to the world, "the gift of racial peace, the utter overturning of the barbaric war of color."[29] The fact that someone as visually and aurally as loud as Garvey could come from such a world could mean one of two things: that Du Bois's assumptions about the Caribbean (hence the globe) were incorrect, or that Garvey was simply a lunatic since his homeland was in fact such a racial utopia. Indeed, a year later Du Bois would write another essay on Garvey, "A Lunatic or a Traitor," in which he concludes by saying that Garvey "should be locked up or sent home."[30]

Winston James "places" Du Bois's perspective in a helpful way:

> No Jamaican, or, more accurately put, no untravelled Jamaican, would or could have written about Jamaica in such terms. This is Jamaica seen through the eyes of a black American; Jamaica as seen by one who has lived in the dark and cruel shadow of Jim Crow and the lynching tree. And although Du Bois perhaps did not notice this—if he did, he did not tell—this was also Jamaica as seen through the eyes of a "light skinned," "colored," Harvard-educated gentleman. This is how the Jamaicans would have seen him, and this is how they would have treated him, and this was bound to have a bearing on how he perceived Jamaica.[31]

In Du Bois's estimation it was Garvey who could not and did not read the specifics of the cultural landscape he encountered upon landfall. Garvey "took no account of the American Negro problem" and attempted to "settle the Jamaican problem in the United States."[32] The UNIA spectacle becomes in this hearing a "foreign"-sounding spectacle that makes erroneous political and aesthetic claims in another dialect and belongs to a distinct history. This is akin to the argument, made by some, that the extreme color-consciousness of Claude McKay's *Home to Harlem* featured an inaccurate and inappropriate importation of Caribbean racial politics into an African American social context. So "Garvey Must Go!" is a rejection of this spectacular intrusion; it rejects the notion of interconnected black histories that was at the root of Du Bois's own pan-Africanism, with its avowal that "the color line belts the world." More accurately, this is a rejection of a pan-Africanism that does not function within the cultural hierarchies within the race that Du Bois establishes in *The Souls of Black Folk* and that *The New Negro* will continue to assume—one in which African Americans had pride of place.

Rejecting this view of an imported struggle, Edouard Glissant in *Caribbean Discourse* contextualizes the intrusion that was Garveyism:

> Ultimately, Caribbean intellectuals have exploited this need for a trickster strategy to find another place: that is, in these circumstances, to link a possible solution of the insoluble to the resolution other peoples have achieved. The first and perhaps the most spectacular form of this tactic of diversion is the Jamaican Marcus Garvey's African dream, conceived in the first "phase" that drove him in the United States to identify with the plight of black Americans.[33]

That Glissant would identify Marcus Garvey and his Universal Negro Improvement Association and African Communities League as the first and most spectacular form of diversion is for him to identify the Harlem Renaissance as the first and most spectacular site of transnational, cross-cultural black engagement since slavery. Harlem becomes a crucial node in a shared imaginary geography as one place allows a group from another place to explore its own concerns via the prismatic refraction allowed by the perspective granted by immigration and via the shared mask of race.

It is worth remarking Glissant's description of Garvey's politics as a "trickster strategy," though he does not specify who or what is being tricked, mocked, or subverted by this strategy. Hill's reading of Garveyite carnival spectacle is also unclear as to this point. This is important to clarify since Garveyism managed to threaten the nationalism of the NAACP perhaps even more than it did the racism of the United States and certainly more than the parochial colonial politics of his home island that forced him and his UNIA to take refuge in the black social world of Harlem. In Glissant's formulation, Garvey's strategy appends itself to the perceived solutions of the African American struggle to formulate solutions that could apply to the culturally and politically less amenable island community. This acknowledges that intra-racial masking and camouflage are as much a part of black cultural politics as they are a part of black political and cultural resistance; the trickster strategy mediates the tensions of a shared racial politics. For despite the clearly pan-African resonance of the Garvey/African American encounter, concealment and diversion exist in the encounter between African Americans and West Indians. Since direct confrontation is not possible on its home turf, this trickster strategy allows one group to hide in the skin of another and attempt to resolve its local political and historical relationships from within the language of another. Glissant slightly smoothes over the tensions and resentments of this cross-cultural, intra-racial encounter and pays no attention to the local reception granted this strategy of diversion; nor does he provide a more complicated reading of Garvey's "identification" with the African American community. However, despite his disinterest in the micropolitics of encounter, he is absolutely correct to describe Harlem and its renaissance as the "landscape of a zone shared elsewhere" rather than as a space of unwanted immigration.[34]

In his essay "Gift of the Black Tropics" in *The New Negro*, the Caribbean writer W. A. Domingo (cofounder of one of the earliest black socialist groups in America, the heavily West Indian African Blood Brotherhood), mapped the tensions of this shared zone, arguing that a sudden lack of priority for their own "insoluble" problems as well as their sudden lack of privilege motivated much resentment among the West Indian immigrants during the Harlem Renaissance. They arrived "in a country whose every influence is calculated to democratize their race and destroy the distinctions they had been accustomed to."[35] Domingo's focus is on the issue of class as it relates to both culture and nationality and is cogently aware of the kinds of intra-racial tensions that Glissant's trickster would perhaps find equally insoluble. For example, the generally more highly educated West Indian immigrants missed their sense of sociocultural and economic privilege when facing an African American community not willing or able to regard them according to that privilege. However, this description of the deleterious effects of racial "democratization" can be used to understand how, to West Indian immigrants, democratization was ultimately a code word for invisibility and an erasure of their specific histories, vernaculars, and cultural codes. Garvey's presence and the presence of the UNIA were appreciated by many West Indians as a refusal of this democratization and an assertion of black difference in a Harlem illequipped to process its internal cultural multiplicity despite the overwhelming presence of it.

Hence a set of competing racial universalisms within this shared zone, with Garvey's claims to race being reduced to his place of origin and Du Bois's similar claims being reduced by Garvey to specifics of his pigment and the shapes and sounds of his monstrous blood. This conflict between the two men and their respective movements represents not just a fracturing of both articulations of a universal Negro or a pan-African movement; it also provides the faint glimmer of another kind of pan-Africanism predicated on radical difference, tension, and the sprawl of histories, languages, dialects, and signifying traditions. It is in Bert Williams that we can hear the traces of this other pan-Africanism in which the black diaspora functions as intersubjective and micropolitical process. Here race exists in the impossible shifting spaces among plural and competitive masks.

Very few scholars of this period are as aware of the competitive tensions between the West Indian immigrants and the African Americans in New York as is Robert Hill. Only Winston James in *Raising Aloft the Banner of Ethiopia* and Irma Watkins-Owens in *Blood Relations* explore these tensions more deeply. Although not pursuing these issues beyond the point of a romanticized nationalism of inclusion, Heather Hathaway attempts to explore these cross-cultural tensions, albeit to a lesser extent, in her *Caribbean Waves*. James and Watkins-Owens both isolate and accept the tensions and differences as constitutive of Harlem modernism. This is particularly clear in James's critique of how West Indians and their forms of radicalism were interpreted by various African American writers, scholars, and political figures. It is also clear in Watkins-Owens's description of the drama of Marcus Garvey's presence:

> The negative reaction of influential members of the black press to what it saw as Garvey's intrusive foreign status and the uncertain feelings such bias evoked in the Caribbean community is important to understanding Harlem's ethnic dynamics. The point here is that the presence of the UNIA leader helped to focus ethnic awareness in ways not so apparent before his organization galvanized such spectacular appeal in Harlem. Garvey was not solely a leader of Caribbean immigrants; he attracted large numbers of black Americans, including politicians who in the early years tried to use the organization's constituency for their own purposes. Although Garvey and his organization promoted internationalism and were enthusiastically supported by wide segments of the native-black community in Harlem, William Ferris also noted that "the Garvey movement, by marshaling the West Indians en masse, made manifest the characteristics in which the West Indians differed from the American Negroes." Garvey and the controversies surrounding him helped to shift the nature of traditional politics to encompass ethnic as well as racial concerns. Still it is important to keep in mind that in Harlem the more fundamental battle was over political space and the economic rewards it afforded, areas which Garvey's leadership challenged on the local as well as the national scene.[36]

Watkins-Owens's text not only acknowledges the intra-racial tensions and articulates them as constitutive; she also argues that the tensions challenged and transformed an African American discourse of identity that was defined solely on the basis of race. Garvey's very loud dialect performance forced the question and problems of micropolitical, ethnic differences within an African American community responding to the general American nativism of the time by closing ranks. She reads Garvey and the complex West Indian presence as being crucial to the establishing "of a new historical development in American urban life—African intraracial ethnic community."[37]

Garvey never became an American citizen; and Watkins-Owens points out that this fact was often the basis of much anti-Garvey rhetoric from the black left, the NAACP, and the African American community. Claude McKay explores how West Indians would often exacerbate "foreign-born"/native-born tensions by making yet other claims on national belonging: "The West Indians are incredibly addicted to the waving of the Union Jack in the face of their American cousins. Of all the various peoples who migrate to America, the West Indians may be classed as the most patriotic to their homeland."[38] His own "addiction to waving" will be explored in a later chapter. This exacerbating of differences would seem to be a simple case of immigrants highlighting their differences and claiming an elsewhere to resist and scorn those who resist and scorn them. However, the very idea that the British Union Jack was a sign of patriotism to their island homelands shows just how complex, cross-cultural, and transimperial these intra-racial interactions were. In The New Negro W. A. Domingo argues that much of the West Indian support for Garvey was actually occasioned by those assaults on his nationality rather than on a support for his program: "The support given Garvey by a certain type of his countrymen is partly explained by their group reaction to attacks made upon him because of his nationality."[39]

In Robert Hill's view, Garvey's role as trickster/minstrel/clown can be claimed within a specific cultural context and for a specific social movement. But the fact still remains that the trickster/minstrel/clown in general is as disruptive of those being mocked as it is of those who assume themselves to be doing the mocking—Esu-Elegbara faces and cuts both ways. Bre'r Rabbit, Anansi the Spider, and the Signifying Monkey, for example, may be products of specific communities, but to claim them as representative of specific communities is very difficult since they are so unpredictable and—as the folk tales all bear witness—are as dangerous as they are beneficial. These figures are as much signs of community as they are of fractures and contradictions within it. Simply put, none of them is always on "our" side and they are often figures of menace and fragmentation as well as subversion and resistance. When Hill links Garvey's masquerade to a specific social movement, one wonders which. The most obvious assumption is that the social movement in question is the broader cause of Negro advancement, which was explicitly

Garvey's focus and the inspiration behind his resistant use of popular spectacle. Yet to root this kind of performance and public subversion in the vital
folk tradition of specifically Caribbean masquerade is to fragment that "social movement" into distinct voices, dialects, and performances all maintained simultaneously. It is to reveal the multiple social, cultural, and political
movements that were masked and often silenced by the term "Negro." Was it
in fact a West Indian–American social movement, or was Garvey using a
specifically West Indian tradition in the cause of the broader "Negro" movement? Hill aptly describes how "like the rebellious Dada movement of the
twenties, Garvey's caricature shows the Janus face of the movement as well as
his aspirations. The carnivalesque aspect of Garvey and the UNIA's rituals
contained an element of dissimulation."[40] Hill's recourse to dada omits a full
accounting of that movement's utter and glorious nihilism, one in which
there could be no advancing of any social movement whatsoever.

But to return to "nature": as we have seen, it was the explicit concern of
Williams's and Walker's minstrel performance and provided the discursive
"root" of both New Negro-ism and Garveyism in that both movements relied
on a biological understanding of their similarities despite a clear misunderstanding of their cultural differences. It is known that different types of
insects and animals within the same species also practice deceptive and
protective mimicry in response to each other. Although it is not true that the
UNIA was specifically a West Indian social movement, clearly West Indians
and their cultural practices and traditions were recognizably dominant within
it, so much so that many remember it as a specifically West Indian movement
when it most certainly was not. This historical fact enables a description of
the dissimulation and parody involved in the UNIA's parade tradition as being
polyvalent. It signified simultaneously against dominant Euro-American racism and African American particularism. This signifying occurred alongside a
strong West Indian desire to transform island particularities into critical
norms which allow for a resistance to what were essentially two forces of
assimilation—Euro- and Afro-American. It also allowed for the maintenance
of a race/class hierarchy between the largely more highly educated West
Indian immigrants and the never quite native African Americans. The parade
thus functioned as a space-clearing gesture, a comic, epic, and exaggerated
ritual of phaneric display. The broader social movement may have been explicitly racial, but it was implicitly transnational as various group aspirations and
signifying traditions engaged each other behind the mask of cohesion that
was race. C. L. R. James's "mimic warfare" was never more apt a description.

But despite being a West Indian like Garvey or anticipating the more strident poetic voice of Claude McKay, Bert Williams's form of mimicry was not phaneric. It was not a statement of aggressive presence, of advertising, and of claiming space. He was "Nobody," an engaging, critical absence for whom the visual field was merely a tool of dissimulation and was already overdetermined by specific and authoritative notions of what constituted "black" in the American imagination. In *The Material Unconscious*, Bill Brown writes of a "spectatorial apparatus, an incitement to visibility and a protection from contact" which "makes visible the need to make the black man and the blackness of the black man visible."[41] Like colonial expositions, the circus, and vaudeville, minstrelsy was very much a part of this "epistemophilia—the pleasure of knowing" which enabled white power to "reproduce difference as alterity" and to universalize its construction of race.[42] Bert Williams slipped through the cracks of this desire, using the African American mask as a sign of truth and plenitude in order to denature it and to secure a space of strategic invisibility. So his mimicry bore a closer resemblance to the allaesthetic, which is a semiotics of silence and of critical disappearance. This latter form of mimicry is ultimately one where kleptoparasitic invisibility requires a sharp and constant awareness of a mask being worn: it does not accept the possibility that the mask and the flesh are one, nor does it imagine for a moment that the web in which it thrives is its own. What we then witness in Bert Williams as a black immigrant and in his stage presence are two distinct yet closely related black performance traditions: minstrelsy and passing. Both are dependent on mimicry, which, as Eric Sundquist says of imitation in general, is "the theoretical cornerstone of racial, as well as artistic, assimilation."[43]

The Color Line and the Black Immigrant Mask

In *Black Face, White Noise*, Michael Rogin writes that the act of "blacking up" and the attendant act of revelation through contrast that comes from the "wiping off" of the burnt cork was "a rite of passage from immigrant to American."[44] Using the example of the Eastern European Jews who dominated the blackface industry in early-twentieth-century American popular culture—Al Jolson, George Burns, George Jessel, Sophie Tucker, and Fanny Brice—he argues that minstrelsy was an "ethnocultural expression" which "served a melting-pot function":

> Far from breaking down the distinction between race and ethnicity, however, blackface only reinforced it. Minstrelsy accepted ethnic difference by

insisting on racial division. It passed immigrants into Americans by differen-
tiating them from the black Americans through whom they spoke, who were
not permitted to speak for themselves. Facing nativist pressure that would
assign them to the dark side of the racial divide, immigrants Americanized
themselves by crossing and re-crossing the racial line. Their discovery of
racial inequality propelled the United States beyond ethnicity by transforming ethnic descent into American national identity.[45]

Blackface, as Rogin asserts, maintains the "color line" in the act of crossing
it. White minstrels—Jewish minstrels—encounter the chthonic void between
mask and flesh and traverse it in the process of "wiping off." What they are
granted on the other side is what is guaranteed by ritual and alchemy: transformation. More importantly for the analysis here, blackface maintains the
binary coding in American racialist discourses by that very profitable invention of whiteness (that transubstantiation into whiteness). This whiteness
has the correlative effect of inventing a blackness that is just as magical yet
much more politically fragile. Of course black minstrels were denied the
patriotic denouement that came with the wiping off of the burnt-cork mask,
for what would be revealed by them in that act was not a stabilizing and
contrastive whiteness but the very impossibility of the melting pot for African
American and Afro-Caribbean peoples—which is to say, more "blackness."
Rather than buttressing a discourse of binary racial coding, Bert Williams's
minstrelsy stressed a much more micropolitical and finely shaded set of
cultural—not "racial"—divisions. It was a minstrelsy not based on visual
contrast at all.

Rogin cites Williams as an artist who was able to "turn self-denigrating
irony against the viewer," though he simultaneously describes black blackface as operating "outside a self-alienating economy of pleasure."[46] It is
precisely this "self-alienation" that gave Bert Williams's performance its kick
in front of both black and white audiences; to paraphrase the comedian, his
humor was prismatic, was derived from seeing himself as others see him. But
overall, there is really no room in Rogin's otherwise trenchant and politically
relevant analysis for the black immigrant voice or experience because Williams's "self alienation" operates outside the binary colorline essential to
Rogin's work and to most studies of minstrelsy. This is partly because Williams was such a rare figure, though it would be fruitful to compare and
contrast the blackface of black American minstrels with the Jewish and poor
white blackface performers. Rather than simply describing black minstrelsy
as self denigration or dismissing it as a desperate but necessary way to enter

into American popular theater, it would be fruitful to explore the various forms of desire embedded in that masochistic self-denigration and the will to self-annihilation coded in this particular use of the mask.

For there is an economy of pleasure in an embrace of one's own stereotype. During a historical moment defined by "positive," "affirming," and tightly self-controlled images and expectations of blacks, one can imagine the threatening and liberating appeal of a black minstrel to a black audience. In light of Du Bois's neo-Victorianism and the middle-class politics of assimilationist nationalism, in the context of the growing hegemony of the black church, this figure is an explicit and sweet threat, much like the pimp or thug or "gangsta" icons in the present-day context of black media masquerade. Considering the success of and the hostility to the black urban primitivism of Claude McKay and Langston Hughes, one can see the territory that the black minstrel stood watch over. These writers tapped into the libidinal and ludic possibilities of "black soul" in opposition to the conservative and rigid vision of race maintained by the talented tenth and its religiopolitical dominance. It was clear to them then as it should be now that the fear and institutionalized rejection of the minstrel is also often used by black political culture to police dissent within its ranks: dissent over "appropriate" modes of representation, "appropriate" forms of sexuality, and "appropriate" manifestations of pleasure and politics and expressive play.

Although Williams was no primitivist—an aesthetic ill-suited for his staunch assimilationist nationalism—his persona did allow for a severe and elaborate mockery of the pretension and pomp of the Negro elite, as exemplified by his epochal performance in In Dahomey. To further explore the potential intra-racial subversion that exists in black blackface would force a re-examination of a notion like resistance, given the possibilities available to the black minstrel. In this context the "stage Negro" could be read as that alien artifact which allowed an exploration of the vague and horrific possibilities of there being inestimable truths locked within its negative stereotyping. On the other hand, this alien artifact could be read as depending on an unpleasant mode of parody to force a reassessment of the political expectations and dominant representations of black people that were maintained by black people themselves, from Garvey to Du Bois, from the masculinism of pan-Africanism to the bourgeois obsessions of "True Womanhood." In other words, what is often being resisted in Williams's black minstrelsy is not only white-generated racial stereotypes but also those cultural traits, habits, and modes of being that did not fit the dominant representation of racial uplift during a time where the dominant politics was driven by the bourgeois desire for consolidation and the self-righteous moralism of appropriate representation.

Claude McKay and Langston Hughes would flirt with the frisson of these stereotypes by re-inventing them as distinct precolonial truths that freed blacks from both the restraints of hypercivilized overindustrialization and the prejudices of an older nationalist (and in McKay's case African American) bourgeoisie. Minstrelsy and primitivism blend in the work of these two dialect poets, as they did in the later work of the Williams and Walker stage shows. In Hughes's words, "the tom-tom cries and the tom-tom laughs. If colored people are pleased we are glad. If they are not, their displeasure doesn't matter either."[47] For him this sound is beating deep within the "Negro soul—the tom-tom of revolt against weariness in a white world, a world of subway trains, and work, work, work; the tom-tom of joy and laughter, and pain swallowed in a smile."[48] This is an example of a sublimated minstrelsy in which Hughes draws directly from the ludic possibilities available to the black artist from the black mask. The final line is telling, reminding us that it is Bert Williams whose Anansi-smile haunts the Harlem Renaissance.

Ultimately, though, *Blackface, White Noise* cannot contain Bert Williams as both black and immigrant because race is continually sounded as a discursive singularity when it comes to issues of language, culture, and politics in North American–centered discourses. Again, as in Rogin, "black" almost always means "African American" just as "black immigrant" and "Great Migration" always signify the South in discussions of the Harlem Renaissance. A passage from Heather Hathaway's *Caribbean Waves* is helpful in addressing this problem:

> because of the propensity toward binarism that dominates racial conceptions in the United States, both first- and second-generation African Caribbean immigrants have been routinely classified by popular, institutional, and even academic cultures as "African American" or simply as "black." But this categorization obviously overlooks key cultural and national differences that have profoundly shaped the interaction between African Americans and African Caribbeaners, and even more seriously risks reducing the plurality of black American identities to a monolithic entity based on skin color alone.[49]

Since Rogin depends on Ann Charters's *Nobody* for his information, he is presumably aware that Bert Williams was also an immigrant. But it is the binary American color line that dominates his reading of minstrelsy. "Immigrant" as a category is maintained in opposition to "black" or African American. Minstrelsy as a product of merely black and white cultural tensions, when it was clear that other ethnic and cultural groups were involved, ultimately reifies the binary chromatism of American culture, which is largely Rogin's point. Yet minstrelsy also challenged the color line by introducing and superimposing multiple forms of difference onto that line, whether they were visible or not. To read minstrelsy outside the color line or on its margins is a more productive way to explore the resistance to bichromatism at work in this example of early-twentieth-century American popular culture. Rogin's phrase "the dark side of the racial divide" should remind us that for Afro-Caribbeans, the color line in America has never been singular. It has instead comprised many cultural and epistemological lines that they must cross, re-cross, blur, and sometimes be blurred by. Its "dark side" is infinitely dark, variegated, and textured with multiple shades of shadow.

Rogin's basic formula—immigrant/minstrelsy/assimilation—provides great insight into how Bert Williams functions within a pan-African, transnational modernism. According to Rogin, after the Irish phase of minstrelsy, the immigrant Jews used the blackface masquerade to displace ethnicity and linguistic difference onto the African American population. If this is true, minstrelsy then requires that African Americans function as the untransmutable core of American assimilation, allowing for what is essentially "white-on-white" passing. In this form of passing, the previous "ethnicity" becomes enforced as homogeneously white after the alchemical transfusion of the minstrel mask. The mask attains the position of the legendary philosopher's stone. Rogin's formula is quite unlike Eric Lott's notion of "cross racial desire," which features a white working-class attempt to criticize and resist dominant white middle-class power by affiliating themselves through minstrelsy with African American working-class culture. If one accepts it, this is a rare but not singular historical instance of whites sincerely attempting to pass as blacks who represented a subversive cultural authority and a romanticized primordial American authenticity.

Considering his immigrant status, Bert Williams could not function in this latter way; but the stage Negro certainly does in his performance of it. There is clearly much love and theft in his black-on-black masquerade, much intimacy, and much distance. Rogin is right to be suspicious of the notion of "cross racial desire" as one should be suspicious of all attempts to see in any kind of cross-racial discursive "blacking up" or "cultural cross dressing" some mystical alchemy of progressive or subversive politics. He emphasizes how power maintains itself through subversion and through the confusion of its own codes: indeed, that may be the great contribution made by American hegemony, the ability to maintain power through the championing and commodification of potentially subversive doctrines such as "freedom," "democracy," "independence," "multiculturalism," and even "identity" and "resistance." Masking occupies a critical place in this intricate mechanism of "self subversion" or self-othering as it has throughout history.

So this is where Bert Williams's minstrelsy can be located: navigating the "blacked up" fractures of American-centered racial nationalisms predicated on binarism and the assimilation of culture by race. Because his minstrelsy was motivated by a heightened sense of West Indian distinctiveness, he could not accept the dominant discursive norms of African American culture, though he did share in the racial essentialism of the time. Like the Jews in Rogin's analysis, Williams's masquerade served to distance himself from African Americans but did not allow him to become white. But unlike the Jews, it cemented an intimacy with African Americans that was politically necessary but tragic in that it required that the history of his own voice be swallowed up into the locally produced authenticity of the community through whose mouth he spoke. That is, until that fateful night on stage in 1915, when his voice broke through the mask. Though because it had been muted so long and had reached ears able only to hear the louder sound of burnt cork, its meanings could only be attributed to the primary mask.

In Bert Williams's own words, his distance from the stage Negro and its language was greater even than the space between African Americans and the racist caricature: "I took to studying the dialect of the American Negro, which to me was just as much a foreign dialect as that of the Italian." Rereading these words after the "outing" that occurred on that fateful moment on the Broadway stage—that precious moment of slippage—one realizes just how far indeed was the space between mask and flesh, tongue and language. The "darky" or "stage Negro" was not only a fiction but a specifically American fiction that served Bert Williams well in his attempts not only to become "natural" but to symbolize both the naturalization of the black immigrant to both American *and* African American culture and the problematics of both pressures and forces. Mastering that icon's words, sounds, and gestures was proof of his new identity as an American—an identity so well performed that it could be taken for authenticity. This authenticity was confirmed not just to white audiences but also to African Americans who could accept him only after he had made public his mastery of their codes, their sounds and gestures, and their vernaculars. Since the discourses of race were structured overwhelmingly by the specific histories and cultural experiences of the African American majority, for the black immigrant to be heard was to speak through their mouths. It was this that Garvey refused to do and this that partly kept Claude McKay on the social margins of the New Negro movement. Yet this cross-cultural, intra-racial mimicry became the source of narrative tension and linguistic genius in his *Home to Harlem*, the primary American text of Caribbean double assimilation.

The sociologist Aubrey W. Bonnett describes this strategy as employed by West Indians in confronting the dual tensions of assimilation by which black Caribbean immigrants were pressured to assimilate into the dominant Euro-American culture as well as into an African American community that was often intolerant of intra-racial distinctions. He uses the term "ethnic alter-casting." To read this strategy alongside the performance of Bert Williams situates his performance within the broader West Indian presence in an African American–dominated Harlem, which is in turn situated within a virulently anti-black political moment:

> Thus, some West Indians professionals finding themselves cast in the black role, may attempt to employ the more profitable universal human being identity, or extremely talented meritocrat—doctor, actor, lawyer, etc. This attempts to shift the focus from the more negative to a positive status. These are the ethnics who would avoid at all costs living in ethnic suburban or urban areas and utilizing ethnic cues. And yet there are others, those who may assume the ethnic West Indian identity before a partisan West Indian audience, a black identity when addressing Afro-Americans, and the larger universal identity (all god's people, human beings, one of humankind, Americans) when facing members of the dominant group.[50]

Although Bonnett mentions but does not at all explore the "intense competition and social conflict that marked [West Indian] relations with Afro-Americans"—latent and unreconstructed nationalisms guarantee that very few are wont to do so—this is the general context of Bert Williams's plural masking.[51] The possible irony in the phrase "finding themselves cast in the black role" goes unchecked here and the gulf behind each gesture of "assuming" another black identity is also ignored as if it were a simple thing and as if there were no repercussions to this black-on-black masquerade. Race makes everything authentic and cohesive in Bonnett's study. He goes so far as to argue for a triumphalist process in which "the black experience—their rite of passage—transforms them into black Americans."[52] Bonnett's reading of this switching of identities would suit Rogin's analysis, except that in this context there is no "wiping off." Instead there is a statement of solidarity, a sharing of the mask which, on the level of political destinies and mutual cooperation, occurred more often than not.

Identity altercasting, however, was used as much to foment this global unity as it was to fracture, evade, and redefine it. The point here is that an awareness of the needs of each distinct cultural audience and an arsenal of gestures, dialects, and other kinesthetic elements were already fully established in the black immigrant community as kleptoparasitic survival strategies. In Bert Williams's case, minstrel theater and vaudeville dramatized "ethnic altercasting." Most prominently, his persona featured the particularly black West Indian process and strategy of passing as an African American through the mastery of black vernacular speech and symbolic/cultural codes. Passing here is not a question of ocular metaphors or visual referents: it is auditory and explicitly performative. The voice is the mask when the flesh looks the same. In Bonnett's words: "For members of ethnic groups with long histories of oppression, the art of identity assumption, switching and altercasting may be highly developed. Indeed, it may be an individual's only weapon in the arsenal of racial defense in a rigid caste society."[53] Could one find a better context for Anansi the Spider and the Signifying Monkey to coexist, flourish, and compete? In this, they establish the parameters of a community as resistant to its own external subjugation as it is toward its own internal orthodoxies.

Mikhail Bakhtin, whose early career is coterminous with the period of the Harlem Renaissance and whose work is unavoidable in this book, writes this of parodic repetition:

> the author employs the speech of another, but . . . he introduces into that other speech an intention which is directly opposed to the original one. The second voice, having lodged in the other speech, clashes antagonistically with the original, host voice and forces it to serve directly opposite aims. Speech becomes a battlefield for opposing intentions.[54]

The immigrant Jews in Rogin's analysis do not clash antagonistically with the "host voice" because that voice sounds white American racism and represents a mask they wish to wear. They instead master its discursive form and remake themselves in the language of its intention. Yet the method of Negro stereotyping that is minstrelsy enables Bert Williams to make that passage from immigrant to American without that "wiping off" necessary to Rogin's formulation. The obvious difference is that the position he would occupy upon arrival through the mask is not the one available to the Irish or to Eastern European Jews; it is not accompanied by the various privileges associated with whiteness, that precious and evanescent commodity produced in and through Anglo-American modernism and fetishized through white minstrelsy. So it would seem best to keep deferring the revelation, best to keep the mask in play and in motion as Esu is known to do.

Bakhtin's notion of a "host voice" evokes Williams's position as an immigrant. Minstrelsy in this context emphasizes an alienation and a critical distance from African American language and culture, white American citizenship, and that troubling signifier that symbolically links the two segregated communities: the minstrel "darky" or the "stage Negro." But given his curious position in an overwhelmingly African American modern movement, one that he supported both by choice and by segregation, it is difficult to locate in Bert Williams's black dialect performance specific intentions opposed across a linguistic color line. Situated in some critical relationship to British colonial power, American imperialism, and African American assimilationist nationalism, Williams was forced to do more than simply subvert race or reveal the constructedness of both sides of a hegemonically produced set of oppositions. Williams's masquerade does not merely establish what Marjorie Garber would call a "category crisis" either, since his cultural cross-dressing is underpinned by a commitment to racial uplift and the very category of race which motivates his performance of the African American subject.

The problem is not that Williams did not parody whiteness, or that he parodied African Americans with the same kind of complex intentions that motivated white Irish and Jewish blackface performers. His critique of and resistance to whiteness was accomplished through his masquerade of African American-ness, and his critique of the latter was not subordinated by his commitment to a mutual advancement and cooperation. He would recuperate an African American discourse of assimilation through parody, yet because it was parody—because he was distant from the subject of his performance—he could simultaneously create space for a distinctly Afro-Caribbean subjectivity at the center of a first-world modernism. In this interpretation of his life and work, this was accomplished by keeping the masks on, circulating them for different parodic and political purposes. To use Ralph Ellison's words, Bert Williams kept changing the joke to continually slip both white and black American discursive yokes.

Masks in Motion: On the Children of Esu

The natural world also features a form of linguistic or dialectal passing. In the sciences of zoology, entomology, and ornithology, this phenomenon is known as "protective auditory memory." Two examples of this are the African crowned eagle, which is able to mimic the territorial call of certain monkeys in order to lure and attack them, and species of insects that are able to mimic the sounds of larger insect species in order to delude and evade predators. It is this latter form of protective auditory mimicry that is sounded by Bert Williams as one of the many voices of the turn-of-the-century American Afro-Caribbean community. This intra-racial mimicry must be read alongside what Locke in The New Negro calls a "protective social mimicry forced upon [the Negro] by the adverse circumstances of dependence."[55]

It is worth noting that a generation before Locke's manifesto, Thorstein Veblen made use of "protective mimicry" in "The Barbarian Status of Women" (1889–90). In explaining the shift from a patriarchal marriage bond based on "seizure" and the forceful capturing of women to a still patriarchal one based on a "virtuous and honorific relation of ownership-marriage," Veblen argues that mimicry allows for the sublimation of one form of patriarchal dominance to another. In his reading, the institution of marriage becomes a ritual of substitution or sublimation where the violence of the encounter of difference—men vis-à-vis women—is transmuted and legitimized. Veblen concludes by stating that "marriage by feigned capture within the tribe is a case of mimicry—'protective mimicry,' to borrow a phrase from the naturalists. It is substantially a case of adoption . . . and as in other cases of adoption, the ceremonial performance is by no means looked upon as a fatuous make-believe. The barbarian has implicit faith in the efficiency of imitation and ceremonial execution as a means of compassing a desired end."[56]

One could perhaps read the UNIA parade as sublimation or perhaps a rechanneling of intra-racial tensions in that it was a cross-cultural social movement/organization in which African Americans importantly functioned but were not dominant. One could also read it as being simultaneously an exacerbation of those tensions since there were those, such as Du Bois, who because of the prominence of West Indian folk forms and dialects could read it as being primarily other. For Locke the Negro's protective mimicry had to be transcended in order for the New Negro to achieve voice or, in Baker's words, national sounding. The mimicry of Bert Williams, however, dared not expose itself because it would be silenced by a national sounding for which only the UNIA was competition. And Bert Williams was no Garveyite, no advocate of separatism. So he essentially controlled his own absence, manipulated his disappearance rather than be actively erased. With Williams, mimicry folded in on itself, which is to say he was able to signify on signifying and transform race into a transnational and self-referential vortex, an ever-shifting space of multiple and simultaneous performances. Henry Louis

Gates touches on this when he describes Esu-Elegbara as "a mask-in-motion, who signifies in ritual by his phallic dance of generation, of creation, of translation."[57]

Yet we needn't go so far in reading Bert Williams's mask, especially since its material effects are manifest in the relationships between the two cultural groups in question. In *The Signifying Monkey* Henry Louis Gates describes what is for this analysis the central problem of how black signifyin(g) is understood and implemented. Although he articulates this problem in a work that also slightly perpetuates that problem, he does trace the need to transcend racial/discursive/parodic binaries back to Africa, a site ironically too often neglected in contemporary Black Atlantic discourse. He writes:

> While other scholars have interpreted the Monkey tales against the binary opposition between black and white in American society, to do so is to ignore the trinary forces of the Monkey, the Lion, and the Elephant. To read the Monkey tales as a simple allegory of the black's political oppression is to ignore the hulking presence of the Elephant, the crucial third term of the depicted action. To note this is not to argue that the tales are not allegorical or that their import is not political. Rather, this is to note that to reduce such complex structures to a simple two-term opposition (white versus black) is to fail to account for the strength of the Elephant.[58]

The use of the iconic monkey figure recalls that term used by African Americans throughout the Harlem Renaissance to pejoratively describe West Indians in Harlem, especially those associated with the Garvey Movement. "Monkey chaser" was the term, and it appears in much of the literature of the period, from the work of Claude McKay to the work of Rudolph Fisher and Wallace Thurman. Du Bois's use in "Back to Africa" of the term "monkey-shines" to describe Marcus Garvey was no doubt meant to signify on this term of intra-racial abuse. Monkey chaser was derived partly from a rejection of the "back to Africa" movement—that is, chasing monkeys back in Africa. It was an attempt to assign to West Indians a lower status on the evolutionary scale because of their foreign-born status and despite their often higher socioeconomic status in Harlem.

Using Gates's mathematics, it is tempting to place Bert Williams in that undertheorized "third space" of postcolonial discourse evoked by both Gates's attention to "trinary" forces and Houston Baker's investigation of Caliban's "triple play" of signification in *Modernism and the Harlem Renaissance*. But unlike both Gates's and Baker's discursive tripling, the "third space" (as also articulated by Homi Bhabha, Teshome Gabriel, and other postcolonial thinkers and critics) does not allow for what is essentially a black nationalism disarticulated from within by its African American and Afro-Caribbean resonances and affiliations.[59] Despite the anti-binaristic implications of his performance, Bert Williams's minstrelsy, Garvey's masquerade, and Claude McKay's internationalism remain committed to race despite being bedeviled by rivaling claims to multiple sites of cultural authenticity and political authority. By stressing performance and masking, both things are possible, flickering according to the needs of an audience or a set of discourses; shifting yet fully committed to each performance as an authentic moment of expression. Also, the dependence on a "third space" is mathematically imprecise. To double a double is not to produce a third. In her reading of Du Bois, Darlene Clark Hine reminds us, for example, that to superimpose gender as well as class on such a paradigm produces, at least, a fiveness: "Negro, American, woman, poor, black woman" (assuming of course the dangerously clichéd naturalization of Negro and poor and/or Negro and woman that characterizes too much academic discourse).[60] The commitment to the possibilities of tripling is also unaware of how "third spaces" in the Caribbean have become occupied by a white or Creole elite who often celebrate "hybridity" as a way to repress a specifically black majority.

To employ Gates's language, Bert Williams's signifyin(g) operates in relationship to both the British and the American Lions, but also to the Elephant-in-the-sitting-room, which may well be African American culture in turn-of-the-century Harlem and now televised and digitized within the media sprawl of contemporary American popular culture. Indeed, the mimicry of African Americans and their vernacular culture by West Africans and West Indians in their home countries might be a sign of a black postmodernism where Bert Williams's mimicry marked a black modernism which had as its totem an African mask but an African American voice. Gates's passage helpfully acknowledges that subversive double voicings and parodic signifyin(g) in the African American tradition are not exclusively products of American racism although they are honed by it. He importantly points out that these techniques of textual exegesis and political resistance exist even in Africa and preclude the politics of race and Western colonization.

"Signifyin(g)," Gates writes, "is black double-voicedness; because it always entails formal revision and an intertextual relation, and because of Esu's double-voiced representation in art, I find it an ideal metaphor for black literary criticism. . . . Repetition with a signal difference, is fundamental to the nature of Signifyin(g)."[61] Despite its pan-African pedigree, he localizes the Signifying Monkey, describing it as "the figure of the text of the Afro-American speaking subject."[62] This icon seems to bear some privileged relationship to Africa: "The Signifying Monkey emerges from his mysteriously beclouded Afro-American origins as Esu's first cousin, if not his American heir."[63] While identifying the New World figurations of Esu-Elegbara—Exu in Brazil, Echu-Elegua in Cuba, Papa Legba in Haiti, and Papa La Bas in African America—he argues that Esu functions as "a sign of the disrupted wholeness of an African system of meaning."[64] Although the very suggestion that a homogeneous, totalizing, or complete African system of meaning existed is problematic, it is true that the black trickster figure after slavery accrues that meaning as well as those already intrinsic to it. In this, Esu becomes a figure of the void, of exile, of endless translation and an endless deferral of meaning.

Yet what does one do if both of Esu's voices repeat, critique, revise, and subvert each other? And given its continental origin, how can Esu and "doubleness" be contemplated outside—or anterior to—the parameters of the binary racial and cultural politics that dominate how doubleness is heard? The parallel semantic universes at work in Gates's argument are the African American and the white—the same ones that motivate Du Bois's veil and his double-consciousness. Yet it is intrinsic to Esu-Elegbara since the deity's presence precedes these parallels and the attendant psychic and cultural splitting they entail. This rooting of black signifying in Africa suggests that the splitting of black subjectivity that marks black modernism and that is articulated by the Du Boisian double-consciousness at the heart of Gates's own readings is possibly a permanent feature of the black diaspora rather than a sign of the Negro-American exceptionalism that Du Bois and Gates intend for it to be. In other words, Esu-Elegbara exists as double *before* slavery and colonization and is always already a sign of an internal polyphony, of other parallel (or multiply doubled) discursive and semantic universes within a "black" discursive field. The fact that "doubleness," "doubling," and vernacular subversion existed before slavery, racism, and the middle passage further questions the status of a double-consciousness and the rhetoric of African American exceptionalism or even an Afro-Caribbean distinctiveness that is rooted in a split subjectivity traceable to racism and slavery. In yet other words, if it was already split, already multiple, what is it now?

But the primary concern is still what to make of that signifying/trickster continuum turned against itself by differential histories of colonization, migration, and race. Even those who speak in doubles bear the risk of undoing themselves in addition to whatever semantic hegemony they attempt to subvert and revise. To engage this internal, micropolitical scenario one can return to *Modernism and the Harlem Renaissance*, one of the few texts to actually theorize black cultural modernism albeit from an ethnoparticular space that often masks itself as diasporic. Houston Baker describes how this specific modernism features a dual strategy of mastering dominant, white forms and cultural codes (even self-denigrating ones) and the display of that mastery by the self-conscious deforming of those forms and codes for anti-racist aims. Using this dialectic of mastery of form and deformation of mastery as a way to explore the meanings of West Indian-ness within this specific modernism, one wonders what it means for the Afro-Caribbean presence in relationship to African Americans and vice versa. As the member of a minority within a minority (who to the former minority functions as a majority), is Bert Williams's minstrelsy a mastery of mastery and a deformation of deformation? Perhaps, but maybe not; yes, but then again no. What these meta-meta-gestures force is a recognition that there is no end to displacement and deferral, revision and resistance. The acts of parodic refusal and the carnivalizing of dominance leave themselves open to an infinite regression which may be indistinguishable from disappearance or acquiescence despite being rooted in a progressive (or radical) politics.

These issues of cross-cultural signifying and material sociopolitical interaction should be contextualized by the encounter between specific icons of black textual history and cultural politics—the African American Signifyin(g) Monkey and the Afro-Caribbean Anansi the Spider. By paying close attention to the shifting masks and vernaculars, affiliations and idealizations at work simultaneously in each vernacular expression, black modernity becomes less a product of the bilateral "counter-culture" described in Paul Gilroy's formulation. The mask must be read laterally as well as vertically and the infinite spaces behind it given as much attention as the endlessly morphing social worlds within which it functions. The relationships here are not only economic, as immigrants threaten and compete with the local community. They ultimately feature a cultural and linguistic contest that does not—or did not—abandon race though each group struggles differently within it.

Anansi and the Signifying Monkey are two of Esu-Elegbara's most tendentious children, and the question of who is "first cousin" is both debatable (since Esu reached the Caribbean first) and inconsequential (since the economy of mythic and oral reproduction has always been digital—all copies are originals). Both of them are doubles of each other and are rooted in distinct black cultures and histories and are signs of black folk/working-class agency as well as epistemic rupture. They also provide strategies of resistance and its less glamorous yet more historically common twin—accommodation, which often is accepted only under the guise of ironic subversion, just as acquiescence is possibly a mask for a ruthless destabilizing of the status quo. But when these icons interact, as they do in Bert Williams's performance and in the work of Caribbean moderns like Claude McKay, Eric Walrond, and perhaps even Nella Larsen and Eulalie Spence, the multiple levels of masking and parody which coexist in one black performance (or in one performance of black) can make that vernacular voice unwieldy due to the political responsibilities of its multidirectional and, in Bakhtin's characterization, "centrifugal" signifyin(g).

This stream of ideas then reintroduces Bert Williams's sadness, his "self-torture," which, as Rogin put it, was the condition of his performing genius.[65] Upon the comedian's passing, Eric Walrond described the sadness:

> Some day one of our budding storywriters ought to sit down and write a novel with a Negro protagonist with melancholia as the central idea. Bert Williams had it. Although it was his business to make people laugh, there were times when he would go into his shell-like cave of a mind and reflect— and fight it out.
>
> "Is it worth it?" One side of him would ask, "Is it worth it—the applause, the financial rewards, the fame? Is it really worth it—lynching one's soul in blackface twaddle?"[66]

In answer to this final question, Walrond concludes that yes, "Bert Williams' tree—to him one of gall—is already beginning to bear fruit, and there is no telling how long the harvest will last."[67] But rather than rooting the tragicomic dread of "Mr. Nobody" in a simplistic racial binary, as both Rogin and Walrond do, it is possible to hear the sadness and melancholy as resulting not only from the limitations of racism but also from black polyphony itself, as both the Signifying Monkey and Anansi the Spider struggle for pride of place behind the blackface mask; or perhaps more accurately, as Anansi the Spider wears the mask of the Signifying Monkey. Certainly Walrond was of a generation that could revel in this transnational polyphony; his work certainly does. But it is possible that his literary voice may have been marginalized in part for being too overly laden with black languages and vernaculars, as well as for being too experimental with multiple black dialects and modes of register; this in a time when race and social realism were almost as synonymous, as were "the vernacular" and African American.

Williams's burden was not simply the black mask but also the burden of too many dialects (American and British Standard English being also distinct dialects in his repertoire). His was a heteroglossia cursed to be continually recuperated by the "centripetal" forces of America's racial polarities, which either sifted out the accents of Caribbean crossings or employed them as signifiers of an "elsewhere" marginal to a primary racial discursive formation. Silence was the only space open to him, and so he colonized it, making it sound a visually imperceptible difference that resisted erasure but courted a protective invisibility. As an icon of black modernist popular culture, Bert Williams presents this question among so many others: how many doublings, repetitions, and metatextual reversals and revisions can be traced in a modernism structured around specific racial soundings, yet fractured by the din of linguistic and cultural variation even in just one language? Also, does multiplying difference lead necessarily to plurality, or can it foment a greater invisibility as certain forms of difference attain a greater priority than others and are then read as homologous with internally marginalized, less visible others?

To hear the full implications of Bert Williams's voice and comprehend its sadness, it is necessary to briefly leave the Signifying Monkey in the trees of New York and return to the mythopoetic web of the Caribbean trickster Anansi the Spider. The tragic, self-torturing (or "self lynching," as Walrond would have it) character of his persona and performance suggests the limits and the cost of subversive performativity. Like Henry Louis Gates, Edward Kamau Brathwaite also traces an Afro–New World tradition of subversive racial signifyin(g) back to Africa. He does it through his reflections on the work of the Barbadian-born, Canada-based novelist and critic Austin Clarke: "Austin Clarke, has been developing what we can only call an Anansi style of the third generation (the first generation being Asante Ananse, the second being Slave/Caribbean spider-man. Clarke demonstrates . . . that in the Black immigrant communities & pressures of the North, Ananse still (has to) live(s)."[68] To give a convenient name to what Brathwaite describes, it can be called the "Anansi Continuum" and includes within it Robert Hill's reading of the UNIA parade as a specifically West Indian cultural form of signifyin(g) within the African American political context. It must also include the work of Bert Williams and certainly of Claude McKay.

Although Anansi and the monkey are sisters (the African tradition being as sexually rootless as today's cutting-edge theories of drag and performativity), they encounter each other as intimate strangers in Harlem. As argued much earlier, it is that encounter that produces a black modernism catalyzed by but not limited to specific national boundaries. Patrick Taylor warns, however, against seeing in Anansi (or in the Signifying Monkey) a necessarily subversive politics and liberatory poetics, a criticism echoed by Marjorie Garber, Judith Butler, Eric Lott, and Richard Burton. Anansi operates outside binaries due to his penchant for inexorable reversals and border crossings and his sexual masquerade. But because s/he is a liminal figure, s/he is also easily counterrevolutionary, though never quite nihilistic. So just as accommodation can be a mask for resistance (as in Baker's reading of Booker T. Washington), resistance can also be a mask for accommodation or even self-destruction. Taylor writes:

> It is this very ambiguity, at once destructive and creative, that is both the power of the trickster tale and its ultimate, tragic limit. The tales articulate a mythical conception of the world as a place of endless and ongoing struggle, of progress and regress, friendship and enmity. This mythical conception has implications for the meaning of the tales in relation to the colonial social and political totality. If there is nothing permanent about the position of the master, there is also no necessary permanence in the community. One perverse implication (from the point of view of the community) is that the trickster-slave may indeed turn his skills against his own people in order to benefit himself and become like the master.[69]

In short, subversive masking swings both ways because they script a world in which all categories are in crisis—including subversion. This is why Bert Williams can only be marginally West Indian since even that site of fixed belonging is thrown into crisis by his relentless and multiple masking. His performative multiplicity threatened to erase even him since he existed in a political world where in the final analysis race was the fundamental determinant.

Considering the black inability to "wipe off" difference as well as the fact that crossings define the path, Taylor finds in race the "tragic limit" of performativity. This can be directly linked to the tragicomic sadness of Bert Williams's persona, one that could not escape itself and could only play with categories, not shed them. Keeping in mind the still socioeconomic and juridicopolitical fixity of white elite power which functions despite its own fetish for masquerade, when the oppressed play with dominant categories, their seeming liberation through performance may be the product of their sudden access to another role—the role of the master without the full power of the master; this while simultaneously performing the role of the slave without the historical innocence of the pure victim.

CHAPTER 4 The Global Economy of Minstrelsy

For the purposes of this text thus far, Bert Williams's intra-racial, cross-cultural masquerade has been framed within the context of twentieth-century modernism: a context in which cross-cultural catalysis is the secret history of racism, and colonialism and immigration the secret history of America's celebrated penchant for self-invention and reinvention. The questions and concerns raised by Williams's performance of race can, however, be traced back much earlier to the initial moments of black-on-black culture contact during chattel slavery, itself the open secret of Western modernity. Before even the "great race-welding" that Alain Locke describes in The New Negro, a modern black subjectivity had already been molded via the radical juxtapositions and collisions of differential black ethnicities and cultural differences.[1] It is well known, for example, that in the crucible of chattel slavery—in the holds of ships, on long overland marches where black slaves were connected by chains, in pens, dungeons, and stables—new languages and sensibilities were forged and syncretized before landfall in the Caribbean, America, Latin America, and Europe.

Arguing against the commonly accepted notion that enslaved Africans

composed a homogeneous and specific "culture" that can be set in opposition to an equally reductive view of "European culture," the anthropologists
Sidney W. Mintz and Richard Price in *The Birth of African American Culture* put it
this way:

> We have suggested that much of the problem with the traditional model of
> early African-American culture history lies in its view of culture as some sort
> of undifferentiated whole. Given the social setting of early New World colo-
> nies, the encounters between Africans from a score or more different so-
> cieties with each other, and with their European overlords, cannot be inter-
> preted in terms of two (or even many different) "bodies" of belief and value,
> each coherent, functioning, and intact. The Africans who reached the New
> World did not compose, at the outset, groups. In fact, in most cases, it might
> even be more accurate to view them as crowds, and very heterogeneous
> crowds at that. Without diminishing the probable importance of some core
> of common values, and the occurrence of situations where a number of
> slaves of common origin might indeed have been aggregated, the fact is that
> these were not communities of people at first, and they could only become
> communities by processes of cultural change. What the slaves undeniably
> shared at the outset was their enslavement; all—or nearly all—else had to be
> created by them. In order for slave communities to take shape, normative
> patterns of behavior had to be established, and these patterns could be
> created only on the basis of particular forms of social interaction.[2]

Such revisionist histories isolate the active process of black cross-culturality
and linguistic catalysis as central to the constitution of the black diaspora.
And in a postnationalist moment, they also allow for a vision of racial dis-
aggregation and fragmentation that is still politically resistant, critical of
essentialism, and motivated by the ideal of reinventing community along
nonbinary lines. In this view it is in the holds of slave ships that what will
become, say, African American or Afro-Caribbean identities will be forged by
disparate and distinct African culture groupings. It is in the micropolitics
of these social interactions that one can imagine cross-cultural, intra-racial
masquerade as a major component of cultural change. For example, one
wonders how many fugitive slaves took refuge in the languages and identities
of other blacks as they evaded the undifferentiating eye of white slavers and
black captors. How many blacks passed as other types of blacks or how many
Africans went hiding in the skins of others? Certainly they were often lumped
together via the racial category; but didn't that only facilitate the poetics and

politics of disappearance, dissimulation, and protective mimicry? Especially since it is the case that not all African cultural groups were enslaved and interacted with in the same ways by whites ever aware of cultural hierarchies and differences during the continental slave trade? And isn't this kind of disappearance and masquerade also at the root of a nationalist poetics of identity despite its fetish for biocultural authenticity?

Group identity or even racial subjectivity in this context must be rooted in a strategic masquerade that evolves as the mask becomes a new skin, as distinct cultural crowds become a race by pretending to be each other or choosing to act (or sound) the same. One can easily imagine any number of possible and likely scenarios where Africans pass for other Africans in order to confuse and subvert the system of racial slavery as well as simply to escape or improve their lot within it. It is on this intersubjective and micropolitical level that a specific black modernism and modernity can be described far in advance of the black transnationalism of early-twentieth-century New York. This is a modernity that doesn't romantically fetishize itself as a counterculture—especially since modernity itself is produced by so many countermovements and countercultures. The very fact of racial slavery is itself a countermovement against the dominant discourse of freedom that marks the discourses of modernity. Primitivism is another example of a counterculture/ movement that is actually constitutive of modernity—as are most contemporary discourses of counterhegemonic subversion and romanticized otherness. This black modern vision of disappearance and intra-racial masquerade provides a history that is behind and within the flesh of modernity itself: heard only by echoes rather than being seen.

Every Darky Is a King:
Fraud, Impersonation, and Pan-African Identities

The modernist version of this kind of social interaction and cultural change is what occurs in Harlem, the global crossroads of black community in the early years of the twentieth century. Esu-Elegbara, after all, is the god of the crossroads, so what better place to find a figure of a globalized African continuum of signifying than here? Bert Williams's masking functions on the eve of a Harlem Renaissance predicated on racial authenticity and on the political authority of that authenticity. Despite this fetish, it is a cultural and political renaissance largely due to the presence of black migrants from the American South, from the Anglophone and Spanish-speaking Caribbean, and, in smaller numbers, from the continent of Africa itself. Minstrelsy—particularly Williams's minstrelsy—adds global significance and transcultural resonance to a form initially rooted in a binary chromatism and in the specifics of plantation slavery. Both the racist and anti-racist fetish for the "natural" were challenged and bolstered by minstrel theater for reasons of its primary conceit—the reduction of identity to a performance and the celebration of performance as the ground of identity. White minstrelsy even at its worst was an engagement with those racialized discourses of American identity, attempting to contain difference within the racial hierarchy of power and to diminish the shock of cross-cultural encounters by dramatizing and controlling them through caricature.

Black minstrelsy as performed by Williams and Walker was the anti-racist interrogation of that engagement. Behind the burnt-cork mask, Williams's accented voice became also the silent voice of a global black modernism that is often eclipsed by the rhetoric of both binary chromatism and African American exceptionalism. His was a voice that refused the noisy and vainglorious spectacles of Garveyism by opting for its own invisibility rather than an aggressive display of its own dialect. After all, since "black" meant African American and "dialect" meant its local vernacular, his parodic use of that voice emphasized that although there was little space for his own dialect in the soundings of race, it could be masked rather than forgotten and its absence controlled rather than erased. And to render the other's voice so artfully, better even than its native speakers—well, that is an immigrant politics of mimicry all to itself, a form of discursive transcoding where the alienation of the kleptoparasitic black immigrant can only be projected through the socially recognizable stereotype and by a faithful sounding of the black native.

Again, to locate a precedent for intra-racial masking and cross-cultural soundings it is possible to go further back than Bert Williams or modernism or even the Harlem Renaissance. It is possible to return even slightly closer to the dawn of modernity by exploring a text like *The Interesting Narrative of the Life of Olaudah Equiano* (1789) for an early example. Although one of the black diaspora's founding texts and one of the most important anti-slavery tracts ever written, it is not the text itself that is of concern here. What is of interest is a minor controversy that attended its publication. Although in his 1967 edition Paul Edwards quickly dismissed the controversy as a ploy of those hostile to abolition (which it more than likely was), Vincent Caretta in his 1995 edition prefaced the manuscript with the controversy. Caretta does not dwell on it, does not explore the matter beyond the conclusions made by Edwards and emphasized by Equiano himself. Yet the controversy is of increasing importance to contemporary discourse because it suggests that the authority of Equiano's narrative, that the force of his anti-slavery polemic, could be undone by the allegation of a black-on-black masquerade.

Here is Paul Edwards in reference to Equiano and the controversy:

> During these years he made enemies amongst those who stood to gain from the slave trade, and it seems to have been these who made charges against him in The Oracle of 25 April 1792 that he was not a native African, but was born on the Danish Island of Santa Cruz in the West Indies. This story was repeated in The Star two days later. However, Equiano was able to produce evidence of his African origins, and the editor of The Star apologized, admitting that the story must have been a fabrication of the enemies of abolition who would do anything to weaken the force of arguments against the slave trade.[3]

The attack in The Oracle is worth reading primarily for the tone that it takes in revealing this information to the public. There is the clear sense in this letter that a great fraud is being unmasked, that a charlatan or a trickster is being revealed as a public nuisance. One is reminded here of the presence of Marcus Garvey on the Harlem stage; he whom the black and white popular press continually described as a charlatan, a huckster, a faux African emperor, a West Indian. The letter partly reads, "there is no absurdity, however gross, but popular credulity has a throat wide enough to swallow it. It is a fact that the Public may depend on, that Gustavus Vassa, who has publicly asserted that he was kidnapped in Africa, never was upon that Continent, but was born and bred up in the Danish Island of Santa Cruz, in the West Indies."[4] Interestingly, toward the end, the writer quotes Alexander Pope's Epistle to Bathurst: "Old Cato is as great a Rogue as You." The attack in The Star reads: "The Negroe, called GUSTAVUS VASSA, who has published an history of his life, and gives so admirable an account of the laws, religion, and natural productions of the interior parts of Africa; and in which he relates his having been kidnapped in his infancy, is neither more nor less, than a native of the Danish island of Santa Cruz."[5] In the Caretta edition, the reader encounters these letters before encountering the narrative itself and hence must first wade through these allegations of inauthenticity and cross-cultural impersonation before engaging a moving attack on the horrors of racial slavery. The reader also encounters Equiano's letter of defense, in which he attacks the "invidious falsehood" of the letters that were intended "to hurt my character, and to discredit and prevent the sale of my Narrative, asserting, that I was born in the Danish island of Santa Cruz, in the West Indies."[6] He goes on to "appeal to those numerous and respectable persons of character who knew me when I first arrived in England, and could speak no language but that of Africa."[7] In addition to this process of a white validation of his African authenticity, Equiano was forced to prove an African-ness rooted not simply in race but in geography. His *type* of blackness was in question. This is remarkable because the assault on his authenticity as an African is an attempt to subvert the global and diasporic focus of a narrative that crucially links Africa, diaspora, and modernity by way of race and slavery. Questioning his origins and placing them somewhere presumably less authentic whittles down a global vision to unrelated component parts.

What is most significant about this need to claim a "real" Africa to ground Equiano's written words is that the letters suggest that to unmask him as an Afro-Caribbean is to diminish the anti-slavery polemic that is *Equiano's Travels*; that by somehow locating a "false" "African-ness" behind the "real" one, the narrative is invalid. Because it stood against multiple layers of legitimation and had then to prove its masklessness, Equiano's narrative had yet another fully acknowledged burden. The question of his cultural—not racial—origins forces the author to prove his culture in order to liberate his race in an intellectual climate where they were, ironically, generally considered to be the same. Equiano prefaced subsequent editions of his narrative with his "To the Reader," a response to both letters. That he felt impelled to begin an already successful book with this defense, even after the newspapers apologized and acknowledged his true origins, suggests that there would always be a need to police and preempt those accusations.

By relocating the controversy to the beginning of the most recent edition of *Equiano's Travels*, Caretta foregrounds the larger issue of cross-cultural, intra-racial masquerade which is a primary product of black-on-black cultural contact. Here it is much earlier in modernity and, although minor, sets the stage for what will erupt in New York at the turn of the century given the radical diversity of its black community. The above reference to Garvey is not incidental. A distinct line can be drawn from Equiano's controversy to the controversy of one Prince Kojo Tovalou-Houenou of Dahomey who in 1924 made his first trip to America under the aegis of the UNIA. In his history of African American, African Caribbean, and black French interaction and "differance," Brent Hayes Edwards appropriately describes Prince Kojo as a "philosopher, lawyer and brazen social climber."[8] In his series of photographs of Harlem during its vogue, James Van Der Zee captures the prince standing between Garvey and a UNIA official. The prince stands elegant and resplendent in a white suit and wearing a hat; the two others carry their hats in their hands as if in ritual deference to him. The two men who flank the prince are clearly staged and posed to emphasize the central presence: after all, it can be no mistake that both of them frame the image by leaning slightly on opposing chairs while Kojo stands without the need for support, his flamboyant wing-tips edging forward. With his hands behind his back and against the background of what looks like a dirty Harlem alleyway, he does convey the image of royalty in exile—a symbol in no way lost on the rank and file of the UNIA. Interestingly, this is one of the few pictures of Garvey in which he is clearly not the center of the image, not clearly the subject of the picture; in fact, one barely notices him. Among the three figures, Garvey is marginalized not only by the fact of Prince Kojo's intensely bright white suit or the sober gravity of the other man's black suit. In gray, his colors matching the washed-out tones of the walls behind him, Garvey is also the shortest figure, and his head tilts slightly upward and toward Prince Kojo. For someone as scrupulous about his media representation and the power of the image, this is more than a little unusual. Another image features Prince Kojo actually sitting on a chair, with a deferential Garvey flanking him, standing.[9]

In *Harlem: Negro Metropolis*, Claude McKay writes:

> Prince Kogo, as a royal native potentate, was honored with a picturesque reception at Liberty Hall, where all the colors of God's fertile imagination were assembled in his honor. He made a speech full of praise for the work of the Universal Negro Association and saluted Marcus Garvey as the leader of the Negro people of the world. . . .
>
> Probably Prince Kogo, overwhelmed by the wonderful reception, was not fully conscious of the political significance of his act. He was no African clown prince. He was an authentic member of the family of Behanzin, the deposed King of Dahomey.[10]

That an authentic African prince would speak to the assembled UNIA and describe Garvey as "the leader of the Negro people of the world" was clearly a coup for the man who, despite his global impact via *The Negro World* and his international popular support, was relentlessly struggling for legitimacy in a context where even West Indian writers, activists, and intellectuals had turned against him. Yet Prince Kojo's support of Garvey was not without its cost. To give Garvey legitimacy was to have his own authenticity assaulted:

Kogo's princely act in acknowledging Garvey's leadership came as an inspiration to the movement at that critical time. But Kogo later paid dearly for it . . . he was ignominiously humiliated. One of the largest Paris dailies published a report on his personal affairs. It stated that Kogo was a swindler and a faker. He was not truly a prince. Posing as a prince of Dahomey he had borrowed large sums of money from people which had never been repaid.[11]

It is worth noting that on this same page McKay situates Kojo and Garvey in the context of high European modernism: "It was the time when James Joyce and Marcel Proust and T. S. Eliot were the intellectual gods."[12] This was a time also where issues of cultural authenticity and value were exacerbated by new means of technological reproduction alongside a colonial poetics of the African primitive. It is also worth noting that before even introducing the allegations of fraud, McKay felt it necessary to hypersignify Prince Kojo's authenticity by identifying him as "no African clown prince." This suggests that "African clown princes" either did in fact exist or were rumored to exist in such a way as to require a certain amount of scrutiny and policing. He further describes the prince as "a rare piece of primitive African sculpture" to complete his description of the cultural and artistic climate where African authenticity was the primary fetish.[13] McKay confirms that Prince Kojo was in fact an authentic member of the deposed Dahomeyan royal family. This defense was deemed necessary because if he were not really a prince, then it was possible that he was not really an African and could be—if not as exotic as a West Indian—then perhaps something much more ignoble: an African American. Yet despite constant proofs of his identity, Prince Kojo never outdistanced the accusation of fraud, and his reputation never fully recovered.[14]

The fact of Prince Kojo being from "Dahomey" and the suspicion of fraud are more than a coincidence considering that the term had been used at least since 1908 by various African performers to describe their stage shows.[15] Of course "Ethiopian," "Congo," and "African" had already been in use in American minstrel shows since the middle of the nineteenth century and numerous black street and carnival characters had been passing themselves off as authentic Africans for generations. A footnote in Bernth Lindfors's *Africans on Stage* provides a good sketch of these practices: it references one "Edgar B. Knight, the Wombwell 'crocuser' ('quack' doctor and herbalist) originally from Demerara, who called himself Abyssinian and dressed in long 'African' robes"; also, there was "Black Dougie, from Jamaica, who worked the British racecourses as an African." From Guyana there was Peter McKay, who posed as "Ras Prince Monolulu . . . who from the 1920s on entertained people at railway stations, racetracks, and in the streets of London."[16] This latter character is particularly interesting given the title "Ras," which appears as the name of a militant West Indian Garveyite in Ralph Ellison's *Invisible Man*; this years before the Rastafarian movement even appeared in New York City or the continental United States. That these and many other such "performances" occurred in England is interesting considering the popular success of *In Dahomey* there in 1903 and the fact that blackface minstrelsy was popular in England up until 1978 with the cancellation of the beloved *Black and White Minstrel Show* by the BBC—the same year it decided to screen the television series *Roots*. In England, where encounters with black peoples were limited, *In Dahomey* was so successful that King Edward VII and the royal family asked for a command performance, thereby establishing minstrelsy in the imagination of British popular culture. At this performance Bert Williams performed his hit, "Evah Darkey Is a King":

> Evah darkey is a king!
> Royalty is jes' de ting.
> If yo' social life's a bungle,
> Jes yo' go back to yo' jungle,
> And remember dat your daddy was a king.[17]

In "Ethnological Show Business: Footlighting the Dark Continent," Bernth Lindfors charts these various performances of African identity by exploring their connection to ethnological display and the rise of the circus. After the Anglo-Zulu wars, for example, circus entrepreneurs actually recruited Zulus for their shows. P. T. Barnum even offered the British government $100,000 for permission to exhibit Cetewayo, the captured leader of the Zulus, known for routing the British army in two great and bloody victories.[18] The British fascination for this specific African group helped kick-start the market for "Zulus" on display throughout the end of the nineteenth century. Yet intraracial masquerade was also crucial to this form of containment and entertainment in British popular culture. As Lindfors points out, "Needless to say, many of these Zulu performers were frauds."[19] From the memoirs of two showmen, we have testimony. A British circus showman writes in his memoir, "I recollect at the time of the Zulu war how one showman conceived the idea of exhibiting a number of Zulu warriors. There was only one drawback—not a single Zulu was at that moment in the country. But drawbacks do not exist for the born showman and a party of ordinary niggers were easily made up into Cetewayo's savage soldiery."[20] An American circus showman adds this transatlantic echo:

In the side show we had a big Negro whom we had fitted up with rings in his nose, a leopard skin, some assegais and a large shield made out of cow's skin. While he was sitting on the stage in the side show, along came two Negro women and remarked, "See that nigger over there? He 'aint no Zulu, that's Bill Jackson. He worked over here at Camden on the dock. I seen that nigger often." Poor old Bill Jackson was as uneasy as if he was sitting on needles, holding the shield between him and the two Negro women.[21]

In subsequent sections of this book, more will be made of the specific kind of specularity at work here between the African American gaze and ethnographic display. It must be distinguished from the colonial gaze or the white European gaze which used ethnographic display in order to both constitute colonial/racial subjects and to establish what both Curtis Hinsley and Anne McClintock argue as a form of touristic display as the colonies were translated into commodities by the market forces which defined the particulars of an American imperial vision.[22] This "other" gaze is important also because it is at the heart of the kind of minstrelsy at work in Williams's and Walker's In Dahomey and the "other" modernisms that are located in Bert Williams's use of blackface. These are modernisms in which a black diasporic vision is articulated and refracted through plural and multiple masking, explicitly as a product of a black ethnographic vision which produced distinct black subjects via the same technologies of touristic display and the consumption of minstrelsy.

But the use of "ordinary niggers" in the place of authentic Africans in fact became so widespread that even naturalists had to declare the authenticity of their specimens. In 1885, one had defensively to prove that the Africans on display were actually Africans, not "as some of the journalists have wickedly insinuated, Irish immigrants, cunningly painted and made up like savages. They are genuine Zulus."[23] It would be fascinating to hear what Eric Lott would make of this alleged Irish impersonation of continental Africans. Even P. T. Barnum—the self-described high priest of "humbug" who was responsible for many such frauds—had to acknowledge this before his own show at Madison Square Garden in 1888.[24] He advertised his specimens as "Two Real African Zulus" not simply to authorize his display in relation to other suspected fakeries but to distinguish this particular display from his own frauds, such as the infamous "Zip, the What-is-it" a monkeylike "missing link" that was often performed by small, microcephalic African Americans.[25] The hyperbolic assertion of the realness of Barnum's Zulus is reminiscent of Bert Williams's and George Walker's billing themselves as "Two Real Coons" to distinguish their performance of authenticity from that of the dominant white minstrel tradition.

For Williams and Walker, the African American stereotype had been filtered through many generations of white impersonation; only their own racial authenticity could be used as an edge in the "mimic warfare" of vaudeville. This, by the way, was not unlike the claim, made by producers of African American culture, of an authentic relationship to Africa as a competitive edge over white moderns, who were already identifying and claiming Africa as the site of their own distinguishing subjectivities and attempts to redefine "the new." For Barnum, his own and so many African frauds made an appeal to authenticity necessary—however, like Equiano's situation, this was not simply a question of race but one of culture, for the blacks on display had to here be differentiated from the *less authentic* African Americans. Lindfors concludes by pointing out that " 'Zulu' thus became synonymous with artifice and disguise. Pseudo-Zulus proliferated, emerging as a stock character type that eventually entered the standard vocabulary of ethnic imagery projected by such powerful media as Hollywood films."[26] David Killingray and Willie Henderson note that by the early part of the twentieth century, "imitating Africans was a well-established practice among black entertainers."[27] Lindfors also explains that in American circus jargon, "Zulu" as a term "gradually expanded its field of reference to include any Negro who participated in the 'spec.' A black laborer or musician employed by the circus could earn a 'Zulu ticket' (a credit slip for more pay) by donning a costume and parading around the hippodrome track in the grand opening pageant."[28]

So by the time of Williams's and Walker's comic spectacle *In Dahomey* and by the time of Prince Kojo's appearance on the UNIA stage, the terms "Ethiopian," "African," or "Dahomeyan" (not to mention "Nubian," "Congo," or even just "jungle") had started to fold racial masquerade within their field of meaning much as did the term "Zulu." It was just five years after *In Dahomey* that a troupe of Sierra Leoneans worked in England as "Dahomey warriors," no doubt exploiting the resonance of that word as established by the Williams and Walker minstrel show.[29] As noted, this masquerade was also a common practice outside the circus or ethnographic exhibitions among black con men and hucksters. For them the exotic authenticity of the African mask enabled a greater degree of social mobility than plain old despised black skin. In *Pan-Africanism from Within*, Ras Makonnen describes how this intra-racial passing/masquerade could work against racism in America: "Once you had discovered this American folly, you would put on your fez and 'pass' like any other white. . . . People might think you were an African prince."[30] In *Invisible Man*, Ralph Ellison will also note this sociopolitical oddity which operates on the plane of the visual only to facilitate a strategic absence: "I recalled a report of a shoe-shine boy who had encountered the best treatment in the South simply by wearing a white turban instead of his usual Dobbs or Stetson."[31]

It is worth noting that this observation strikes the text's nameless hero after he hears a powerful declamation by the multiply masked Reinhart, he who existed in "a vast seething, hot world of fluidity."[32] Ellison's representation of Reinhart explicitly depends on both minstrelsy and the classic trickster figure. This child of Esu declaims, "BEHOLD THE SEEN UNSEEN/ BEHOLD THE INVISIBLE."[33] The observation also occurs right before the narrator accepts the strength of this politics and puts it to use not only in relation to white America but in relation to those other blacks who root themselves in nationalist discourse of presence: "I felt that somewhere between Rinehart and invisibility there were great potentialities."[34] He realizes something about this strategic possibility that is of use in this work's exploration of black cross-cultural contact and signifyin(g) during modernism; it enables a recovery and a redefinition of alternate modalities of resistance in a rhizomatic postmodern era: "Not only could you travel upward toward success but you could travel downward as well; up and down, in retreat as well as in advance, crabways and crossways and around in a circle, meeting your old selves coming and going and perhaps all at the same time."[35] That this politics of masquerade is already the parodic product of double-consciousness within the specifically African American context—signifyin(g) within signifyin(g), something also central to African American feminism—is important. It reminds us that every local articulation of race is itself shot through with its own parodic undoing, its own masquerade. However, to return to the cross-cultural politics of the fez and the turban, the primary equation here in both Ellison and Ras Makonnen is fascinating: *black skin plus African costume equaled social whiteness.* This emphasizes how much American racism was dependent on the cultural specificity of and a deep historical intimacy with African Americans.

Killingray and Henderson also state that during this period "for black entertainers to pretend an African origin and to append a 'royal' title was not uncommon in Britain or the United States."[36] Every darky could then become a king and claim an abstract historical and racial origin as well as a nifty costume and grandiloquent title as the source of royalty. For a white audience perhaps nothing was more comical and exotic than the notion of Negro royalty—something that mocked nobility and sociocultural hierarchy while serving to further debase the Negro. But one can imagine that to a black viewer, beyond this racist mockery were traces of a desire for power and nobility, a kingdom and a nation. The various titles by which Garvey described himself and UNIA notaries as having great suzerainty over Africa—for example, Duke of Nigeria, Overlord of Uganda, Empress of the Nile, and Lord High Potentate of Africa—should be read in line with this history; after all, such titling was an established popular tradition in theater, carnival, and the street con game and was a desire buried deep in the hearts of the black oppressed. Garvey made this performance politics but could not strip it of its ridicule. Bert Williams would exploit its ridicule to make it cultural politics. As we will see, In Dahomey features songs like "Leader of the Colored Aristocracy" and "On Emancipation Day" which mock and celebrate the notion of black nobility and power while simultaneously suggesting that the very notion of such a thing as impossible was intolerable. Du Bois's description of Garvey and the UNIA's public spectacles by way of a reference to Bert Williams then makes sense given that the international success of In Dahomey preceded and prepared the way for those street and cultural performances in which Africa was the mask for multiple and competing local intentions.

For confirmation that black intra-racial passing was a thriving strategy during the Harlem Renaissance, one can turn to the work of such Caribbean writers as W. A. Domingo and Eric Walrond. In his "Gift of the Black Tropics" in The New Negro, the former alludes to those black immigrants who were "too dark of complexion to pose as Cubans or some other Negroid but alien-tongued foreigners."[37] Language functions here as the cultural border, not pigment; passing as a strategy is then opened up to include multiple vernacular directions within the skin of race. Although Domingo does not say this, it is clear that only an "African" masquerade would be available to these black immigrants because of the color of their skin, where their lighter-skinned peers could pass as Italians, Latin Americans, or Egyptian/Middle Eastern exotics. But the primary point here is that Domingo acknowledges that the act of intra-racial passing and masquerade was common during Harlem's vogue. West Indian writers seemed particularly attuned to this issue. Throughout his work, Eric Walrond identified and criticized those among the black immigrant community who "passed" as other types of blacks. In his marvelous essay "Vignettes of the Dusk" he describes this process of black-on-black passing as "philological assimilation," which recalls the "ethnic altercasting" mentioned previously.[38]

Philological assimilation, however, entails the power dynamic at work between African Americans and Afro-Caribbeans, whereas ethnic altercasting is primarily concerned with the flexibility of discursive possibilities among bi- or tri-dialectal immigrants. In an interesting take on Walrond's term, this poly-dialectical context was claimed by the West Indian aviator Hubert Fauntleroy Julian, who immigrated to Harlem in 1921. Dubbed "the black Lindbergh," Julian was the first black person to obtain a pilot's license. As Ann Douglas writes in *Terrible Honesty*:

> White journalists loved Julian for the colorful copy he provided, but they invariably cast even his most heroic exploits in terms of updated minstrel comedy, presenting him as a boastful and too stylish Zip Coon figure. Dignified reminders from Julian, "No monkey business with this story. It's very serious," were of no avail. Like many West Indian and American blacks, Julian used two forms of English; he called it being "ambidextrous." In addition to various European and African tongues, he spoke both Standard English and a mixture of West Indies and Black English; journalists liked to parody what they saw as his linguistic confusion.[39]

No monkey (chaser) business indeed; there was little space in the popular imagination for this confident and destabilizing (yet colorful) version of Mikhail Bakhtin's "polyglossia." Yet the white American attempt to recuperate the linguistic "excess" that was Julian's always media-savvy persona as a form of minstrelsy is no surprise. However, Walrond was very aware of the "dialectical oppression" experienced by black immigrants in a Harlem where the African American vernacular was the status quo and West Indian English was mocked and marginalized.[40] As he wrote in 1935 in "White Man, What Now," reflecting on his migration to America:

> I went on to New York. I settled in the Harlem Negro quarter. I found the community fairly evenly dominated by Southern Negroes and West Indian emigrants. A wide cleavage existed between the two groups. The West Indian with his Scottish, Irish or Devonshire accent, was to the native Black who has still retained a measure of his African folk-culture, uproariously funny. He was joked at on street corners, burlesqued on the stage and discriminated against in business and social life. His pride in his British heritage and lack of racial consciousness were contemptuously put down to "airs."[41]

Walrond was wise to see this cleavage in terms of the larger racial dynamic which ultimately motivates the masking and intra-racial performances with which this chapter is concerned: "The white man in America, strangely, does not consider the West Indian a 'nigger.' He is to him a 'foreigner.' "[42] An argument could easily be made that Walrond's stunning book *Tropic Death* has suffered by reason of his own "foreignness" in a climate where African American literature and cultural production were prioritized. The text depends on various West Indian dialects, languages, and settings in a literary renaissance where "the South" is the dominant site of "home" for blacks and where the African American vernacular is the more marketable sound of "the folk." One could extend this argument to include Claude McKay, whose success as a poet and novelist came primarily after he suppressed his Jamaican dialectal specificity in order not to become "universal," as Edward Kamau Brathwaite suggests in his deeply flawed but historically essential *History of the Voice*, but to perform a much more marketable and audible African American-ness. This is, in fact, precisely the argument of this book's closing chapter.

Forging the Dark Continent: An African Savage's Own Story

An intriguing example of the kind of intra-racial and cross-cultural passing/masquerade being discussed can be found in the life and work of a man who, at the same time as Garvey's Prince Kojo, made quite a career for himself as a Dahomeyan prince. In this case ethnic altercasting is linked clearly to both vaudeville and ethnographic display; and "philological assimilation" is turned back to not Africa but a commodified performance of its absence. Prince Bata Kindai Amgoza Ibn LoBagola was the author of *An African Savage's Own Story*, an autobiography first published in *Scribner's* magazine in 1929 and in book form soon thereafter. We have David Killingray and Willie Henderson to thank for unearthing and unmasking LoBagola, since his book was forgotten after having been widely dismissed and discredited upon its publication. In its time the "autobiography" was compared to Rene Maran's *Batouala* (1921), the first black novel to win the French Prix Goncourt. However, the narrative, style, and language have more in common with Edgar Rice Burroughs's *Tarzan of the Apes* than with *Batouala* or even *Equiano's Travels*. Knopf, LoBagola's eventual publisher, already had success publishing the work of Walter White, James Weldon Johnson, Langston Hughes, and Carl Van Vechten; so the presence of this racial "forgery" in the midst of a literary renaissance obsessed with racial and cultural authenticity is too good to be true.

LoBagola's story is an essential text of its time because it shows just how much intra-racial masquerade occurred not only on the margins of the "great race welding" that was the Harlem Renaissance but also in the shadows of the undifferentiating gaze of white ethnography. Like Bert Williams, Lo-Bagola provides the link between "ethnological show business"—the display of "foreign peoples for commercial and/or educational purposes"—and a heteroglot pan-African politics and sensibility.[43] Such impersonation is undertaken in relationship to the "spectatorial apparatus," as Bill Brown would have it, that "incitement to visibility and a protection from contact" which "makes visible the need to make the black man and the blackness of the black man visible."[44] It is the stress on race as a visual form of knowing that is exploited here as a mode of strategic disappearance. To become an "African" was in some ways a partial escape from race by asserting a cultural specificity and authenticity that may or may not have been one's own. However, to call oneself a "prince" was also to ennoble that site of racial/cultural origins and, in both cases, to blind white spectatorship and its desire for visual fidelity. In other words, one could pass in the other direction and in such a way that one would disappear into a fictional authenticity and operate cannily from within it.

An African Savage's Own Story strangely parallels Equiano's Travels and Batouala. It begins with an exotic West African setting—one that was both imaginary and produced by an untrained ethnographic vision. The first few sections are rich with folk tales, strange customs, and details of social life, and the final chapters are curious compendiums of ethnographic material. In the first section, "A Savage Home in the Ondo Bush," Ibn LoBagola tells us that he was born "in the village of Nodaghusah, six hundred miles north of Abomey Calavi, once the capital of Dahomey, and about forty-five days' walk north of the Gulf of Guinea, and three days' walk south of the native city Timbuktu. The country is in the Sudan, in the sphere of influence of the French Colonial Government."[45] According to his telling, the term "Dahomey" does not come from the natives of that savage bush, although it is in the local vernacular. "Dahomey" as a name for this space between bushes arises from his particular subculture: the "B'nai Ephraim," or as called by the natives, the "Emo-Yo-Quaim."[46] His people are the "strange people," the "Black Jews of the Ondo Bush" who arrived in the land of "Da-Ome" (Good Water) almost two millennia earlier. It should be noted that Equiano, in his Travels, on a number of occasions likened the natives of his Africa to Jews. Ibn LoBagola writes:

> How this name left our present country and drifted to the coast, I have never found out, but Dahomey is the name of the country on the coast. It did

not take long, according to our rabbis, for the natives on the east and west of us to find our snug little place. They surrounded us and wrested from us the village that our people had made, and set up their own rule. We were never a fighting people, and we were easily subjugated. But we lived on in that same place, and we have seen many changes, but we have remained always the same, preserving our law and guarding our sacred Torah with our very lives.[47]

Traveling to Africa after the destruction of the Temple in Judea, the "strange people" migrated to Morocco only to leave after encountering even greater persecution. From there they migrated to Timbuktu, where they "were not treated badly, but we were not content to live under the rule of desert tribes any longer than was necessary."[48] After so many of them died from impure water, they decided to stay in a "bush" that had good water despite being surrounded by "wild beasts, elephants, leopards, lions, monkeys, and reptiles, the horned viper and the boa constrictor, and thousands upon thousands of hook lizards. This was the place we decided to make our home, because we were free when we came upon it."[49] This depiction of LoBagola's "bush" is in marked and spectacular contrast to Equiano's highly romanticized description of the "charming fruitful vale" of Essaka.[50] Ibn LoBagola, unfortunately, says nothing about the evolving and mutating racial character of this migrant people; he says nothing about their skin color and what happens to it as they travel for so long and for so far and for generations engage and encounter radically distinct cultural and ethnic groups. He tells nothing of the politics of passing as survival/subterfuge, which is nothing new to the Jewish Diaspora, although he does claim that "purity in blood" is the root of their nobility.[51] What is important here is that this description of his authentic identity, which he maintained throughout his life even up until his famous conversion to Roman Catholicism, establishes Ibn LoBagola's ethnography as being produced already by dislocation, from a marginalized, migrant not-quite African perspective there in the heart of savagery. Despite his attempt to cloak himself in an authenticity that was eventually revealed as false, it is important to note that this "African-ness" in his own telling is ultimately not "African" at all.

It is obvious that these earlier sections of *An African Savage's Own Story* borrowed heavily from the numerous travel narratives and popularized adventure tales of the time in which the African background is rendered as pure fantasy. Where Equiano spends much of his time attempting to rationalize and demystify "primitive" Africa, Ibn LoBagola seems to often revel in its savagery to emphasize his own personal narrative of transcendence in the context of a general civilizing. Because these earlier and contemporary adventure tales were about dark and mysterious Africa, even the most outlandish representations could be accepted as authentic, or at least believable. "Africa" stood for literary fantasy, for an utter fiction of romance, exploration, and escape—in short, as a landscape it was always already a literary forgery that contained and helped to control the administration and domination of "the real." No two writers express this better than H. Rider Haggard in England and Edgar Rice Burroughs in America. In terms of cultural impact and iconic influence, their respective "Africas" have been much more significant than those of Sir Richard Burton, John Speke, or even Joseph Conrad's favorite, E. D. Morel, and LoBagola's favorite, David Livingston.

One could easily read Burroughs's *Tarzan of the Apes* series as not just the extension of a Haggardian vision but the American appropriation of that colonial envisioning of Africa to signal a discursive if not formal colonial control as one empire succeeds the other. The "Africans" in *Tarzan of the Apes*—many of whom are literally lynched in this novel after Tarzan learns how to use a lasso—are very clearly African Americans who, now free, are depicted as reverting to wildness and savagery. Ibn LoBagola's Dahomey borrows heavily from the traditions of colonial travel narratives and colonial adventure fiction, just as his performance of African identity borrowed heavily from the science of ethnography and the art of popular fiction. To his credit there is a good amount of ethnographic detail and quasi-anthropological investigation in the autobiography along with the very obvious elements of adventure melodrama. But the words "savage" and "horrible" appear far too often in this narrative for it to be anything more than pulp fiction; moreover, there are just too many titillating and overexaggerated descriptions simply to impress the 1920s audience.

Ibn LoBagola's racial politics, however, is clearly at work in those sections in which he observes that the native traditions and local cultures are far superior to those he would later encounter in the West. For example, after comparing African polygamy with Western monogamy, he concludes, "one wife with divorce and alimony is not so wholesome as twenty wives with neither divorce or alimony. The wild men in my country do not know anything about alimony; it seems to me, alimony is making a lot of civilised men wild."[52] Also, "You could not blame me for the habit of telling the truth; I was on the way to becoming civilised, but I was not yet quite civilised enough to tell lies."[53] One is reminded here of one of Du Bois's darkest statements in *The Souls of Black Folk*, where double-consciousness is linked directly to double-dealing: "The Price of Culture is a lie."[54] There are many such observations in LoBagola's narrative, though they are perhaps less moralistic than the ones that proliferate throughout the anti-slavery polemic of *Equiano's Travels*. Another such moment of relativism comes when he describes how white men were seen and imagined in the Ondo bush, in a passage similar to Equiano's description of the European slavers who he is initially convinced are cannibals. Ibn LoBagola writes:

> As for me, I never saw a white man in my country. When I was a child, as far back as I can remember, and that must be when I was about four years old, I heard talk of white people, but it was never clear whether white people actually lived, or whether they had become extinct. I welcomed the thought that they had died out. All I could hear my mother say was that if white men should come across us, they would eat us raw. She said they fed themselves only twice in the year, and that then they ate their young if they could not get the young of other people. My mother said that white people came like witches, from no one knew where; they just appeared and disappeared. They were formed much differently from our own men; every white man had only one of everything: one eye, in the middle of the forehead, one leg, with a great wide foot, fan-shaped, so that when he lay down, the foot acted as a sunshade. A white man had no visible nose, and his mouth was large and could be made much larger at will. He lived on raw human flesh and could be seen in the bush just before and just after the rainy season.[55]

Obviously Ibn LoBagola is very much aware of the politics of myth and fantasy and how much myth and fantasy came to bear on the white colonial view of Africa and Africans. Africa as a site of fantasy, darkness, a continent of monsters is here overturned in a relativistic gesture where the European reader encounters himself through the eyes of an authentic savage—or, a black persona masquerading as an authentic African savage who uses that masquerade as a strategic, critical position. Just to make it clear that he is quite aware of this gesture and of his reversal of the tropes and topoi of colonial narratives of African monstrosity, LoBagola writes:

> Now, what could you expect us children to see, when our parents told us such things? Especially when they were supported in their stories by men who had been accustomed to going away to different trading markets? Some of these men had seen white men, but they knew nothing about them. That is reasonable, because I know even in these Western countries, where everyone

is supposed to be wise, some provincial folk know that wild black people exist, and many have seen them, but they do not know much about them. I venture to say that they talk to their children in no uncertain terms of "niggers," as the black men are called here.[56]

This politicized pseudoethnography must be situated in relationship to Lo-Bagola's own description of his work as an "itinerant entertainer and vaudeville artiste, informant to anthropologists, lecturer on African 'culture,' convict, and soldier in both the United States and Britain."[57] His perspective and its political impact are produced by a life in which race is encountered and experienced in multiple ways and in a panoramic social landscape that few African Americans of his time and generation could have had access to. Not only was he a native informant; on his way to West Africa he actually described himself as an anthropologist as well as a "British Colonial Subject."[58] Later on in his narrative he would confess, "To tell the truth, I had no idea what I was saying . . . So I followed instructions and simply played to the gallery."[59] Talk about plural masking and double voiced signifyin(g): Ibn LoBagola was an even more multiple mask-in-motion than Bert Williams and used the mask to make much more noise, escaping perhaps much deeper into the strategic fiction of African identity.

Bert Williams's only experience in Dahomey was onstage. Although it is not described in his "autobiography," LoBagola did spend some time in West Africa. He told the Naturalization Service in 1934, "I went to London and was there several months and went to Dahomey, West Africa. I stayed there and traveled in the bush north of Dahomey until 1912, when I returned to Scotland in May, 1912."[60] The autobiography states that he was advised to emphasize for his audiences that he was not from any specific part of Africa but from "Dahomey" simply because in the world of vaudeville, as in the world of minstrel theater, it was a well-known topos : "people would not believe me if they did not know where the place was. I got thorough instructions."[61] In tracing LoBagola's life, Killingray and Henderson write that he "followed the path of many traveling 'Africans,' to be found performing and struggling in every corner of the world, and at times being 'studied' and exhibited as creatures of exotic, and often imaginary, cultures."[62] He was an example of how a "purveyor of ethnographic data and popular entertainment blended into one."[63] For Ibn LoBagola scientific knowledge of race and vaudeville performance were no different from each other. To be a cultural informant was literally to be a performer. To be a native was to be onstage; to be an African was to wear (multiple) masks. To lie was to entertain, but given Ibn

LoBagola's constant critiques of racism, colonialism, and white supremacy, it was also to return the white ethnographic gaze by opting to *only seem* like its product in order to safely gaze back. As Curtis M. Hinsley writes in his study of the 1893 Columbian Exposition in Chicago, "Where the gaze can be returned, specular commerce becomes uneasy."[64]

In line with this relation between ethnography and intra-racial masquerade, Shane Peacock explores the display of Zulus by P. T. Barnum and others during the late 1800s after the Anglo-Zulu wars in Southern Africa. This sets the stage for LoBagola and for Bert Williams and George Walker, who in 1894 would do exactly the same thing as the notorious "African Savage" and take on the personae of exhibition Zulus years before becoming successful on the vaudeville stage. Peacock writes, "it was not uncommon for Victorian promoters to exhibit 'exotic Africans' who were really from places like Hoboken or the Bronx."[65] His wonderful essay "Africa Meets the Great Farini" tells the story of an African American from North Carolina who was over seven feet tall. After approaching a museum in circa 1882, he was remade into a "Dahomeyan Giant" by a theatrical costumer and coached to forget his ability to speak or understand the English language. This masquerade was so successful that he was then passed on to a sideshow where for many seasons he "posed as a Dahomey giant, a Maori from New Zealand, an Australian aborigine and a Kaffir. This man's success was the initiative for a score of other Negroes, who posed as representatives of any foreign races the sideshow proprietor wished to exhibit."[66] Bert Williams's own penchant for playing other kinds of nonwhite ethnicities in his minstrel performances is very much a part of this much larger tendency in American sideshows (and perhaps cultural discourse) to collapse all forms of subordinate otherness into one.

LoBagola's masquerade is thus merely a part of a long tradition of both black-on-black minstrelsy and a commercial form of ethnic altercasting. Black performers participated in this form of racial commodification simply because the white market for extreme racial and cultural difference was lucrative in an era in which those spaces and people once located as "exotic" and "distant" to the white imagination were becoming dangerously banal and easily accessible. Not only were these performances a sign of American imperial provenance; they represented a colonial consumer malaise at the root of American "produce imperialism." It was the white gaze that was being exploited by these commercial displays, a gaze so overdetermined and conclusive in its knowledge of otherness that it was simply begging and paying to be deceived. For example, when "The Great Farini" premiered his "Friendly Zulus" in England before bringing them to America, he did so at a theater well known for blackface shows and minstrel vaudeville—the site of racial fraud and impersonation.[67] At the end of his long career displaying exotics, The Great Farini took charge of England's widely popular Moore and Burgess Minstrels. During this period, the line between blackface and the display of "real" Africans was therefore porous and fluctuating, maintained by the increasingly ill-fitting garb of race and exploited by the pseudo-coherence of the category which maintained itself in two primary ways: by the overwhelming desire for it to fit and by the frisson produced by the possibilities of deception.

By the time of Ibn LoBagola's stint in England there were already many African-themed or black shows in popular theater, where the legacy and memory of the Williams and Walker troupe was still very much alive. According to Killingray and Henderson, In Dahomey had become the name of a popular troupe and LoBagola did perform on the vaudeville stage as "The Fire King of Dahomey."[68] An African Savage's Own Story describes Ibn LoBagola's first encounter with "other" blacks as a spectator at a French colonial exhibition:

> During the whole time that I had lived in Scotland and in England, I had never seen another black man. I remembered seeing blacks from Dahomey on exhibition in the Dahomey village in Paris when my young master had run away with me; but before then, and since then up to the time that I am speaking of, no one had ever mentioned to me that there were black people living in the world outside my own land, Africa.[69]

Although this confessional autobiography is largely a fiction, it is important to note that the transatlantic encounter of black intra-racial, cross-cultural differences is here mediated by colonial exhibitions. It is curious that this fact is conveyed a mere page after LoBagola writes of his entrance, however innocent, into the world of ethnographic show business and racial display/ performance while in England:

> In New Brighton I met a woman, a Mrs. Collins, who traveled in a show. She owned a traveling cinematograph show and induced me to go with her to attract people to see her show. I did not see why I should not do as she asked and, in fact, I thought it would be fine sport; so I went along. Her people taught me how to dance, and then they dressed me up in a white suit and made me dance on a platform outside the show. By traveling with the show I saw many towns in England.[70]

But it is in America that he supposedly becomes much more dependent on that form of performance for his living. It is in America that ethnographic show business makes him famous as performer and ultimately as a lecturer on the university circuit—a distinct form of vaudeville: "I secured many engagements on the vaudeville stage. My picture appeared in a motion-picture weekly and I was heralded far and wide as 'The Fire-proof Man.' A vaudeville circuit gave me bookings through theatres all over the eastern part of the United States, and it seemed as if my star were in the ascendant."[71] LoBagola claims to have danced and performed in an early silent film and to have become the darling of the media; he went from performance to performance shifting his stories and his costumes to suit the crowd and their interests. From America to Europe to Africa to vaudeville to the University of Pennsylvania; from the department of anthropology at Oxford to dressing in feathers, playing with fire, and landing in prison; from accusations of fraud to multiple charges of pedophilia and child molestation: this was the trajectory. And he never removed the mask.

It is during this period working in America that he claims to have first encountered racism: "Now I was confronted for the first time in my life with the problem of colour. Up to that time no one had ever mentioned my blackness to me; it had not been thought of, so far as I knew, except as a curiosity. The thing that puzzled me now was that I was not spoken of in the new country as a black man; I was called a 'coloured' man."[72] He avows that he went to America partly out of an eagerness to "help civilise the people there."[73] But his first encounter with the problem of color? What does it mean for this African American performer, wearing a complex ethnofictional African mask, to tell us that it is in America that he first encountered racism and the color line? And this especially after he has described his relationship with his "master" as a young boy in Scotland, seemingly without irony: "We loved each other, just as a master loves his pet dog, and the dog loves the master."[74] This statement comes in the chapter entitled "Taming Begins," in which LoBagola perversely romanticizes the process by which he is transformed from a jungle "monkey" into a semi-civilized Scottish lad. When as a young boy he returned to the Ondo bush from Scotland he was scolded by his native father for his affection for his "white father" and his confusion about his racial persona: "Don't you know that you cannot be white and black at the same time?"[75]

The text is full of such race and color tensions, far in advance of LoBagola's fictional landfall in segregation-era America. An awareness of American race-relations in fact suffuses the text and informs and motivates its sometimes powerful and oftentimes bizarre take on early-twentieth-century racism and colonialism. It seems clear that the narrative ultimately saves its ire for the racism of Ibn LoBagola's "authentic" home, for America: this was the place where he was most scarred by not only racism but also relentless allegations about his sexuality and his inappropriate relationships with underage white boys. Early in the narrative he exclaims, "I love my native country, I love my savage people; but at the same time I am forced to hate my own customs, the customs of my father. I am neither white nor black, I am a misfit in a white mans country, and a stranger to my own land."[76] Which native country? Which savage people? What kind of stranger? What customs? What kind of misfit? Here the levels of doubling, alienation, and marginalization seem far too extensive to be contained without some form of ruthless and relentless masking. Some form of intra-racial passing is absolutely necessary as a tortured psyche folds in upon its own fictions.

Like Equiano and Prince Kogo, LoBagola was hounded by accusations of his inauthenticity, accusations that his story was a fraud and his specialist's knowledge of Africa purely fiction. Not that it mattered much to the exhibitors and those who engaged him for lectures; many of them knew that to an audience hungry for the exotic, the mask was as good as flesh, provided it was costumed, painted, and situated in an ersatz natural (or authorial academic) setting. Not that it mattered much to LoBagola, who at times seemed much less interested in racial or cultural fidelity than were his contemporaries in the Harlem Renaissance. Yet LoBagola, like Equiano and Prince Kojo, protested vociferously, knowing that in an intensely racist climate the mask was much safer than flesh and allowed much more freedom: "People all over the country try to show that I am deceiving people in this story of my life. They have told me to my face that I never saw Africa; that I was born somewhere in western Pennsylvania or in some place in the South."[77]

The introduction to An African Savage's Own Story echoes the controversies surrounding Equiano's Travels as encountered in Caretta's edition. It also reminds one of Ras Makonnen's description of the subversive politics of the "fez": "Ibn LoBagola's costume is usually the costume of any well-dressed American, but on occasion he wears a red fez and sometimes a loose robe, neither one of which, he says frankly, has anything whatever to do with his native land . . . he wears fez and robe merely for effect."[78] After all, says the introduction, here reminiscent of the various descriptions of Bert Williams, "He is a born mimic and delights in entertaining."[79] The introduction asks,

"Is the Story True?," primarily for reasons of the disbelief that attended Ibn LoBagola and the publication of *An African Savage's Own Story*. This disbelief derived in part from the racism of the time, which was still unsure about the literary ability of blacks—especially untutored blacks from a ferocious and savage bush. And that is precisely what Ibn LoBagola exploited: that racist disbelief, which, though still rooted in ethnic pseudoscience, was nevertheless hungry for that science to entertain:

> From a scientific point of view, attention is attracted to this African savage's life story for two reasons: his unequalled presentation of authentic African folk-lore and tribal customs; and the remarkable development, psychologically, of a naked bushman into a man of ability in civilization. That a naked bushman should develop into an author is certainly remarkable; it is a long step from being an unclad savage in the Ondo bush to being a professional writer.[80]

To make his case and respond to his critics, the African savage, like Equiano, provided "a great number of letters, recommendations, official records of military service, and photographs of himself at various ages and by giving the names and addresses of people who corroborate what he says."[81] Of course, these were all forgeries.

After unveiling Ibn LoBagola as Joseph Howard Lee, born in Baltimore in 1887, Killingray and Henderson suggest that for this poor African American to play "the alien African prince" enabled him to "thumb his nose at 'Jim Crow' laws."[82] This is the same point made earlier by Ras Makonnen and Ralph Ellison; though for West Indians in an African American city and renaissance, passing as African Americans would be their way of thumbing their noses also at Afro-Yankee parochialism while simultaneously maintaining their own problematic sense of cultural superiority. In this way African otherness enabled one to maintain pride of culture while simultaneously accepting the anti–African American racism of the time and the attendant logic of white supremacy. The "uneasiness" that Curtis Hinsley describes in relation to "specular commerce" is an uneasiness with regard to the specular racial categorization upon which both racism and African American nationalisms depend. It is a dis-ease akin to the "category crisis" that Marjorie Garber describes in the politics of drag and cross-gender performance because it fragments the racial category and its supposed political affiliations along cultural, linguistic, and national lines. It is more complex here, however, because the poles of difference in Garber's theorizing—male and female—

begin from the assumption of essential difference. This category crisis is rooted in a fundamentally assumed sameness: African and Negro.

Killingray and Henderson conclude their "outing" of LoBagola by locating a politics in this masquerade, one vastly different from that allowed by Afrocentric or even pan-African appropriations of African identity, which almost always imply a transnational if not essentialist solidarity:

> By adopting an African identity LoBagola was able to exploit his blackness in a way that opened doors that would otherwise have been closed to an African American. In the process he was able to fool a whole range of professional people in the white establishment. Undoubtedly he was exploited, but he also exploited others by his talent for imitation and presentation. As such he entertained at a high standard before large, appreciative, and sometimes critical audiences.
>
> LoBagola's African persona, while both flawed and frequently challenged, was successfully maintained . . . his African "mask" represents an imaginative flight, an escape into a fantasy world, lived out as real. His attempt to justify his own deep-seated confusions and inner tensions by claiming to be a "savage" outsider has pathetic appeal. In one powerful image he can gather together the various fragments of his life in a way which both asserts his dignity and shifts the blame: a fractured and disturbed life made coherent, but not healed, by an appeal to an African identity. . . . LoBagola's autobiography well illustrates his ability to entertain and to charm, as well as to manipulate.
>
> . . . LoBagola played the African prince, a fire-eater, a savage bewildered by modernization, the clown, and much else, but he could also turn his hand to the straight act as singer, Scottish comic, or if necessary, the urbane and disciplined speaker who entranced high school students and well-heeled members of smart bourgeois clubs and confraternities. . . . For an African American to do this consistently in his own country while pretending to be an African says a great deal about his talent. LoBagola did come up against racial hostility and abuse, but he met this by boldly maintaining his stage life and by claiming that he was an African and not a black American.[83]

The description of all of the personae that LoBagola/Lee had at his disposal only emphasizes how much of a strategy ethnic altercasting was for this man for whom racial performance was life. Bert Williams at least tried to maintain a difference between the personae on and off the stage. Indeed, he went so far as to publicly acknowledge that even the name Bert Williams was a fiction:

"Nobody in America knows my real name and, if I can prevent it, nobody ever will. That was the only promise I made to my father."[84] Eric Ledell Smith guesses that this reticence might have involved a family secret. However, Marjorie Garber notes in *Vested Interests* that historical records reveal that it was almost a common practice for cross-dressers to conceal their "true" identities up until their deaths and beyond.[85] What this suggests is that the secret of Bert Williams's persona was more than just the fact of his masked West Indian identity and suppressed vernacular. The absence of a real name was a statement of control over his history and identity in a culture where he rose to stardom but was never ever quite at home; where he achieved success via a persona that he could profit by but which was not his own. The absence of the name—the concealment of the name—functions to keep alive the fracture between race and culture, his distance from the African American community alongside his commitment to a more abstract racial uplift. To be nameless is to keep the masks in play far beyond his era, his generation, and his time on stage: it is to control his own invisibility and to stage his own disappearance.

LoBagola, on the other hand, can be named, identified, and psychoanalyzed. What can be discovered in the story of Joseph Lee is a politics of racial inauthenticity, one of masquerade in which the knowledge of how hegemonic racial categorization works allowed this strategy of self-erasure, of disappearance through and as performance. In other words, like so many others before him and so many others who worked in the interstices between vaudeville and "ethnological show business," Joseph Lee was a minstrel, but one who worked outside of the bichromatism that had come to define the form. As such, he and the countless others who wore the African mask for a variety of purposes showed how global the impact of that American cultural form was and how far blacks from all over the world could go in implementing it for strategic purposes in the shadow of race. Lee, however, was not interested in the moment of contrast enabled and emphasized by the ritual of "wiping off," or in this case revealing the culture beneath the race. That he could follow the trajectory of the Jewish minstrels in their strategic use of blackface to attain a form of social whiteness was impossible, as it was for Bert Williams. LoBagola was trapped because the only thing close to whiteness was in keeping the mask on, in hiding the "ordinary nigger" behind the performance of regal African identity and allowing the tropes of exotica to free him of the restrictions placed on African Americans. Defending his "stage life" while offstage was a way of extending the performance, expanding it so that its norms and conceits could be employed to supersede the extreme social and political limitations of the "real" world.

Globalizing Blackface: Mimicry, Countermimicry, Carnival

That minstrel theater, vaudeville, world fairs, colonial expositions, and the early circus were very much a part of the same cultural and political complex only broadens and enriches historical conceptions of minstrelsy. And that the black mask and the black voice both function within the growing global sprawl of American imperial influence as a complex sign of the "authentic" and of American cultural, technological, and economic power only empha- sizes the scope of racialized masking during the era known as modernism. Yet the space behind the mask was always contested because it was forced to contend with differences within as well as differences without, hierarchies behind the mask as well as institutionalized racism and racial terror out there. Minstrelsy was globalized because of the increasing influence of Amer- ican culture on nations such as imperial Britain, where the discourses of American slavery and British colonialism were conflated by way of the ritu- alistically staged representation of the Negro. It was also globalized by the appropriation of the form by colonized black nations and communities eager to engage and construct a transatlantic conversation between and among different black populations. This conversation was one in which they could re-present themselves through a transnational language of race and a tradi- tion of performance that, although based on bichromatism and the racial psychoses of slavery, did not limit them to merely the negation of whiteness.

Minstrelsy and its dramatizing of the various meanings of race were, then, not a set of concerns limited to the coteries of Harlem's renaissance or even to those who preceded Harlem and made its cultural explosion possible. Nor was minstrelsy a popular cultural phenomenon only in the United States and England. Because the aesthetic of minstrelsy could so spill off the stage and become prominent both on the periphery of these various sites of performance/exhibition/containment as well as within privileged sites of black resistance, it is impossible to not see and hear the tension of black skin under black mask as in fact constitutive of another kind of black modernism. This was a modernism that was international but saw itself within a self- generated simulacrum where race signified identity as much as it did disguise and where the stage became ultimately a metaphor for the diaspora itself. Minstrelsy became a virtual space that connected various black communities throughout the diaspora who spoke to and of each other via blackface perfor- mance. However, what links minstrel theater, vaudeville, world fairs, colonial exhibitions, and circuses and carnivals is ultimately the politics of colonial specularity in which the white gaze constructs its subjects according to the various needs of American imperialism and its rising tides of power. The critique of that specularity by the technique of fraud, impersonation, and invisibility is also the secret history of black minstrel theater and of a politics that even Black Nationalism could not represent or contain or dare to acknowledge.

As Anne McClintock, Jeffrey Richards, and others have argued, colonial forms of specularity produce and are in turn produced by a particularly modernist commercial gaze which transforms "the other" into postslavery commodity and the rational Western self into consumer. In other words, it marks the transformation from the direct colonial rule of the British and other imperialists to the cultural colonialism of the United States in which representation, reproduction, and symbolic meanings accomplish much more than territorial domination could. The use of race in this context of display and performance was no doubt a graphic example of just how wide-ranging the new world market was and how many objects, subjects, sounds, and differences it could contain within its field while maintaining the comfortable, traditional power dynamic in which the white consumer was guaranteed symbolic if not literal control. The black use of blackface or an ersatz Africanity is a direct response to that specularity and establishes a break from it and the kind of knowledge it produces and maintains. However, this very same black-on-black masking and the levels of cross-cultural impersonation it requires and implies produces a distinct form of black global spectatorship that exists alongside, under, and against that colonial specularity in complex ways.

A passage from Veit Erlmann's "Spectatorial Lust: The African Choir in England, 1891–1893" is worth quoting at length since it articulates these tensions of representation and discusses them in South Africa—the home of real Zulus who themselves appropriated the blackface tradition. After so much consideration of representations of Zulus and "real" Africans, it is fitting to begin a discussion tracing the African and Caribbean use of the minstrel mask here, with a nation that took bichromatism to its most tragic and absurd legal ends in its practice of apartheid:

> Needless to say, Africans in South Africa, too, had acquired detailed knowledge about Europeans, given the latter's long-standing presence and dominance in South Africa itself. And ironically, it was again minstrelsy that served as the principal medium of cross-cultural imagination and self-definition. English and American minstrel troupes had been touring South Africa from as early as the 1850s, and throughout the latter half of the century

most South African towns . . . had a thriving minstrel scene. Blacks soon absorbed the format and the aesthetic of the minstrel stage so that by the 1890s most mission schools . . . sponsored their own minstrel performances. Thus, the aesthetics of the minstrel stage not only enabled whites to fantasize about blacks, but in turn also helped blacks to define themselves in opposition to whites. Because the constrained conditions of imperial rule restricted black parody of white behavior to more hidden means of expression, Africans often had few alternatives other than manipulating the representations whites had created of them. Although much of this cross-cultural trafficking of images and fictions of race remains obscure at this stage, one figure of the minstrel stage seems to have been particularly crucial in providing a template for such re-inscriptions. In one of the many ironic twists of the global, interracial imagination, black South Africans transformed the "coon," the fashion-conscious, urban, emancipated black male, into a hero. Beginning in the 1920s urbanizing Zulu-speaking migrant workers reworked the songs and dances associated with the minstrel stage into their own distinct blend of modern "town" music called isikhunzi. As crucial and counterhegemonic as such African attempts at the definition of a positive self-identity may have been, it is this promiscuous mix of mirror images that made up the consolidated symbolic world of the empire. And it was this peculiar racial unconscious of the world's fair, the exotic show, and the minstrel stage that not only formulated their own grammar, but also produced new modes of perception, new regimes of visuality.[86]

To briefly contemporize this material, it must be noted that the legacy of this global cross-pollination of minstrelsy is still alive in post-apartheid South Africa. The well-known and explicitly touristic "Cape Town Coon Carnival" is a New Year's celebration that explicitly conflates blackface (or, more accurately, the use of whiteface) with a carnival aesthetic. One point must be made concerning Erlmann's observations, as it helps strengthen the more general point about the black indigenization of minstrelsy and adds more prisms to the promiscuous mix of black polyvalent signifyin(g) through blackface masking. It is even more promiscuous than represented by Erlmann through an all-too-local reading of South African minstrelsy, especially since the new regime of visuality he historicizes and theorizes was based on deception, fraud, and multiple layers of impersonation. The "symbolic world of the empire," since it was being enacted and performed through blackface, was broad enough to include not just the local binaries of black and white, Zulu and Afrikaaner. Minstrelsy was a symbolic picture of the world itself and its power relationships, particularly for those on the fringes of a modernism that was defining itself more and more within the all-too-narrow shores of the Atlantic.

In the case of South Africa, minstrelsy was also about Europeans (as opposed to Afrikaaners), Americans, and African Americans who were symbolically inseparable from even the worst of racist characterizations. Knowing how culturally polyglot black South Africa was, the Zulu claim on the reinvented "coon" must have had some impact on other black ethnicities also crouching in the shadows of that era before formal apartheid. Obviously these other black ethnic groups had to negotiate their relationships with the Zulu's while simultaneously struggling against both Afrikaaners and European whites. The "new regimes of visuality" as a by-product of the "peculiar racial unconscious of the world's fair, the exotic show, and the minstrel stage" must be defined, then, not simply by the white construction of the black other or the black subversion of that construction. It should account for the layers of cross-cultural, intra-racial impersonation endemic to the local claim on the global form. The "scopic regime" of this "ethnographic modernism," as James Clifford would call it, includes also a black-on-black specularity that depends on its formal invisibility (the invisibility of black mask on black skin) in order to explore transnational, intra-racial relationships also mediated by the structures of power that make colonial specularity possible. It allows one group of blacks to pretend to be another group of blacks and in so doing to attempt to remove themselves from a regime of knowledge that constructs and contains them simply by their relationship to whites.

It is this "other" specularity that is of primary concern in the remainder of this chapter. To return to the colonial exhibition or exotic shows: those African Americans who found themselves staring at Africans on stages, in cages, or in pseudoauthentic recreations of a "natural habitat" were engaged in a complex and much less stable discourse of history, self, culture, and position. Obviously, this is not to say that they all read the African other in the same way, nor is it to argue simplistically that the black gaze is inherently subversive or political or anti-colonial—the complexities of LoBagola are merely one example of the impossible liberties of black minstrel masking. Instead it is to identify and historicize a different form of specularity that becomes much clearer (though not much simpler) during the Harlem Renaissance and the urban primitivism of the African American and Afro-Caribbean intelligentsia, to say nothing of French Negritude. But even if African Americans did read this African other in exactly the same way as did most modern white Americans—as exotic, alien, degraded, or desirable bodies—this sameness was unwieldy with historical difference. For an African American viewer to occupy the space of white colonial specularity would require a good deal of positioning. The African American "self" here in question is directly in conflict with the pleasures of a white bourgeois spectatorship predicated on its not being black or African; this, of course, is akin to the pleasures of white minstrelsy, pleasures formally ritualized in the moment of "wiping off." But here the caged African other intrudes on the social constructions of that African American "self" in a racist society by threatening it with similitude and the specter of a lost authenticity and perhaps a strong sense of moral responsibility. Indeed, the presence of that African "blackness" threatens the African American spectator's construction of self since that construction is in part and at that time rooted in a desire to distinguish itself from that which is caged and on display. Even if that kinship or phenotypic resemblance were denied by the African American spectator, the strength of that denial would be the excess that differentiates the black viewer from the white.

Despite and because of these contradictions and tensions, minstrelsy's strategic potential for the global black community at the turn of the century and beyond is illuminated by the various types of blacks who embraced the black mask for so many different reasons. This blackface strategy could be deployed due to the fact that the very notion of Africa was by the turn of the century both a sign of the "authentic" and a synonym for masking, or intraracial, cross-cultural masquerade. With all of this in mind, one wonders about the time LoBagola spent "in Dahomey." One wonders about the time he spent wandering through colonial West Africa with only his wits and his penchant for performance to guide and feed him. One wonders these things because not too long after LoBagola claims to have left "Dahomey" and its environs to return to Europe, a form of West African minstrelsy became popular with the arrival of the recorded black voice by way of the phonograph and "race records." Now, there is no proof that LoBagola directly influenced comedians like the Ga minstrel performers Williams and Marbel who worked in Accra in the mid-1920s and the Sierra Leonese comic troupe Collingwood-Williams and Nichols.[87] It is, however, documented that LoBagola performed in Lagos, Nigeria, in 1911–12 to rave reviews. There is also no proof that Bert Williams directly influenced the West African minstrels as he did the Trinidadians; however, the presence of the name "Williams" in both of these prominent West African black blackface troupes is more than a little tantalizing. One wonders if the name "Williams" had attained the kind of iconic and commercial significance that a name like "Smith" would in the era of black women's blues singers ushered in after Mamie Smith's "Crazy Blues." Certainly after the arrival of the "Empress of the Blues" herself, Bessie Smith, and the success of Clara Smith, Trixie Smith, and others, many so-called Smiths suddenly popped up in vaudeville and on blues recordings. Nick Tosches makes the same point about the name "Emmett," which was adopted by turn-of-the century white minstrels in homage to the great Dan Emmett, the founder of the very first American minstrel troupe.[88]

It is, however, worth thinking about the presence of continental African minstrelsy as well as Caribbean minstrelsy at the turn of the century, since the form as argued thus far speaks not simply to the bichromatism of American or British race relations but also to the interactions of various black colonial subjects with each other throughout the African dispersal. Minstrelsy functions as an emergent site of a black, transnational discourse which ranges from direct appeals to a solidarity beyond cultural distinctions or divergent histories, to an assertion of difference in which the mask emphasizes the performance of race within the specific dialects of culture. According to the work of the scholar/musician Edmund John Collins:

> Black minstrelsy, which appeared in America during the 1840s and later became incorporated into vaudeville and burlesque, found its way to Africa by the end of the nineteenth century. According to David Coplan, writing about South Africa, "the final development of coloured street music into a professionally performed accompaniment to urban dancing took place under the influence of black American minstrel styles heard in nineteenth century Cape Town and the Eastern Cape."[89]

Before even the coming of the phonograph or of recorded song, the apparatus of blackface had made it to an Africa still struggling under European colonial rule and its rigidly Manichean racial hierarchies. Indeed, it becomes the ground source of an indigenous musical culture. Ragtime music was hugely popular in the streets of West and South Africa during this period and its cultural influence was profound. Many local bands began to perform ragtime and early jazz music and began to incorporate instruments typical of minstrel theater into their music. Instruments like the musical saw and the swanee whistle were appropriated by West African orchestras and early recording artists. Closer to the "Dahomey" of black Western mythologies, black minstrelsy in Ghana made a powerful impression on the local culture still struggling with and against formal colonial domination. The African American vaudeville team of Glass and Grant was brought to Accra in 1924 and then moved on to Lagos in 1926 and was the primary influence on the aforementioned local performance troupes.[90]

Performing minstrel classics like "Nothing Could Be Finer than to Be in Carolina," "The Gold Diggers of Broadway," and "Alexander's Ragtime Band" in cities like Lagos and Accra, these performers brought and translated the mythic theatricality of America's Harlem Renaissance to the space that had always been a myth in the African American community. Here in "Dahomey," Harlem and black Americans were all the rage—and it was assumed that blackface was in fact a representation of actual African Americans, not necessarily white fantasies of race and sex. Because of this understanding or creative misrecognition of minstrel theater, blackface could easily be appropriated into the realm of West African fantasies of liberation. In this prismatic context, America could ironically signify liberation via the black mask—a mask that was connected to African American music, the presence of Garvey's *Negro World*, and other bits of information about the burgeoning New Negro movement and black "first world" success stories. The fact of translation is important to emphasize. Blackface operated outside the specifics of American race relations and plantation/Jim Crow cultural economies, so it was made to address and signify upon the specifics of colonial Ghana. For example, "Black minstrelsy had its rural Jim Crow and Jumbo Chaff in contrast to the slick urban Zip Coon and Dandy Jim. Likewise Ghanaian concern has its urbane Kofi Sharp and Tommy Fire in contrast to the rural 'bushman.' "[91] But because these local meanings and double-meanings were being directly produced by a West African specularity in which African Americans were the imagined site of performative authenticity, cultural power, and ideological resistance, there is embedded in the specifics of Ghanaian minstrelsy the traces of a simultaneous conversation with the United States and its own racial economies.

In the Caribbean we can witness how this transnational movement of minstrelsy leads to a carnivalizing of the minstrel tradition. In his wonderful *Calypso Callalloo*, Donald Hill writes:

> Minstrel shows toured the United States, and some traveled to South America and the Caribbean, where they were very popular. Although there had been blackface routines throughout the Americas before, the arrival of blackface minstrels from the United States in the late nineteenth century gave the stereotypes renewed popularity and focus. Vaudeville troupes, in which the blackface characters were only a part of a larger cast of entertainers, also toured the Caribbean.

In Trinidad, American-style blackface routines were added to Carnival and were called minstrels or the Yankee band. There mask was part black, part white. This Carnival masquerade was accompanied by a band consisting of guitar, vera, bones, and banjo that played American folk or popular tunes.[92]

The "part black, part white" politics of Trinidadian masquerade will be discussed later; but to flesh out this transnational appropriation/translation of American minstrelsy, Hollis "Chalkdust" Liverpool's *Rituals of Power and Rebellion* is very helpful. During the early period of the urban masquerade tradition in Trinidad, the presence of American blackface was prominent *alongside* the African masking themes and motifs which were popular during the late nineteenth century:

> The period was also marked by the introduction of the "minstrel" masquerade, as revelers copied the Yankee minstrel shows that were popular in the United States at the turn of the century. In the United States during the first half of the 19th century, black-faced White performers as minstrels, using the African-American dialects, portrayed comical images of Africans. In order to appear authentic in their presentations, they sang the songs of the enslaved people, used the humour of African Americans and absorbed African rhythms and dances. Minstrelsy then symbolized White superiority by "emphasizing the peculiarities and inferiority" of Africans. By 1865, African-American minstrels began to make modifications to their images: by the late 19th century, they developed distinctive features of their own. They resurrected the songs of the enslaved as well as the "Negro Spirituals," mocked White planters and focused on the joys of freedom.
>
> The Trinidad revelers imitated these American minstrels, but instead of blackened faces, they whitened theirs over a black charcoal base, laced red spots on their cheeks and wore the "Uncle Sam costume of scissor-tailed coat, tight striped trousers, white gloves, and tall beaver hat.[93]

The year 1865 proved significant for the presence and practice of minstrelsy in Jamaica. That it is the same year in which Liverpool located the black appropriation and modification of minstrelsy that allowed the black mask to focus on "the joys of freedom" is too eerie to be coincidental, considering the events in the Anglophone Caribbean at that time. Here the minstrelsy being imitated in Trinidad—the African American countermimicry being mimicked—is linked explicitly to an African American politics of subversion and resistance. This "freedom" is clearly not intended to be the ludic and libidinal freedom typically associated with what Houston Baker calls "the psychodrama of the minstrel mask"; it is a freedom linked to political emancipation and racial deliverance, but it was masked in the discourse of the ludic.[94]

Liverpool also discusses those many minstrels in carnival for whom black-face was an explicit act of pan-African solidarity: "in the 1920s and 1930s, minstrels identified with the resistance movement of African Americans in the U.S., and with race pride. . . . It was a way of reaching out to the African Americans in urban North America who, like the lower class in Trinidad, were deprived of voting rights. It was to remind the Africans in Trinidad that 'despite our tribal or ethnic differences and localities, we all belong to one race—the human race.' "[95] Yet despite this final gesture toward racelessness and toward the transcendental category of the "human," these minstrels "sang 'slave songs' from the plantation and painted their faces white in mockery of white Americans who were darkening theirs."[96] It is interesting to note that rather than simply place a white mask on their black faces they would first lay down the burnt-cork mask and then add the white makeup. This suggests that they were aware of the details of the convention, one that demanded blackface before they could erase it by adding another layer of color. This ritual was almost the opposite of the "wiping off" ritual described by Rogin in Blackface, White Noise, which emphasized the visual and thereby cultural contrast that would allow Jews to become "white." In this case, the foundational layer of black was seemingly there only to emphasize the presence of that which was being erased or critiqued or perhaps politically emphasized. Invisibility by application and an erasure by addition, by supplementation; reversal by layering and the emphasis by the revelation of an antecedent mask: at work here are the poetics and politics of Bert Williams.

Considering that the culture of carnival was steadily feeding immigrants to New York's own Harlem carnival, it is amazing to witness how the blackface stereotype could transmute into Uncle Sam. This is a stunning example of the subversive appropriation of a racist appropriation. And that Uncle Sam would be the target of Trinidad's satirical ire only reaffirms the global presence of an American empire that would station military troops there during World War II and remain there until the nationalist fervor of the early 1960s led to independence in 1962. However, despite the critique of "whiteness" and the political affiliation with an Americanized "blackness" visible in Caribbean and West African minstrelsy, African Americans still did and do signify the utopian space at the end of black immigrant dreaming: America. Blackface here functions as an interruption of the discourse and symbolic power of the British Empire while "America" becomes reduced to two things: its racism, but also its promise of freedom by way of the iconic presence of African Americans whose journey to claim the space behind the mask is metaphorized as a journey toward freedom and a greater visibility. From the black diaspora, the black mask functioned as a sign of cultural power, with America signifying a carnival wherein such reversals could seriously come to pass.

A few things should be emphasized about blackface in Trinidad. Again, the appropriation of the form occurred after African American minstrels had already begun to modify and distinguish minstrelsy and themselves through it. It was the black minstrels who added to the subversive mix of colors and costumes that were a colonial carnival. Second, this use of blackface occurred during an intense period of Caribbean out-migration, which brought Trinidadian performers to New York and back, thereby cross-pollinating both carnival and calypso and the performance and political culture of black New York. Third, this is the era in which calypso had already become a recorded form, with much of the recording done in New York City and sent back to Trinidad with touring musicians and itinerant calypsonians. The "Jazz Age" was not without the sound of calypso simultaneously transforming the transnational social spaces of Harlem. Finally, this critique of white American blackface performers was simultaneously a critique of American racism and the pigmentocracies of Trinidad itself. The mask was made to signify transnationally and cross-culturally. It was as much about American race relations as about the colonial Caribbean, as much about the declining British Empire as it engaged the rising imperial ambitions of America. In the shadow of this polyvalent signifying, the mask addresses and contains an emergent pan-African sensibility that transcended, critiqued, and supplemented the fetishized space of Harlem by refracting the black gaze within its own racial and transcultural frame of reference.

In the way that the vernacular blues and jazz culture of the Harlem Renaissance enabled its literary and artistic efforts, the presence of calypso, carnival, and Caribbean vernacular culture impacted the "little Renaissance" of Trinidad's modernism. This small but not minor modernist movement is an example of the process by which, as Edouard Glissant describes, writer-intellectuals were forced to contend with the "language of the street" being "forced back down our throats."[97] In light of the increasingly dominant culture of carnival and calypso in the early part of the twentieth century, these scions of nationalism threw in their lot with the urban masses and in doing so defined a new form of radicalism not predicated on the colonial-nationalist fear of any soundings that promoted an indigenous self-perception. These so-called Jacket Men for the most part made up the small cadre of writer/intellectuals of the Trinidadian renaissance of the late 1920s and early 1930s, suddenly empowered by vernacular soundings. This group most notably included C. L. R. James, Alfred Mendes, and Alfred Gomes, the editor of their journal *The Beacon*, which consistently argued for both the validation of a distinct West Indian culture through carnival and calypso and for a general indigenization of culture through a synthesis with these new vernacular forms. As Reinhard Sander describes, the *Beacon* group advocated writing

> which utilized West Indian setting, speech, characters, situations and conflicts. It warned against the imitation of foreign literature, especially against the imitation of foreign popular literature. Local colour, however, was not regarded as a virtue by itself. A mere occupation with the enchanted landscape of the tropics did not fulfill the group's emphasis on realism and verisimilitude in writing. Realism combined with and supported by the Trinidadians' social and political ideology resulted in fiction that focused on West Indian characters belonging to the lower classes. The group around Trinidad and *The Beacon* consisted essentially of middle-class people, with a slight racial preponderance of white Creoles and expatriates; but they as well as those middle-class members who were of African or Asian descent, or what is more likely in Trinidad a mixture of any of the major races, "made contact" with Trinidad's lower classes in the pages of their magazines.[98]

Calypso, carnival, and steel bands were all major obsessions of *The Beacon's* writers and intellectuals. And as was the case for the New Negro movement which inspired them, it was the vernacular that linked these writers to the products of Trinidadian working-class culture and which underpinned all attendant cultural phenomena. In their assault on the "intellectual dropsy" of the colonial middle class, dialect was the primary weapon.[99] Of course the notion that authenticity either resided in or emerged from "the folk" or the working class was not exclusive to this small modernism. And although Africa is not explicitly articulated here as embodied by the folk and made audible in its language, there is still some trace of countermimicry in that the performance of the vernacular is here an antidote to the "aping" of the foreign. This use of "the folk" is one of the things that links this modernism to global currents of literary and political thought in the twentieth century along with incessant Caribbean out-migration throughout this period. Hazel

Carby points out, for example, that the Trinidadian renaissance is and must be connected to both the Harlem Renaissance and international proletarian literary movements for which "realism" was also a question of "folk speech" and folk/popular culture.[100]

But as Glissant suggests, this appropriation of the vernacular voice on the part of the "little Renaissance" wasn't an obvious step in their evolution as artists and activists, nor was it the eruption of authenticity that later critics would describe. It was a response to the pressure of the suddenly dominant urbanized folk culture. C. L. R. James himself admits in *Beyond a Boundary* that he "was fascinated by the calypso singers and the sometimes ribald ditties they sang in their tents during carnival time. But, like many of the black middle class. . . . I was made to understand that the road to the calypso tent was the road to hell."[101] Derek Walcott is even more critical of this process of "appropriating" calypso and the carnival complex for the sake of an Afro-Caribbean literary modernism: "But carnival was as meaningless as the art of the actor confined to mimicry. And now the intellectuals, courting and fearing the mass, found values in it that they had formerly despised. They apotheosized the folk form, insisting that calypsos were poems."[102] His is the language of the apostate, for whom the religion of the vernacular could never ease a consciousness committed to fragmentation as poetic and political strategy. His is the language of the aesthete, whose politics is ultimately produced by the rootlessness of trickster promiscuity rather than its nemesis: nationalist orthodoxy and its fetish for place. Again, there is little talk of Africa in the work of this movement. For them the vernacular with its cultural apparatus was prized for its potential for newness, which made it less a product of the indigenous—fixed in time and easily identifiable as romanticized or vilified other. Instead it was a mode or a practice of indigenization, a product of a new authenticity resistant to colonial representations and systems of value and meaning.

One of *The Beacon's* editorials from 1933 makes clear how the vernacular would lead *from* mimicry to the indigenous. The very notion that mimicry could produce the indigenous and was merely a transitional stage is the primary point here:

> The day will come when we, like America, will produce our Walt Whitman; then, and only then will the movement towards an art and language indigenous to our spirit and environment commence. One has only to glance through the various periodicals published in this and the other islands to see what slaves we still are to English culture and tradition. There are some who

lay great store by this conscious aping of another man's culture, but to us it seems merely a sign of the immaturity of our spirit. It is an ailment that is, however, only temporary, and we look forward to the day when it will be no more.[103]

Despite that lack of direct interest in Africa in the *Beacon* group, for Walcott this primary gesture toward the folk is linked to nationalism by virtue of its dependence on a countermimicry in which the elite (nationalist, bohemian, or otherwise) mask themselves in the vernacular. What Walcott sees in the nationalist claim on the folk as the direct conduit to Africa is a similarity to the claim on carnival as a sign of direct access to the folk—this even though the latter is often depicted as the ultimate anathema to the essentialism of the former. In "What the Twilight Says" (1970), Walcott writes: "The romantic darkness which they celebrate is thus another treachery, this time perpetuated by the intellectual. The result is not one's own thing but another minstrel show."[104] In this reading, the black-on-black minstrelsy first articulated as a political gesture by the *Beacon* group is one which consciously apes the folk rather than the European in order to reinvent the native. It is then deconstructed as minstrelsy by Walcott a generation later for its dependence on the falsely mimetic and the appropriations and fantasies of class privilege. Walcott seems indifferent to the very possibility of a counterpolitics of minstrelsy *within* the language of minstrelsy/mimicry itself. An even more class-conscious description and dismissal of *The Beacon*'s intellectuals and their relationship to carnival comes from the great calypsonian Attila himself:

> And now the cultural resurgence which the early post-depression years were witnessing, bringing into being *The Beacon* literary magazine, had drawn the native intellectual, chafing under his yoke, to the kaiso as a moth to a flame. All barriers were down and inhibitions forgotten as middle-class society filled the tent to hear Tiger sing "Money Is King."[105]

Attila suggests here that perhaps it was the "carnival complex" that ultimately appropriated and assimilated the Trinidadian literary renaissance—as it could be argued that minstrelsy ultimately usurped African American modernism from within, becoming so prevalent as a strategy, a sign, and a gesture that the mask disappeared into flesh. Attila triumphantly claims that the "chafing" which describes Walcott's well-known poetics of division and doubt—preceded of course by Countee Cullen's "Heritage" and Paul Laurence Dunbar's "We Wear the Mask" or perhaps even Du Bois's *The Souls of Black Folk*—could be transcended or contained by the din of the carnival.

So by the time of this minor but not insignificant Caribbean renaissance, carnival, calypso, and the vernacular were no longer marginal elements in a colonial anticolonialist coming of age. Those colonial forms had triumphed from the bottom up and were well on their way to becoming postcolonial national institutions. In Gomes's words:

> It is as if these native minstrels have preserved a flair for what is basic in humour which their more sophisticated brothers and sisters have lost some-where along the path of becoming educated. We have only been educated to the point of not being eager to recognize our surroundings: we have yet to reach the point where our education will suggest to us that it is not complete without recognition of the roots from which we have come.[106]

As seen here, the struggle to claim vernacular culture in the Caribbean re-volves around the definitional tensions of the minstrel figure: as naive pro-ducer of native song and sound, and as comic blackface stereotype in a global economy of racial masquerade in which vaudeville, burnt cork, American racial spectacle, and carnival become linked through a transnational move-ment of black dialects. As noted earlier, Donald Hill points out something that contextualizes the latter: "In Trinidad, American-style blackface routines were added to Carnival and were called minstrels or the Yankee band. Their mask was part black, part white."[107] He also isolates the most important influence on the Caribbean minstrel tradition: Bert Williams, who "influ-enced many Caribbean vaudevillians including Sam Manning, Bill Rogers, Phil Madison, Johnny Walker, and Ralph Fitz-Scott," though there is no evidence that he ever toured there.[108]

Because of its dependence on the African American use of the minstrel mask, the "part black, part white" sign of the Caribbean minstrel is re-mapped. It is part black because of Bert Williams and other black minstrels from the American stage, and part white because its racial politics is not the same as that which produces American minstrelsy. The sound here is dif-ferent, having been refracted through the African American use of blackface in the context of white racism and the Trinidadian use of black- and whiteface explicitly in the context of carnival. Some of these performers like Sam Man-ning, Phil Madison, and Bill Rogers were as well known in Port of Spain or Guyana as they were in New York City, having recorded and performed there. It is safe to say that their minstrelsy was directly informed by a study of performances in the United States as well as by performances of touring minstrel shows. So it should not be surprising to have found certain vernacular trademarks of African American minstrel sound in one of the carnival tents some loud early-twentieth-century *J'ouvert* morning.

Among the Caribbean vaudevillians working in both the United States and in Trinidad, and significantly influenced by Bert Williams, were Johnny Walker and Ralph Fitz-Scott. The aforementioned Sam Manning was one of the—if not the—first American calypsonians who "introduced Caribbean comedy and calypso to Harlem audiences."[109] Although born in Trinidad, Manning was never known to work in the calypso tents. His fame came from Harlem and his audience was largely Caribbean-born Americans for whom calypso music was as much the sound of a global modernism and cultural countersignifyin(g) as were jazz and the blues. According to Roaring Lion in his *Calypso*, Phil Madison was actually the first to bring vaudeville theater to Trinidad during a time when calypso was struggling for local recognition and respect. Ironically, vaudeville arrived from America via a much more circuitous routing. Because "carnival was tabooed by the upper classes since emancipation," vaudeville was accepted, coming "all the way from what was then British Guiana, and took over the shows throughout the island."[110] Madison was himself a Guinean who arrived in Trinidad in 1908 and returned in 1912. After Madison teamed up with the local performers Johnny Walker and Berkely, vaudeville became the dominant form of Trinidadian popular theater; and it became unwittingly the tool of the middle class that had worked hard to suppress the indigenous forces of carnival by way of a celebration of the racialized performance traditions of an imperial America in blackface.

These Caribbean performers also toured throughout the Caribbean during the early years of the twentieth century, further spreading the poetics and politics of blackface performance as it arose in plantation America and began to incorporate the local inflections of its colonial vernaculars. But before the widespread success/appropriation of carnival in colonial Trinidad, it was the vaudeville/minstrelsy complex that claimed precedence in Trinidadian popular culture. As Roaring Lion tells it: "Before that the center of attraction was vaudeville, Black and White Minstrels that became known during the two days of carnival as the 'Yankee Band.' Even certain popular musicians with well established bands refused to accompany calypsonians in those days."[111] Here in colonial Trinidad the mimicry of an imported racial discourse and performance tradition was employed to suppress a local racial discourse and performance tradition. Lion even argues that it wasn't until island musicians were sent to record in the United States and their songs became hits on

Broadway that local musicians and middle-class patrons began to socialize with or take seriously the calypsonians.[112] Because masking is the common strategy of both traditions of racial performance and because each tradition can be used to signify the other, a necessary blending was quickly enabled. Lion assesses the relationship between vaudeville and carnival this way: "at one point in time, both had to work together, the calypso being at a disadvantage, and hoping to use the vaudeville in order to get a stronger foothold in the theatres."[113] Both had to "work together," meaning simply that both wore each other's mask in order to occupy each other's space while simultaneously maintaining their own.

In his redoubtable *Calypso and Society in Pre-Independence Trinidad*, Gordon Rohlehr further blurs the line between the calypsonian and the black vaudevillian and minstrel. Since "American vaudeville had become popular in the second decade of this century . . . calypsonians of the twenties would either . . . function as both calypsonians and vaudeville entertainers, or have to compete with the extremely popular vaudeville shows which were staged in cinemas. It would be a decade before these same cinemas allowed the staging of calypso shows."[114] Interestingly enough, it was the phonograph that allowed calypso to displace American-style vaudeville from Trinidadian popular culture: "It became necessary to team up with the vaudeville in order to present the calypso throughout the year. But after Sa Gomes took over the calypso recording business it was no longer necessary to do so. Our records did the trick for us, and the calypso quickly replaced all other shows in Trinidad."[115] Eduardo Sa Gomes was one of the major patrons of calypso during the 1920s and 1930s. He owned one of the earliest Trinidadian recording studios and became a dominant figure in nationalizing the commercial potential of calypso and in marketing it internationally. It was he who, before opening his own studio in Port of Spain, had financed the travels of calypsonians and Caribbean musicians to New York to perform and record gramophone discs to be shipped back to Trinidad for carnival.

Beyond his significance to the Caribbean American community, Sam Manning was notorious for being the traveling companion of Ashwood Garvey after she had left Marcus Garvey under charges of infidelity. The two of them would eventually collaborate on the successful play *Hey, Hey*, which premiered in New York in 1926 and was performed in Caribbean dialect. This play could be read as an interesting riposte to both Williams's and Walker's *In Dahomey* and Marcus Garvey's "Back to Africa" in that it concerns, in the words of Irma Watkins-Owens, "two dissatisfied husbands who divorce their wives and are determined to find their true soul mates in Africa. After much adventure and searching, the men locate two women who have the necessary qualifications, only to discover they are their ex-wives, who have preceded them to Africa."[116] Harlem theater reviews did in fact celebrate *Hey, Hey* as a sendup of Marcus Garvey and the UNIA. Manning and Ashwood Garvey continued to integrate Caribbean themes and vernaculars into Harlem popular theater until they migrated to London, where they opened a successful nightclub and restaurant. To further seal the connections between minstrelsy, vaudeville, carnival, and pan-Africanism, their restaurant became well known as a gathering place for numerous pan-African intellectuals, including C. L. R. James, George Padmore, and Kwame Nkrumah.[117]

Minstrelsy in Jamaica has an even more dramatic history. It was exported to Jamaica during a key historical moment of extreme racial tension, one where the races were polarized, where the metropole/colony relationship was threatened, and where violence was common. It was a climate so volatile and violent that it even managed to infect the attitudes of the Victorian intelligentsia and further add to the growing insecurity over the management and maintenance of the colonies. In his *The Jamaican Stage, 1655–1900*, Errol Hill describes the presence and impact of blackface minstrelsy in colonial Jamaica. Because of the year in question, minstrelsy and British colonial domination are clearly much more intimate than what has been shown via the theaters and street culture of late Victorian England earlier in this analysis:

> A new dimension in popular entertainment was introduced when the first quartet of minstrels to visit Jamaica arrived from New York in July 1865. . . . Although the so-called Negro Songs had in the past been rendered as supporting items to dramatic plays, this quartet was the first professional group to introduce Jamaica to the blackface minstrelsy that had become immensely popular in America during the second half of the nineteenth century. Other troupes would soon follow: the Original Georgia Minstrels in 1869, the Christ Minstrels in 1872, and Edwin Browne's Minstrel and Novelty Company in 1884. They established a tradition of blacking-up to portray comic stereotypes of the black man that Jamaican comedians of the populist theatre adopted and maintained into the Bim and Bam era of the 1950s and 1960s.[118]

Blackface minstrel songs had already appeared on the Jamaican concert stage by 1849, when local musicians and music professors presented at the New Court House in Kingston a locally produced version of "Ethiopian songs and glees."[119] Considering the impact of the radically pan-Africanist Rastafarian movement in Jamaica a few generations later, the use of the term "Ethiopian" is more than a little interesting. This movement, as is well known, is noted for appropriating and ultimately performing a romanticized and essentialist "Ethiopian" identity. This identity initially functioned as a militant critique of colonial and neocolonial Jamaican race relations before unraveling into a hazy parody of itself via its appropriation by an island tourist industry that, like its music industry, would eventually become indistinguishable from its nationalism. As Robert Hill points out in "Dread History," his seminal essay on the early Rastafarian movement in Jamaica, although it reached full flower in the late 1920s and 1930s, the broader currents of "Ethiopianism" which preceded both Garveyism and Rastafarianism had been present in Jamaica from the turn of the century.[120] The overlap between "Ethiopian" as a sign of political affirmation and "Ethiopian" as a sign of Afrocentric mimicry is as important here as it is in the context of "Dahomeyan" or "Congo" or "Zulu" in the United States and Britain.

But it wasn't until the fateful year of 1865 that an American blackface performance "of the true Ethiopian minstrel style" was given in Spanish Town.[121] Errol Hill writes that it would take twenty-three more years, with the arrival of "the Tennessee Jubilee Singers" 1888, for Jamaicans to be introduced to "authentic American blacks who had no need for the blackface makeup."[122] That the appearance of this new form of theater and performance was in 1865 is remarkable considering that it was the year of the Morant Bay Rebellion, known also in America and Britain as the "Governor Eyre Controversy." This rebellion or controversy politically split the Victorian intelligentsia and in many ways signified the movement toward formal independence in Jamaica that came almost a century later. Briefly, this controversy concerned the response of Edward John Eyre, the temporary governor of Jamaica appointed in 1862, to the challenging of colonial authority by emancipated blacks. These challenges to colonial authority were largely over questions of taxation, poverty, land reform, and racism as the newly freed Jamaican blacks aggressively claimed equality in an island where they vastly outnumbered whites. These were organized challenges, and blacks made their case against the planters and local magistrates alongside members of the local mulatto elite such as George William Gordon, a highly regarded critic of Governor Eyre and a deacon who had long sided with the black peasantry.

The violence erupted most viciously in the town of Morant Bay, where hundreds of blacks clashed with volunteer guards, killing dozens of mostly white men. In reprisal, Eyre instituted martial law and his men killed more than 400 Jamaicans, wounded 34, flogged hundreds more, and thoroughly devastated local villages. Gordon was found guilty of high treason and promptly hanged. In England the "Eyre Defense Committee" was initially chaired by Thomas Carlyle, author of the notorious 1849 broadside "On the Negro Question," which was later reprinted as "Occasional Discourse on the Nigger Question" (1853). In this particular polemic, the author of the great *Sartor Resartus* seems deeply indebted to some form of minstrel representation of blacks that could be traced back perhaps to the figure of the harlequin, since it would be some time before actual American minstrelsy reached England:

> Do I, then, hate the Negro? No; except when the soul is killed out of him, I decidedly like poor Quashee; and find him a pretty kind of man. With a pennyworth of oil, you can make a handsome glossy thing of Quashee, when the soul is not killed in him! A swift, supple fellow; a merry-hearted, grinning, dancing, singing, affectionate kind of creature, with a great deal of melody and amenability in his composition.[123]

It must be said that this representation is quite culturally specific in its use of "Quashee," that being a term used to signify Caribbean blacks, despite Carlyle's overwhelmingly generalized racism. However, it is also worth noting that in Carlyle the category of "soul" and the notion of performance are both deployed in an explicit attempt to politically disempower Caribbean blacks. The "soul" of Quashee is musical and merry, and his essence is performance and entertainment—not self-governance or independence. In response to the overreactive violence of Governor Eyre and the support of the British government for his actions, the "Jamaica Committee" was formed led by John Stuart Mill, whose "The Negro Question" had been published soon thereafter and in response to Carlyle's travesty. The Jamaica Committee was able to get Eyre removed from office though no charges of murder were ever leveled against him or his men. He in fact received a generous pension and had his legal fees paid by the British government.

One can only wonder what the responses to minstrelsy were among the polyglot audience in colonial Jamaica during this period of severe colonial and racial tension. Unlike the minstrel theater of the United States, which operated largely in the context of legal segregation, minstrelsy in the Caribbean played to mixed audiences who were separated in terms of seating but who all watched the same shows simultaneously. But of course what they watched may have been the same, but what they saw was notably different. West African minstrels also performed for a polyglot audience, not only a racially diverse one but also one comprising multiple local African ethnicities. Minstrelsy in this context was partially a way to create a unifying discussion and symbolic discourse of race where the imagined African American presence could mediate the multiple local black ethnicities. After all, the carnival complex manifests various social, historical, and cultural contradictions and conflicts ritualized through masking and theater simultaneously. Each experience of carnival differs based on the social and political register within which each experience or subculture functions. This is what Richard Burton means when he asserts in *Afro-Creole* that in carnival there are many mini-carnivals.

Minstrelsy, then, especially when separated from the bichromatic cultural politics of the United States, registers on multiple levels within a polyglot community still under formal colonial control. The same of "ethnological show business." Clearly the white spectator makes something much different of the African "specimen" than does the African American spectator, who experiences a distinct form of spectatorship given his or her position in the hierarchies of race and power. Whether their response is one of outrage or humiliation, scorn and/or psychic distancing, that gaze and its products are as important to American "produce imperialism" as they are to African American nationalism and what were the growing discourses of pan-Africanism.

CHAPTER 5 *In Dahomey*

It is time now to return to the waning years of the nineteenth century, when Bert Williams and George Walker were a few years away from celebrity and less than a decade away from *In Dahomey*. We return now to California, to San Francisco in 1894, where in the midst of an economic depression the city decided to mimic the success of Chicago's World's Columbian Exposition of 1893 that featured the display of native peoples from all over the world—the high point of American ethnological show business. Shane Peacock concludes his fine essay on the exposition with this observation: "At Chicago in 1893, public curiosity about other peoples, mediated by the terms of the marketplace, produced an early form of touristic consumption."[1] As an American display of increasingly globalized consumption patterns, this exposition helped mark and ritualize the transformation from the colonial hegemony of the European empires to the new forms of international power and control that would distinguish the American century. Of this exposition, lauded as "the greatest fair in history," Hazel Carby has documented the much more critical African American response to this ritual of the nascent American century:[2]

> For black Americans it . . . symbolized "not the material progress of Amer-
> ica, but a moral regression—the reconciliation of the North and South at the
> expense of Negroes." At the time, black visitors expressed their resentment
> at their virtual exclusion by renaming the fair "the great American white
> elephant" and "the white American's World's Fair"; Frederick Douglass,
> attending the fair as commissioner from Haiti, called the exposition "a
> whited sepulcher." The Columbian Exposition embodied the definitive fail-
> ure of the hopes of emancipation and reconstruction and inaugurated an age
> that was to be dominated by "the problem of the color-line."[3]

This response is an example of a distinct African American spectatorship at
work simultaneously alongside yet against white touristic consumption. Ida
B. Wells would also register strong complaints about this exposition. This
form of spectatorship is aware of and produced by the intimacies between
American colonial exploitation and domestic racism, anthropology, and racial violence.

However, Frederick Douglass's specific response to the Dahomeyan Village that was recreated and displayed for the Chicago exposition is worth
exploring further since it is more complicated and ambivalent than suggested
in Carby's analysis. Its ambivalence is a telling example of the space between
an African American spectatorship and the Dahomeyans who become and
remained silent interlocutors in this conversation between African Americans
and the ideological formations of segregation-era America. Knowing the
intimate relationship between representations of Africa and the social and
political treatment of African Americans, Douglass felt that the presence of
the Dahomeyan Village existed "as if to shame the Negro" and functioned to
"exhibit the Negro as a repulsive savage."[4] In *To Wake the Nations*, Eric Sundquist quotes from Frank Leslie's *Popular Monthly*, where this equation between African savages on display and free American Negroes was explicitly
being made for and by white spectators: "Sixty-nine of them are here in all
their barbaric ugliness, blacker than buried midnight and as degraded as the
animals which prowl the jungles of their dark land. . . . In these wild people
we easily detect many characteristics of the American negro."[5] At the opening
of the Dahomeyan Village, however, Douglass would applaud the Dahomeyan dances, which in his view "were all on the same principle, if not quite
so well developed, as those of people living nearer to civilization."[6]

In a later response to the Exposition, he made this plea: "Measure the
Negro . . . not by the standard of the splendid civilization of the Caucasian.
Bend down and measure him—from the depths out of which he has risen."[7]

For Douglass, still ensconced within the turn-of-the century binary of civilization and barbarism and still victimized by the assumption of African savagery, the Dahomeyan Village was an outrage in part because it reminded him of the horror of cultural origins. In this case, the way African Americans were struggling to be seen in America was harmed by the seemingly "authentic" representation of native Africans; the political struggles of the former were seen by Douglass as being subverted by the flagrant African-ness of the helpless other blacks there on display. Ultimately the critical response of many African Americans to the Colombian Exposition and its representations of Africans and other nonwhite peoples owed primarily to the tacit acknowledgment that these representations of Africa lent legitimacy to legalized segregation which had been officially countenanced in 1896 by the Supreme Court's *Plessy v. Ferguson* ruling. On the global front it was clear also that these representations of Africa and "Africans" provided "support for American economic penetration of the African continent."[8] This latter concern is present in Williams's and Walker's *In Dahomey*, where the line between Broadway spectacle and African fantasy is blurred to comic and parodic and ultimately subversive effect.

Carby also mentions that as a part of the "discourse of exoticism that pervaded the fair," alongside a panoply of nonwhite peoples African Americans were also "included in a highly selective manner as part of exhibits with other ethnic groups which reinforced conventional racist attitudes of the American imagination."[9] The contiguity of all of these differences is fascinating and, were it possible to imagine the absence of the organizing principle of white colonial specularity, one could produce a curious reimagining of twentieth-century cultural history. The seemingly less controversial San Francisco Mid-Winter Exposition was held in Golden Gate Park, far on the margins of early-twentieth-century black modernist political activism and far from the glories of Chicago or Paris or New York. Ann Charters writes that "the Exposition wasn't much of an enterprise as World Fairs go, relying mostly on a small midway, a ferris wheel, donkey rides, band concerts, stalls selling sponge cake, and a scattering of exhibits, including one of Chiquita, the smallest woman in the world."[10] In this small-time scenario the replica of the African Dahomeyan Village with its imported Dahomeyans was definitely a main attraction. But representations of Africa and Africans at all of America's world fairs were central to the success of the fairs themselves: "So interwoven were fairs and African shows that by the beginning of the twentieth century it was difficult to imagine a world's fair without some kind of display

featuring Africans."[11] Indeed, the Dahomeyan Village at the Columbian Exposition in Chicago "set the standard" for all subsequent fairs, expositions,
and no doubt carnivals.[12]

The Infinite Mask: Passing for the African Self

But who or what were these "Africans," these popular figments of the touristic imagination featured at these fairs, expositions, and carnivals? In " 'Darkest Africa': African Shows at America's World Fairs, 1893-1940," Robert W.
Rydell asks a question that interrogates the ethnographic fiction of the world
fairs with the secret history of masquerade, intra-racial deception, and, ultimately, black minstrelsy: "By the close of the 1930s, however, a subtle shift
had occurred. American fairs continued to represent Africa, but not with
Africans. What happened?"[13] What happened was that African Americans
were employed to stand in for Africans, to perform as Dahomeyans for an
audience that presumably couldn't tell the difference or for whom the difference was negligible since the line between black mask and black skin was
often imperceptible. Knowing how interlinked are the desires for ethnographic authenticity and the secret desire to be potentially hoodwinked and
deceived, much of the audience enjoyed this frisson between what Sally Duensing, in her exploration of museums and the mechanisms of anthropological truth-making, calls "artifacts and artifictions."[14] This kind of fraud was
not something that only happened toward the end of the period that Rydell
explores. Even before Williams's and Walker's performance at the Midwinter
Fair, it was obvious to many that one of the ways to recreate your own
homegrown ethnography was by way of minstrelsy. LoBagola and many other
performers attest to this. Rydell quotes an 1893 handbook which suggests
that "these distinguished foreigners should be impersonated by quick witted
young men . . . with blackened faces and fantastic wooly wigs. . . . Wild war
dances, songs, and cake-walks should be arranged as entertainment."[15]

To insert the specularity of two erstwhile black minstrels into this spectacle of a nascent American globalization is to listen beyond the narrative of
"touristic" commodity culture in order to hear a critical response that differs
from the response of Frederick Douglass and that comes in the form of a
counterethnographic minstrel masquerade. This is not to suggest that the
black spectator is innately immune to touristic consumption or the sublime
pleasures of American globalization and its narcotic logic of commodity
fetishism—which, as we know from Marx, is dependent on the misrepresen-

tation of real social relations and a transmutation of actual social contradictions into their fantastic resolutions in the realm of representation: that is,
masking. To think about the black spectator in this context is to explore
the twinned yet differential politics of consumption and identity formation
at work as the black subject optically consumes and ultimately reproduces
through mimicry the caged and living African object. In this case—the case
of Williams and Walker—this consumption/reproduction does not view the
"authentic" African subject as the object of mockery but as a recuperated icon
of nationalist reclamation predating the UNIA or even Alain Locke's "The
Legacy of the Ancestral Arts." And unlike Frederick Douglass's reading of the
Dahomeyans, this specularity in turn performs "the African" which exists
already in the exoticizing logic of both colonialism and capitalist commodification in order to erase it—much in the way that the American "darky" was
steadily being erased by the performance of Williams and Walker.

In his 1906 essay "The Negro on the American Stage," George Walker
recounts the fateful encounter with "authentic" Africans which would help
inspire both him and Bert Williams to "get away from the ragtime limitations
of the 'darky' " in order to "save ourselves and others."[16] He writes:

> In 1893, natives from Dahomey, Africa, were imported to San Francisco to
> be exhibited at the Midwinter Fair. They were late in arriving in time for the
> opening of the Fair and Afro Americans were employed and exhibited for
> native Dahomeyans. Williams and Walker were among the sham native Da-
> homeyans. After the arrival of the native Africans, the Afro Americans were
> dismissed. Having had free access to the Fair grounds, we were permitted to
> visit the natives from Africa. It was there, for the first time, that we were
> brought into close touch with native Africans, and the study of those natives
> interested us very much. We were not long in deciding that if we ever reach
> the point of having a show of our own, we would delineate and feature native
> African characters as far as we could, and still remain American, and make
> our acting interesting and entertaining to American audiences. . . .
>
> Managers gave but little credit to the ability of black people on the stage
> before the native African element was introduced.[17]

This "native African element" was the product of a desire to ennoble the
African since the African as acknowledged by colonial specularity was the
debased ur-Negro which even Frederick Douglass feared. It was no secret that
this and other hostile and racist notions about Africans were also deeply
embedded in African American and Afro-Caribbean popular thought as a

result of the potent legacy of colonial education and racist indoctrination. According to Eric Ledell Smith, it was this intra-racial ambivalence toward Africa that caused Williams and Walker to set *In Dahomey* only partially in Africa despite their initial plans to do otherwise.[18] As he writes in his biography of Bert Williams, "Williams and Walker were taking a risk by using an African theme in their musical comedy. Many black Americans in 1902 wished to disassociate themselves from Africa. Black performers and producers knew that although white people would be amused by onstage portrayals of African people, black people would be offended."[19] Tension would come from the other side of the racial binary as well. One of the first reviews of *In Dahomey* lamented the changes that resulted from the decision to focus on Africa. The reviewer was nostalgic for "pure" minstrelsy, arguing that the show's lack of "plantation songs" proved that it lacked "true black music"; it also had too much sophistication, itself a sign of corruption: "most of the music is by a negro composer, but by a negro writing under 'white' training, influences and inspiration. . . . But where are the distinctive nigger tones?"[20] The reviewer certainly didn't realize that if it were true that the composer had "aped" " 'white' training, influences and inspiration" then *that* would have been the authentic act of minstrelsy. By *In Dahomey* the "distinctive nigger tones" had already given way to a wider politics of masquerade in which the black mask as worn by Bert Williams was the only legacy of minstrelsy remaining yet was the sly mask for a covert politics of escape from the limited possibilities of black representations in and of America. Another critic would also complain that "one thing is missing. . . . There is not a real 'raggy' coon song in the entire show."[21]

These latter criticisms eventually forced Williams and Walker to add the cakewalk: "In their effort to break with the minstrel-show formula, they had omitted the cakewalk finale, or 'walkaround'."[22] Much negative criticism focused on just this absence, particularly during the show's smash tour in England. They decided to add this traditional dance soon after the show's debut and before their command performance for King Edward VII. And despite the show's attempt to expand the limits of the representation of the Negro beyond the plantation and take it "back to Africa," it was forced to locate itself in a more familiar space: Florida, or the well-known topos of the American South. It wouldn't be until *Abyssinia* that Williams and Walker would be able to pull off a stage show set fully on the African continent. This less successful play was set in the context of a highly romanticized imperial Ethiopia. It appeared in 1906, three years after Pauline Hopkins's serialized novel *Of One Blood* (also set in a highly romanticized imperial Ethiopia) appeared in *The Colored American Magazine*, a magazine to which George Walker was a contributor and for which Hopkins was the literary editor until 1904.

Despite these tensions, to mimic and appropriate the gestures, sounds, and clothing of Dahomeyans was a way for Williams and Walker to wage war with the racist stereotypes that were celebrated and disseminated by the colonial expositions and that were rampant throughout the wider society. These stereotypes and symbols, as seen in Frederick Douglass's response, had filtered down into the African American self-image. Through minstrelsy they could critique ethnography and anthropology in the realm of theater and vaudeville: science was here deconstructed in the realm of black popular culture. Williams and Walker were also able to burlesque the Afro-diasporic longing for and imagining of that enduring sign of absence and cultural power called "Africa." Despite this common political impetus, both men did have distinct motives for their African impersonation. Although his above-quoted words ring with the strident militancy he was known for, George Walker was a very practical man. Ann Charters points out:

> Walker may have felt he was a great innovator, but what he accomplished was really just a more elaborately mounted vaudeville farce. In a way he was restricted by the theatrical standards of his time. . . . Walker was further hampered by his own personal limitations, however. He may have liked to think of himself as a courageous pioneer, but rather than developing a thoughtful conception of "native African characteristics," what he actually produced was closer to a superficial theatrical novelty. He had only the vaguest notions about Africa and was totally without interest in a strong identification with the country. Operating as a shrewd business man, Walker realized that the public had had enough plantation shows in the previous century. He wanted to try something new, looking forward to increased box office sales as much as increased respect for the Negro entertainer.[23]

For Walker the "country" called Africa was largely a commodity that could supplant the waning symbolic value of "the South" and/or "the plantation" in a black modernism that was increasingly urban—therefore prone to its own nostalgic primitivism, but ambivalent about continuing to root that nostalgia in the home of slavery and Jim Crow. Of course, it was the very artificiality of this "theatrical novelty" that enabled Williams and Walker to parody and mock so many things alive in a culturally heterogeneous black community held together as much by the limitations of their skins as by their complicated relationship to the mythic and discursive space called "Daho-mey," or Africa.

Bert Williams, on the other hand, was deeply moved by his encounter with the Dahomeyans. It inspired his lifelong interest in reading and studying African history and anthropology alongside his known adoration for Aris-totle. In a 1912 interview with *Green Book Magazine*, we are told that Williams

> has devoted some research to the history of the Negro race and his copy of John Ogilby's *Africa*, published in 1670, is, I believe, one of the five still extant . . . In showing it to me one day, and commenting upon the numerous kingdoms that flourished in Africa centuries ago, Williams said: "I suppose that with this volume, I could prove that every Pullman porter is the descen-dant of a king."[24]

In other words, his song "Evah Darkey Is a King" from *In Dahomey* could be heard and read as a counterhistorical and counterethnographic statement, especially since it was the goal of ethnography, anthropology, and history to prove and maintain the very opposite. So once again (with gusto):

> Evah darkey is a king!
> Royalty is jes' de ting.
> If yo' social life's a bungle,
> Jes yo' go back to yo' jungle,
> And remember dat your daddy was a king.

Being fully aware of how contemporary Afro-centrism fetishizes the notion of African royalty and regality—from the Harlem Renaissance–era work of the Jamaican historian J. A. Rogers to Martin Bernal's *Black Athena*, from Marcus Garvey to Molefi Asante—Williams's comment seems comically pre-scient, but subversive also in its maintenance of an ironic and self-mocking sense of humor absent in those names just mentioned.

It is worth revisiting Williams's "The Comic Side of Trouble" in light of this fateful encounter with authentic Dahomeyans, since that moment of black transnational and transcultural spectatorship is cited by both Williams and Walker as the creation myth of *In Dahomey*. Williams writes that "the man with the real sense of humor is the man who can put himself in the specta-tor's place and laugh at his own misfortunes."[25] In this case one imagines oneself as an audience to the caged self, witnessing one's own behavior or tragedies from a distance and from that distance employing humor as a palliative to tragedy. As discussed much earlier, this is not entirely other to Du

Bois's formulation of "double-consciousness," which is in its way a bridge between the centuries. Ridicule or victimization are not described as problems for Williams's persona, though race is of crucial import to the politics of his mimicry. Humor in his thinking is produced by a creative self-alienation where one not only laughs at oneself but, given that the spectator function is necessarily occupied by another person—usually of another color—one joins others in laughing at oneself: "Nearly all of my successful songs have been based on the idea that I am getting the worst of it."[26]

In the political economy of blackface, Williams suggests that the "Negro" with the "real" sense of humor is the one who must occupy the position of the white viewer. This "Negro" must consume and comprehend the complexity of racial stereotyping and, in laughing, must distance the "self" from the political and historical impact of those very stereotypes: "It was not until I was able to see myself as another person that my sense of humor developed."[27] Here double-consciousness serves a therapeutic function. Here a split subjectivity employs its divisions to maintain an affective equilibrium instead of an organic plenitude. Although later in "The Comic Side of Trouble" he will draw from classical modes of tragedy and comedy to describe his method (most importantly, the use and significance of the scapegoat), Williams's stress on the spectator rather than on the victim—the viewer rather than on the viewed—is curious considering that the spectator-function is what has always been denied the colonial/racial subject. His privileging of the spectator is a claim on a position of narrative power, authority. Within the Western logic of individuality, it is also a claim on subjectivity that must be viewed in the context of racist dehumanization. To claim the role of the spectator is to project oneself on the other side of one's oppression and gaze back at the caged black self as a fiction. It is as if Williams is fully aware of this historical limitation wherein "the Negro" exists merely as an object to be scrutinized and constructed from without. However, by claiming that spectator function and diffusing its racist humor with one's own, one could elude and evade that gaze by silently supplanting its meanings with one's own.

Yet this must surely be different when both the viewer and the viewed, the racial subject and the racial object are of the same race but from distinct cultures. Clearly the power differential between black object and the, say, African American or Afro-Caribbean subject strangely parallels the white spectator as he or she views the African. It is of course not possible to explore what the Dahomeyans—at least the ones who were actually from Africa—saw while staring at the African Americans who were in turn staring at them and contemplating the twisted, transnational logic of slavery and colonialism, gazing upon them with equal degrees of awe and loathing, fear and fascination. No doubt their reading of the African Americans was filtered through their own micropolitics of race, culture, and language and no doubt the world tends to become more binary—here and there, us and them, me and you— when behind bars. But in general Bert Williams did base his performances on mimicking those who were the most unlike him, so perhaps therein lies a description of his more intimate relationship with the Africans. Remember Williams's words: *"I took to studying the dialect of the American Negro, which to me was just as much a foreign dialect as that of the Italian."* Also, as he writes elsewhere:

> I try to portray the shiftless darky to the fullest extent; his fun, his philosophy. There is nothing about this fellow I don't know. I must study his movements. I have to. He is not in me. The way he walks; the way he crosses his legs; the way he leans up against a wall, one foot forward. I find much material by knocking around in out of the way places and just listening. Eavesdropping on human nature is one of the most important parts of a comedian's work.[28]

This "eavesdropping" is facilitated by the cross-cultural, intra-racial dynamics of this performer who made much of his not being either African American or Dahomeyan. However, for Bert Williams the shared intimacy of skin color, the politics of assimilation (double or otherwise), and the poetics of racial masking enabled a portrayal and in retrospect the construction of an authenticity that was much purer than raw, observable phenomena or crude biological fact.

In My Castle on the River Nile: Popularizing Pan-Africanism

Boston: September 22, 1902. The advertisement for the very first documented performance of In Dahomey reads:

> Hurtig and Seamon Present the Pioneers of all Colored Organizations, the Comedians Williams and Walker and their company of fifty people. The Most Costly and Colossal Production ever given by a Colored attraction—3 act musical comedy In Dahomey. Carload of Beautiful Scenery and Mechanical Effects, New Music, Pretty Girls, Funny Specialities, Gorgeous Costumes and A Large Chorus of Well-Trained Voices. One Continuous Laugh from Rise to Fall of Curtain.[29]

Despite the progressive description of this troupe of black performers as a "Colored Organization" as opposed to "Ethiopian Delineators" or any of the phrases traditionally used to describe the "coon shows," this is not too far from the language of the carnival or sideshow barker. Yes, there is the promise of scale, color, pomp, and the exotic, and yes, there is the promise of something unlike anything ever seen; something that because it is produced and controlled by Negroes is even more rare than its scale, its color, and its setting. In suggesting that the Williams and Walker show is a "Colored Organization" the advertisement connects it to and equates it with other such organizations making their names known in the climate of early black American modernism, most notably Du Bois's Niagara Movement, the forerunner to the NAACP founded in 1903.

As "pioneers" this description suggests that Williams and Walker were doing work as significant as that of other more explicitly political organizations agitating for assimilation and against Jim Crow. An article in *Theatre Magazine* published after the premiere of *In Dahomey* sums up its political significance by also identifying the epochal political presence of this performance organization:

> The recent production of 'In Dahomey' at the New York Theatre was largely in the nature of an experiment, since it was the first time that a piece written by Negroes and performed by Negroes, had been admitted to the boards of a Broadway theatre. The unquestionable success of the enterprise is likely to result in renewed and more ambitious efforts in this direction.
>
> Messrs Williams and Walker, the comedians who head the organization, have been popular performers in the cheaper class houses for several years and Bert Williams has long enjoyed the reputation of being a vastly funnier man than any white comedian now on the American stage.[30]

By situating this activism in the realm of performance and culture, the flyer and the *Theatre Magazine* article anticipate the much more explicit politics of the Harlem Renaissance. This movement, as Alain Locke would elaborate in *The New Negro*, took very seriously the space of culture and the strategies of performance in the struggle for racial liberation despite its deep ambivalence for the minstrelsy that would literally clear the stage for the presence of more self-conscious black image makers and cultural workers. However, the tone taken in the advertisement is reminiscent of what one would expect from those ethnographic shows that were linked so intimately with the circus complex in early-twentieth-century America. The advertisement could have been written by P. T. Barnum himself, who despite his profitable displaying of various Africans and African Americans did consider himself a progressive in matters of race. He was in favor of both abolition and equal rights for Negroes and occasionally spoke out on these issues, though they were admittedly marginal to his general concerns. Barnum is important here because he, like Bert Williams, makes complete the connection between ethnographic display, minstrelsy, and commercial theatre. He is important also for his politics that make clear the intimacy of abolition, exploitation, and that white desire to publicly display blacks to "represent" various political and aesthetic positions. This, of course, ranges from the left to the right on the political spectrum.

It is and was obvious that there was very little in the play In Dahomey itself that could provide black and white audiences greater insight into "Negro" origins or African cultures or history. Although the play has its didactic moments, education wasn't its primary or even secondary concern. Written by the in-house team of Will Marion Cook, Paul Laurence Dunbar, and Jesse Shipp, the performance was without question an elaborately mounted vaudeville farce with very little in the way of the legitimate "native African element" that George Walker was obsessed with and committed to portraying. In his words, however, that element was the liberating corrective to classic minstrelsy:

> The departure from what was popularly known as the American "darky" ragtime limitations to native African characteristics has helped greatly to increase the value of the blackface performer on the American stage. . . .
>
> Managers gave little credit to the ability of black people on the stage before the native African element was introduced. All that was expected of a colored performer was singing, dancing, and a little story telling, but as for acting, no one credited a black person with the ability to act.[31]

That the "native African element" is directly connected to (or in fact is) the "ability to act" is a priceless insight and returns Walker back to "Africa" via a simultaneous poetics and politics of both mimicry and authenticity (or of mimicry as authenticity). However, the question of Africa in this play and at this time in black cultural dialogue was primarily a question of sociopolitical and historical legitimation. In this dialogue racial authenticity and cultural authority inheres not in Africa itself but in some self-motivated relationship to that colonially overdetermined signifier. In his account of the play, Eric Sundquist notes this crucial element in Williams's and Walker's stage performance. Their work, he argues, represented the central "paradox" of race in turn-of-the-century American black leadership:

> Could the race advance culturally or ever be accorded equal political and social rights without discarding the traces of its enslavement and African origins? . . . Corresponding to the question of civil rights, then, was another: What life and what historical memory were "authentically" black? What was "genuine" in the tradition and what not?[32]

Another question must be added to the ones asked by Sundquist, one which frames all the others: Did the "Negro" in fact have a singular "culture" as understood by the ideologies of the time? The African American debate around identity had to fixate on Africa simply to address this larger question; this was after all a climate where race implied nation but where America certainly could not function as the easy site of Negro nationhood. The two performers and the show itself represent these important paradoxes and tensions but are ultimately dismissed by Sundquist primarily for their total lack of connection to any "real" Africa or any materially adumbrated theory of racial retentions. Ann Charters is also dismissive of Williams's and Walker's use of Africa, considering how rooted their work was in vaudeville, minstrelsy, and parody. However, *In Dahomey* and the black blackface of Bert Williams must be situated in relationship to these questions about Africa, history, retentions, and culture which were rife within the discursive climate of early black modernism as well as in the general obsessions of Anglo-American modernism. After all, behind the layers of parody, comic buffoonery, and the diminishing burden of blackface, that was what their plays were largely *about*. These conversations were in fact being staged for a massive popular audience in the politically safe language of popular farce.

None of Sundquist's questions and observations is far from what was being achieved in the play *In Dahomey* itself. In it Africa was certainly not real but a discursive space constructed to enable a simultaneously local and global critique by way of a black imagination that was diasporic in its reach. The play makes good on Du Bois's observation: "The Color Line belts the world." As described by Sundquist, these turn-of-the-century debates over Africa were largely internal and national cultural questions and concerns. They are specifically American inter- and intra-racial political questions in which Africa becomes a mediating sign, the linchpin of the debate over the Negro in America and the echo of distant origins that makes all political positions in the racial debate possible. Garvey and Du Bois would stress the global significance of these questions by directly linking the struggle for civil rights in America with the struggle against colonialism in Africa and in the Caribbean. For both these pan-Africanists, Africa, even as a symbol, had a material impact on an increasingly imperial United States in its treatment of blacks in America and throughout the world; and as a symbol, it also made moral, political, and material claims on its dispersed children. The proverbial "hands of Ethiopia" were reaching out not only for metaphysical and verbal support but also for material satisfaction and political justification. Because these claims were embedded in memory and dream, and because they were already masked by a deep black ambivalence toward Africa and its meanings, they were in turn best addressed via metaphor and masquerade. It is the deliberate falseness and unreality of the Africa presented in In Dahomey that allows it to function as a complex interrogation of its subject and its moment.

Sundquist's brief discussion of the play does not imagine just how much the presence of a West Indian performer and an awareness of distinct black cultural and historical differences could impact a reading of In Dahomey's colorful faux-African masquerade. The black modernist dream and construction of Africa is here motivated by the presence of black cultural, linguistic, historical, sexual, and political differences—differences clearly mediated by white power and spectatorship, but which prioritize the black viewer. For example, the material presence of black immigrant groups in New York, many from the Caribbean and some from the continent itself, is symbolized by the minstrelsy of Bert Williams, who was always the "not quite" black (that is, African American) everyman. Yet in the play he literally becomes heir to both symbolic spaces: the "South" and Africa, and as a Caribbean subject he unites them. So the fact that the question of local civil rights was intimately connected to historical questions of racial origins is not as interesting as the fact that the question of authenticity was posed not simply in relationship to origins but in relationship to other culturally distinct, historically differentiated groups of blacks. By the opening of In Dahomey, Africa had already been fed through the diaspora simulacrum, its multiple meanings already refracted and doubled and redoubled so that it could only function as a dream-fiction of maskless-ness, as something external to representation. This anteriority—this primordial absence—could only be evoked through the chthonic ritual of masquerade.

Despite the obsession with the "genuine," the "natural," and the authentic which were assumed and verified by the blood-logic of race that underpinned the minstrelsy of Williams and Walker, that these performances being grounded by intra-racial cultural differences suggests that there was more to Africa than authenticity, or more to authenticity than "Africa." Achieving the "native element" was never the point despite George Walker's grandest pronouncements, though his notion of African retentions and cultural continuity were decidedly essentialist and explicitly performative, as we have seen. A return to the "native" was also never the point for Bert Williams, considering his great hopes to relocate black origins not in the romantic murk of primitivism, as would be the case with some Harlem moderns, but in the spectacle of power and authority by means of a fixation on precolonial, African nobility—as in every Negro was a king. With this performance Williams and Walker stretched the possibilities of minstrelsy via this nascent pan-Africanism despite being limited to comedic performance. As the performance advertisement both promises and encourages, the play, despite its politics (or perhaps, to deflect attention from its politics), should be and will be "One Continuous Laugh from Rise to Fall of Curtain." *In Dahomey* did get them to Broadway—which was the point. Here Bert Williams was recognized by most critics, reviewers, and fans as the premier comedian in America, regardless of race. That he was able to achieve this success as an individual artist (black and West Indian) via the mythic and promiscuous trope of Africa, well, that too was the point.

Considering how little unbiased information about the continent was available to the black audience for a Williams and Walker show and considering how much ambivalence about Africa existed among the black population, it is unlikely that an authentic representation of the continent would have worked, in any case. It is a struggle to even imagine the kind of Africa they could have presented at that time without the constraints of minstrelsy and comedic performance. Sticking with the conventions of vaudeville exotica better allowed them to address Africa in the language that was most familiar to the audience: the flexible language of myth and desire, of absence and metaphor and poetic masking. The language of power was also addressed in the quasi-Africentric vaudeville performance of *In Dahomey*, because through this representation of Africa many of the intra-racial contradictions and tensions of African American society were being highlighted, dramatized, and satirized. These issues of desire, myth, power, and absence constitute the "native element" of the black diaspora in its purest form, and through comedic performance it was stripped of its trauma. Given an emergent global, pan-African presence abroad and non-American black immigrants in the city's own backyard, during the modernist era Africa became increasingly a

sign of intra-diasporic contestation in New York. Common origins become
secondary to differences; however, differences become masked by the essentializing logic of race, which was the only thing available and which would
ultimately privilege African Americans and their shifting and complex views
of race and Africa. It is of no marginal historical significance that "the very
first full-length musical written and played by blacks to be performed at a
major Broadway house" featured these issues.[33]

Sundquist calls In Dahomey one of Williams's and Walker's "back to Africa
farces."[34] Years before George Schuyler's still-too-painful-to-canonize satire
of the African American "colonization" of Liberia, Slaves Today (1931), In
Dahomey cannily identified how a general cultural obsession with African
American powerlessness in America manifested itself in the desire for power
in Africa. It explored how a desire for roots and authenticity could lead to a
maintenance of exploitive intra-racial hierarchies all in the name of racial
solidarity. Years before Marcus Garvey, this play mocked and lampooned the
vainglorious spectacle of a "back to Africa" movement as well as the complexities implied by the very notion of return. It is uncannily prescient in its
critique of the excesses of Garveyism by way of its explicit attention to issues
of power, hierarchy, and exploitation within the race. It addresses those
forms of intra-racial exploitation that often wear the mask of nationalism and
racial uplift as pride becomes dogma and the local black "self" uses race to
legitimize the culture and class biases embedded in the languages of repatriation and anti-racist struggle.

The idealized representation of Africa in the play was also important as it
worked against the traditional "jungle" stereotype that was prominent in
racist mythologies. Rather than provide a dark, ignorant, dangerous, and
chaotic continent, Williams and Walker provided the kind of light and harm-
less exotica that had already been popular in mainstream vaudeville. This
particular representation of the "jungle," because it was so fantastical, musical, and colorful, would be influential for the urban primitivism of the African American cultural elite during the Harlem Renaissance, from Langston
Hughes—nephew of George Walker—to Josephine Baker and Duke Ellington. Hughes even writes in his autobiography The Big Sea that he missed an
important exam during his term at Columbia to attend Bert Williams's funeral in 1922, the same year he repeatedly saw Shuffle Along. This play would
not have been possible without the success of In Dahomey. This important
event in Hughes's life suggests that the generation of high Harlem nationalist
primitivism was more than willing to pay homage to him who was the father
to both their reclaimed and reinvented vision of Africa and to their ambiva-

lence toward minstrelsy. Even Carl Van Vechten, years before becoming the most celebrated negrophile on the Harlem scene, had been deeply entranced by the work of Bert Williams.[35]

Using *In Dahomey* as a convenient marker for generational transformation, perhaps it was here that the subsequent generation of black artists learned that Africa could be commodified as a spectacle which could help them claim cultural capital in the climate of Anglo-American modernism and its aesthetic scramble for Africa. Perhaps it was also here that they witnessed just how far the mask could be stretched in the attempt to create an authenticity of their own. One even wonders if the pomp and ceremony of Garvey's UNIA was in some way directly indebted to *In Dahomey* and its innovative use of black spectacle. Although Marcus Garvey wouldn't arrive in Harlem until 1916 and his UNIA wouldn't be established there until the following year, "back to Africa" ideas had become fully established in the urban folklore of black Harlem—so established that they were ripe for parody and mockery.

Briefly, the plot of *In Dahomey* features a dishonest group of investors in Boston who propose to establish a haven for oppressed blacks in Africa. They dispatch the fast-talking hustler "Rareback Pinkerton," played by George Walker, to Florida, where he masquerades as a prince of Dahomey in order to convince hundreds of African Americans to join his colony. He entices them by singing songs such as "My Castle on the Nile" and "On Broadway in Dahomey Bye and Bye." The former song had been a hit in their previous show *Sons of Ham*, which also featured a few scenes set in Africa. In this play Williams had worn the costume of a Zulu warrior, performing the song along with "My Little Zulu Babe" and the truly bizarre "The Phrenologist Coon." In "My Castle on the Nile" Rareback attempts to seduce African Americans with their very own dreams of wealth and power and aristocracy:

> In my castle on the river Nile
> I am gwinter live in elegant style
> In laid diamonds onde flo'
> A baboon butler at my do'
> When I wed dat princess Anna Mazoo
> Den my Blood will change from red to blue
> Entertaining royalty all the while
> In my castle on the river Nile.[36]

The "castle," the "diamonds," the socioeconomic transfusion, and the "royalty" not only function as Rareback's enticement of the socially and economically oppressed African American masses; they also provide an image of

Africa that is itself mocked by the song. The "baboon butler," "princess Anna Mazoo," and the anomalous absurdity of a European-style castle on the river Nile: these images are being ridiculed, but at the same time their power to manipulate is being stressed. Also, the use of the vernacular to mock this obsession with aristocracy serves to strengthen the play's critique of how Africa was being constructed and imagined by a powerless black audience who aimed to project their dreams of power against the backdrop of a fantasy of reclaimed racial origins.

In his attempt to exploit his own people, Rareback/Walker is accompanied on his travels by the simple-minded and endlessly jovial "Shylock Homestead," played by Bert Williams. Homestead is unaware of his part in the scheme, which is partly to bilk a wealthy and senile old African American of his riches under the guise of repatriation. The theme of repatriation, by the way, turned out to be much more significant than either Williams and Walker may have thought. It was echoed in the tragic fall of Marcus Garvey and his indictment for fraud, which was connected to the Black Star Line of ships that were the vehicles by which blacks in the diaspora would have sailed back "home" to Dahomey. The theme was the topic of the 1932 film The Black King (also known as Harlem Hot Shot), which is said to be a satire of the Marcus Garvey movement years after Garvey's deportation. The theme was also employed by Chester Himes in 1965 in Cotton Comes to Harlem, where once again the potent dream of liberation left African Americans vulnerable to exploitation by their own. A transatlantic echo sounded in colonial Jamaica, where in 1959 Claudius Henry, one of the founders of the Rastafarian movement, was arrested and jailed for selling false passages back to "Ethiopia" which were marked with the tantalizing slogan "no passport necessary."[37] So not only had "Africa," "Ethiopia," "Dahomey," and even "Zulu" come to signify black-on-black masquerade or a general inauthenticity; it seems that the very desire to return "back to Africa" was also becoming linked to fraud and exploitative doubling/double talk.

One could easily argue that one of the reasons In Dahomey was able to make it to Broadway was because it seemed to do what the white press was already fond of doing: mocking blacks, burlesquing Africa, and ridiculing the very notion that blacks could survive away from whites and in control of their own political destinies. It also seemed to exploit the general stereotype, which held that black-on-black exploitation and greed made black social, economic, or political empowerment impossible. True enough, but it was not likely that a musical comedy that attacked whites directly, mocked white philanthropism, and burlesqued the various forms of white Africa-philia would have made it to Broadway at the turn of the century. One wonders if even a play seriously celebrating the possibilities of independent black nationhood or African leadership would have been appealing to an African American audience who more than likely preferred Africa only as a colorful and exotic evocation. That the turn-of-the-century white audience would have difficulty consuming a play that seriously and directly addressed them should go without saying. Yet because the play focused explicitly and exclusively on black dreams, black fantasies, and black political desires, because it used minstrelsy to transcend minstrelsy, it was able to explore intercultural relationships and reimagine the position and possibilities of the "Negro" in a new century. Through this, "Africa" the dream was granted a creative, aesthetic, and political validity in black popular culture that it had never had.

This stress on the intercultural politics of the black world is why certain critics assaulted its authenticity. They lamented that *In Dahomey* was "not so distinctively a darky play" while others resented its refusal to be what it was expected to be: "when white folks are to be amused by the colored race, they want characteristic entertainment, and not an imitation of the musical comedy."[38] These performers dared to mimic mainstream musical theater while only pretending to perpetuate minstrelsy. The *Boston Globe*, while disliking the play, saw clearly its political strategy, describing it as an attempt at "getting the 'real colored show' out of extravaganza and into legitimate comedy."[39] The reviewer for the *Evening Transcript* was more sympathetic, noting that "the composer has succeeded in lifting Negro music above the plane of the so-called 'Coon Song' without destroying the characteristics of the melodies, and he has provided a score which is likewise unusually diversified."[40] This music, it is important to note, was described by George Walker as "purely African" or more precisely as "Americanized African songs," in reference to such songs as "My Zulu Babe," "My Castle on the Nile," and "My Dahomean Queen."[41]

Eric Sundquist is correct in dismissing these claims on Africa as being "hardly creditable"; yet this is only if one accepts the turn-of-the-century discourse of racial authenticity as the barometer for cultural expressions that are explicitly and implicitly performative.[42] The play's assertion of the African Americanization of Africa is a statement arguing for cultural retentions years before that argument would gain strength and confidence in the anthropology which would undergird the work of the New Negro generation. Examples of this include the work of Zora Neale Hurston's mentor, Franz Boas, and the ideas of the grand white progenitor of French Negritude, Leo Frobenius. Indeed, Du Bois's *The Souls of Black Folk* is much in line with this notion of cultural retentions as manifest in "Americanized African songs," which informs his discussion of the historical trajectory of the Negro spirituals toward the end of the book. George Walker's view was of course much more romantic than the views of these anthropologists. Yet it assumes enough of a historical and cultural continuum to justify a performance of an authenticity that would erase the pre-existing and prevailing view of Negro origins that argued that African retentions were a sign of global Negro degradation. Walker's view forms a solid critique of that latter argument, which held its claim to truth by dint of its being articulated and repeated in the Euro-American imagination and used to justify segregation, Jim Crow, and colonization.

In Dahomey authorized itself via an Africa that was necessarily an imagined space of freedom, where the racial norms and political hierarchies of the United States did not exist and where the "nigger tones" of plantation soundings were inappropriate and sounded increasingly inauthentic. The racist dream of containment that was the topos of the plantation was here replaced by a global vision of migration and voluntary movement signified by the imaginative space of Dahomey. In the play, blacks chose to go there and were free to travel regardless of their nefarious intentions. There is no mention in the play of there being any white resistance or constraints on their travel to or interaction with Dahomey whatsoever—indeed, the mechanisms and motivations of the play have absolutely no dependence on white power, permission, or control. This is evident in the flimsy and inconsequential plot, which begins in Africa, moves to Boston, moves to Florida, and then back to a Dahomey that may have been an exoticist fiction, but then again so were Florida and Boston.

In the narrative these spaces are occupied by powerful black businessmen, grand black society events, colorful costumes, and a panoply of highly romanticized black quasi-aristocratic social types. The play features Dahomeyan governors and crowds of warriors, members of colonization societies, a "Chinese" cook, criminals and intelligence officers, colonists, a black woman journalist, a street fakir, bootblacks, numbers of society ladies and gentlemen, and multiple perspectives on the issue of immigration/repatriation. For example, although it is clearly a fraud, many of the characters believe quite strongly in "back to Africa" and the conclusion of the play suggests a tacit endorsement of the dream of return. Since the entire play is staged in the imagination of blacks struggling to see themselves as both internally and internationally powerful and against a larger historical and geographic backdrop, there is no space of the "real" against which to compare this fantastical Africa.

The movement between and among these various spaces was as liberating as was the fact that as far as we know, from this historical distance, all the characters—but for one—were without the burnt-cork mask. Regardless of their social and cultural roles in the play, only one wore blackface. And that one was Shylock Homestead, Bert Williams, who, as the play reveals, is the heir to the Florida fortune, becoming the leader of black communities in Florida and in the Dahomey colony. The flimsy plot concludes when Homestead, discovering that his dear friend Pinkerton is a crook, donates the remainder of his fortune to the Dahomey colony in a symbolic gesture that prefigures and supports the pan-Africanisms to come. Despite the humor and the farcical nature of the performance, a gesture like this was no joke, considering just how fraught the identification with Africa was in the minds of the black audience. Also, in a play that featured a cosmopolitan and socially complex black world, the only trace of the "nigger" or the "darky" or the "coon" was the masked Bert Williams *who turns out to be the hero.* In a play that emerges from a tradition that dictated that blacks could be onstage only behind the minstrel mask and in the context of racial travesty, this lone mask gave the play legitimacy in the minds of white spectators and enabled the other black performers to operate without it. Williams in blackface was the aesthetic and political pivot of the performance, guaranteeing the white audience its familiar sense of control via the tropes and figures of minstrelsy, while at the same time allowing the black audience to look beyond racial travesty and explore the alternate worldviews enabled by cross-cultural performance.

Of course, this had been happening in the Williams and Walker shows long before *In Dahomey.* In fact, there is no record of George Walker or his wife Ada Overton Walker ever wearing burnt cork. They were forever constrained by the roles and meanings established by blackface, but the actual minstrel mask itself became the special purview of Bert Williams. He wore it so that the others didn't have to, balancing the weight of its legitimacy with his personal sacrifice. His hit song from *In Dahomey,* "Jonah Man," written with Alex Rogers, was very like his signature tune "Nobody" in that it articulated the sentiments of the comically down and out figure Williams played so well. Like that previous song, it articulates also the anguish of one who is burdened by the mask and whose tragedy derives partly from his full awareness of this necessary role as the scapegoat for all "darkies":

My luck started when I was born,
Leas' so the old folks say.
Dat same hard luck's been my bes' frien'
To dis vary day.
When I was young, Mama's friends—to find a name they tried.
They named me after Papa—and the same day papa died, Fo'—
I'm a Jonah, I'm a Jonah Man,
My family for many years would look at me
And den shen tears.
Why I am dis Jonah
I sho' can't understand,
But I'm a good substantial, full-fledged
Real, first-class Jonah Man.[43]

The significance of the burnt-cork mask had been diminished by Williams so
mastering it that it became literally his own. He became a projection of the
last "darky," that tragicomic figure from a plantation myth that was being
juxtaposed against a globalized myth of Africa. And in that juxtaposition, the
figure becomes increasingly incongruous, its centrality ever more tragic.

Although the micropolitical and theoretical significance of In Dahomey may
not have been directly acknowledged by Williams's audience or by any scholars and critics from or of that moment, it is possible to see in the play's
opening a genuine debate about spectatorship and cultural ownership. Because Africa and "back to Africa" were its central topics and because it debuted
in the context of de facto segregation, the political and cultural tensions of
the opening night were complicated. The show opened and first ran in
Boston, but it was in New York at the relatively new and architecturally stunning New York Theater that its significance was most deeply felt and where the
audience—or rather, the audiences—engaged each other. Eric Ledell Smith
writes that at the New York premiere, "Blacks vied with whites for the best
seats in the house, some offering to pay more than the dollar price of the
orchestra seats."[44] They were physically barred from access to these seats and
shunted over to the much less hospitable gallery section. Feuds erupted, and
by the next morning the New York Times was describing the conflicts in terms of
a potential "race war." Despite the fact that African Americans ultimately lost
out in the battle for the best seats—though special provisions were made for
the black elite classes—newspapers declared "the race problem was most
successfully handled" at the opening of In Dahomey, noting that both the issue
of segregation and the performance were equally newsworthy.[45]

What Eric Ledell Smith's account does not address, however, is precisely why a black audience already familiar with the segregationist practices of Broadway would decide suddenly to vie with whites for privileged seats in a new theater. What would possess them to stride so confidently into the orchestra and boxes that were known to be reserved exclusively for white patrons? The answer probably has to do with the reputation of the Williams and Walker shows, which were already successful, legendary, and iconic on the African American performance-circuit. For the African American audience, regardless of the space within which *In Dahomey* was being displayed, it was a "black" show because Williams and Walker played largely but not exclusively to "black" audiences. In other words, it was their show, and to be treated as second-class citizens at their show was more intolerable than it would have been at a standard Broadway performance, that is, a "white" show. Their spectatorship bore with it the weight of the entire history of the black appropriation of minstrelsy. For the white audience, this "Most Costly and Colossal Production ever given by a Colored attraction" complete with "Carload of Beautiful Scenery and Mechanical Effects, New Music, Pretty Girls, Funny Specialties, Gorgeous Costumes and A Large Chorus of Well-Trained Voices" was their entrée into the very possibility of an "authentic" black expression. This black expression was, of course, mediated and controlled by the form and structure of white Broadway spectacle. For the white audience, the other's "authenticity" is always a product of their own discursive and socioeconomic control—a white artifact. To have to step down to blacks in the audience would have threatened that mediation, which was the surest sign of power and crucial to their pleasure.

On Broadway in Dahomey Bye and Bye: Cakewalking the Continent

It is in the songs of *In Dahomey* that all the issues thus argued are made clear, though it must be acknowledged that much of what occurred onstage to inflect or transform the given textual meanings is not available. The play's actual performance of race and diaspora is evanescent, present only to the immediate audience and the gestural and symbolic conventions of its moment. But because it was such a broad satire of political positions within a black transatlantic community, and because its various meanings were not intended to be subtle or opaque, its general attempt to critique the internal hierarchies and subhegemonic power structures in the African American community is in fact nakedly expressed. For example, a decade before

Eugene O'Neill's *The Emperor Jones*, complex issues of power, repatriation, self-exploitation, and nationalism are present most powerfully in the lampooning of the African American "Colored Aristocracy." This subculture is directly named and satirized in song and in dance. The song "Leader of the Colored Aristocracy," for instance, features lines such as these:

> To be the leader of the color'd aristocracy,
> Is my ambition . . .
> I have a longing just the same as all the quality,
> For recognition . . .
> . . . I'll drill these darkies till,
> They're up in high society's hypocracy.
> They'll come my way, To gain entrée,
> To the circles of the color'd aristocracy.
>
> Now to establish swell society for color'd folks,
> I have a yearning . . .
> And from the high-ton'd 'ristocratic white folks how to lead,
> I have been learning . . .
> All that I need is lots of dough,
> For that regulates the social scale, you know,
> 'Twill put me in position to make the proper show,
> As the leader of the color'd aristocracy.
>
> And then I'll drill these darkies till,
> They're up in high society's hypocracy,
> They'll come my way,
> To gain entrée
> To the circles of the color'd aristocracy.[46]

The satire is obvious, its bite not diminished by its humor but its politics made possible by its comedic expression. The voice here is a national voice, or rather, the voice of a minority within a minority that claims unto itself the power of a transnational sounding. Notice how the obsession with racial and historical "recognition" is conjoined with the lust for aristocratic power. The speaker equates this "longing" for power with the longing and lust of whites who represent sociocultural and economic "quality." To assimilate is to share in the problematic desires of the dominant class and culture; it is also to perform, to wear an expensive social mask in order "to make the proper show." Note also how the desire for recognition and the desire for power are both underpinned by a discourse of racial pride and assimilation, as racial uplift, callous social climbing, and the obsession with power become synonymous. In this play, assimilation and self-exploitation become one, and the critique of white hegemony is articulated as a product of the envy of a rival, marginalized sub-hegemony rather than a universalized cry for equity and justice.

To be more precise about the tenor of the satire, "High society," despite a full acknowledging of "hypocracy," is not the destiny of all black people or African Americans in general. The issue of class as a fragmenting social reality is at the core of this critique of black exceptionalism which isolates a specific group of power brokers who exploit the hazy universalism of race. "High society" is the destiny of the "color'd aristocracy," those who will be dubbed the "Talented Tenth" the following year by Du Bois and whose socioeconomic, cultural, and moral standards will be asserted as normative. To contextualize this song, a brief diversion into the secret history of pan-Africanism will be helpful. In his fine and controversial essay "W. E. B. Du Bois and Black Sovereignty," Cedric J. Robinson puts this "hypocracy" in helpful, materialist terms. What is crucial about his analysis is how it links— as did *In Dahomey*—local intra-racial hierarchies with the problematic dispensations of global power along the lines of race:

> Like their European predecessors in the eighteenth and nineteenth centuries, and their contemporaries in the twentieth century all over the world, the Black middle classes—that is, the Black intelligentsias of the United States, the Caribbean and Africa—were captives of a dialectic: on the one hand, their continued development was structurally implicated in the continued domination of their societies by the Atlantic metropoles; on the other, the historic destiny of their class was linked to nationalism. Put bluntly, the future of the Black middle class was embedded in the contradictions of imperialism.[47]

Robinson is good to extend this critique to the black, colonial middle classes in the Caribbean and Africa as well as in the United States; however, it is important to note that this same class, because of the intensified contradictions of its position as a colonial, comprador intelligentsia, would eventually struggle for, gain, and institutionalize the ambiguous freedoms of the post/ neo/omni-colonial era. These contradictions produce pan-Africanism itself, which attempts to resolve them from within a globalized sense of African commonality that has yet to fully address its own internal class, national, and cultural biases.

Robinson's essay is primarily focused on how the pan-Africanism reflected in Du Bois's being so located in his class position was able ultimately
to serve the needs and interests of the colonial, American state and the
emergent neocolonialism of the Firestone Corporation. Du Bois, he argues,
"blinded by the elitism characteristic of his class prerogative, fell prey to
American colonialism."⁴⁸ At this time Du Bois's pan-Africanism was not yet a
Marxist pan-Africanism, so he like Garvey believed that it was possible to
liberate Africa within the ideological and socioeconomic relations of industrial capitalism. His blind support of the Firestone company as well as the
dominant Americo-Liberian community, which had been arriving from the
United States as early as 1822, resulted in part from a belief in the civilizing
capacity of African Americans, whom he described as "missionaries of culture for their backward brethren in the new Africa."⁴⁹ It is well recognized,
though often ignored, just how exploitative and violent this example of repatriation was—one wonders if the quick disappearance of George Schuyler's
Slaves Today from the Harlem Renaissance canon has something to do with its
reckless identification of African/African American tensions as central to a
black political modernism. As Robinson goes on to argue, the bourgeois
contention over Liberia was waged implicitly against the Garvey movement,
which had long set its sights on repatriation to that specific nation, which
was formally established in 1847. Garvey, after all, had a much stronger
ideological hold on the emergent nationalisms of the continent than the
NAACP could have ever dreamed of, the result, largely, of the popularity and
significance of his *Negro World* paper.

If Du Bois then represents a black, New England bourgeoisie, an Afro-
Victorian sensibility which could do nothing less than universalize its marginal position in the face of an unruly folk, then Garvey represents a Caribbean
immigrant petit-bourgeoisie which made incursions on white supremacy in
America, on European control of the African continent, and on African American exceptionalism. Both these positions staked claim to the ultimate signifier of racial authority and authenticity that is Africa and each were threatened
by the other's deployment of that signifier, since each refused to see in their
divergence a broader definition of its meanings. By the time Du Bois was
appointed as the representative of the United States at the inauguration of the
Americo-Liberian president in 1924, Garvey had already fallen into disfavor
and was barred from Liberia. Robinson suggests (and finds documents to
support) that Du Bois's appointment by President Calvin Coolidge was made
largely to block the UNIA's plan to relocate and base itself in Liberia as well as

to throw the United States' support behind one black position while silencing another more contentious one. Robinson's analysis is as follows:

> Interestingly enough, during the same period in which Du Bois was quite evidently warning American officials and Black Americans of the "visionary" schemes of Marcus Garvey, he was importuning the American government and American capital to support his own versions of Liberian development. To Secretary of State Hughes, Du Bois had inquired of federal protection for Black venture capital. . . . This, of course, was precisely the relationship between the State and private capital which had precipitated the occupation of Haiti which had begun in 1915. Apparently, Du Bois' immersion in the ideology of the State had hidden this consequence from him.[50]

None of this discussion is meant to privilege the Garvey position and to dismiss or attack the Du Boisian and NAACP perspective. It is simply to draw out the competing black global tensions over Africa and to see in this intra-racial scramble for the continent a crucial set of issues and contradictions there within the global dynamics of race, class, and diaspora. *In Dahomey* had anticipated, mocked, and critiqued these global contradictions of black, diasporic leadership and the nascent ideologies of pan-Africanism almost two decades before they materialized there in Africa. Because it could not explicitly critique the colonial discourse of race, American racism, and white supremacy, the play opted to hone its criticism of the internal dynamics and contradictions of a black world seeking to both find and invent itself beyond the borders drawn and quartered by imperialism. And because it was limited to humor and comedy, it mocked what seemed acceptable to a white audience: blacks' treatment of each other.

Returning to "Leader of the Colored Aristocracy": the movement up the social and cultural ladder in a racist society is here achieved by a willingness to "drill these darkies"—other blacks—as if they were slaves, drill them so well that they will "come my way, To gain entrée." For "darkies" to still desire "entrée" to this system of power and privilege despite being so drilled suggests that this particularly harsh logic of assimilation has been fully indoctrinated and that the system of power it depends on has been naturalized in African American subjects. In fact it had become so naturalized that the only way to work against it was from within: to explicitly and parodically celebrate it, rooting it out with a self-immolating, painfully ironic grin:

To get in high society,
You need a great reputation,

Don't cultivate sobriety,
But rather ostentation.[51]

Assimilation is here rendered as socioeconomic verticality, and its bene-
fits are primarily derived from power itself, however garish and unjust. Of
course, Garvey's obsession with ostentation was not geared toward acceptance in high Anglo-American or white society—for him that was what made
him more "authentic" than Du Bois and the members of the NAACP who
seemed too hungry to curry the favor of whites. He instead favored a parallel
realm of black nobility, power, and distinction that was a mirror image—a
photo negative, perhaps—of white imperial power. It is difficult not to hear
and visualize Marcus Garvey in a song like *In Dahomey*'s paean to a gendered
continent, "My Dahomean Queen":

When I become a King
All the Jingle bells will ring
While thro' the streets on palanquins we're borne
'Twill be the grandest thing
Just to hear the Natives sing
As loyally they fall before my throne
Caboceers will be our sentry,
'Rabian Knights will be our gentry,
The wonder of the twentieth century.[52]

But these songs, as well as "On Broadway in Dahomey Bye and Bye" and the
famous "Evah Darkey Is a King," still work as a critique of that Garveyite
desire to transplant a black aristocracy to Africa. This is a fantasy in which
"natives" sing, liberated by a black empire, eager to throw themselves loyally
before its power. Even though the Garveyite vision would come years after *In
Dahomey*, it is historically positioned by the play as the culmination of and
logical conclusion to those turn-of-the-century "back to Africa" ideas that the
play itself parodies.

As suggested earlier, Du Bois's description of Marcus Garvey and the
UNIA parades as Williams and Walker shows was prompted in large part by
the huge and iconic success of *In Dahomey* and the other "back to Africa
farces" that paved the way for Garveyite pan-Africanism and its use of spectacle. The play serves a prophetic function, depicting a vision of "back to
Africa" that critiques Garvey in advance, as well as reflecting the kind of
contradictions and bloody paradoxes that had already emerged in the African
American "return" to Liberia the previous century. After all, both Garvey and

Du Bois did in fact believe that African Americans would in various ways have to "pacify" or "train" backward natives, were they ever to return to the continent. Garvey would describe this process in "Africa for the Africans" as the benevolent "colonization of Africa by the black race," while in "The Hands of Ethiopia" Du Bois speaks of the "benevolent domination of Africa."[53]

That this critique of black elitism and the obsession with power—learned, the song tells us, as leadership from the "high-ton'd 'ristocratic white folks"— is established through an Africa of the imagination and via minstrelsy is remarkable. Africa as a mythic space produced by fantasy and cross-cultural doubling allows a local critique of intra-racial hierarchies which use racial uplift to justify black-on-black exploitation. By wearing an African mask, the face of African American society is refracted and the seemingly legitimate structure of its racial politics is unmasked and deauthorized by that gesture. What must be stressed is that all of this takes place in reference to an African colonization scheme. This emphasizes the contradictions implicit in the term "colonization" as articulated by erstwhile anti-racist and anti-colonial blacks. As "Leader of the Colored Aristocracy" suggests, the black claim on Africa is merely a claim on a space where the power that is denied them in the United States can be manifested: where darkies can become kings and natives can become darkies; where reversals of identity and mistaken identities serve to underscore a structure of domination that is ultimately rooted in the imperial and racialized power dynamics of the United States. By way of this intricate performance of intra-racial masking the structural forces of whiteness and American imperial power are identified and manifested.

But the song "On Broadway in Dahomey Bye and Bye" takes seriously the very gesture toward an Africa of the imagination that would liberate African Americans from the limitations of the world shaped by colonialism and policed by racism. The imagination was perhaps the only place in which freedom, opposition, and exploration could exist unfettered. And the mask was that which deflected visual policing and scrutiny with a grin in order for the imagination to pursue possibilities other than those available by and through the status quo. "On Broadway in Dahomey Bye and Bye" presents an explicit and imaginative vision of black repatriation—not to a literal "Africa" but to a black simulacrum which features an even deeper critique of the very desire to return and re-invent "home." It begins with a supposition: "If we went to Dahomey suppose the King would say / We want a Broadway built for us, we want it right away."[54] The "we" articulated here are clearly African American. For them Dahomey is the site of freedom from racial oppression but also of an aristocracy that parallels the race and class structures of the West. It also guarantees "them" a hierarchical privilege in relation to the natives found there. Since this latter observation eerily echoes the experience of Liberia and the American Colonization Society, one can't help but wince while chuckling at the complexity of a resistant nationalism that manifests itself as a mere shadow of colonialism. As the song asserts near its end, "None but the Royal blood can qualify."[55] In this, the biogenetic logic of race is deployed to articulate internal hierarchies and a global political dispensation that is sanctioned by the mask of American racism.

To build this new Broadway, conscription is again necessary, as in "Leader of the Colored Aristocracy": "We'd git a bunch of natives say ten thousand or more" to complete a spectacle rivaling perhaps only the pyramids, or, less dramatically, "Wid Banyan trees build a big department store."[56] Ironically, what is encountered in this simulated Africa is a desire to simulate America: Dahomey wants its own Broadway—not its own past, but a future defined by a fantasy of America. As the song continues it becomes clear that this "America" envisioned by the ersatz Africans is an America which has already been re-imagined by African American culture as well as white American stereotypes of African American culture: "We'd sell big Georgia possums some watermelons too / To git the coin for other things we'd like to do."[57] Although clearly a parody of capitalist exchange which emphasizes the significance of race in this mode of exchange, the song still takes seriously how deeply implicated the black desire for freedom is in these contradictions of race, capital, and imperial power. Suddenly Africa becomes not only a colonial suburb of America but one re-imagined and domesticated by African Americans. Cedric Robinson's reading of Du Bois and the Firestone Corporation should be remembered here.

As "On Broadway in Dahomey Bye and Bye" shows, the African American desire for freedom and empowerment could easily be manipulated in such a way as to facilitate greater American economic and cultural control of the beleaguered continent:

> On Broadway in Dahomey Bye and bye
> We'll build a Bamboo Railway to the sky
> You'll see on the sides of rocks and hills,
> "Use Carter's Little Liver pills."[58]

This song is sung right after Rareback Pinkerton promises Shylock Homestead that if he likes Dahomey well enough, he'll "buy it for you."[59] As made clear in the stanza, the Broadway transplanted to Dahomey could never equal the "real" Broadway and could only be a bamboo replica of industrialization. Yet it would still be a worthwhile space for the advertising of American commodities. Despite this quite complex yet absurd vision of an American control produced by an oppressed African American desire for freedom and power in Africa, the song also mocks the system of power in America itself. The false utopia of Africa is held against the all too real dystopia of the United States. For example, the police and legal systems are burlesqued thus:

> On Broadway in Dahomey bye and bye . . .
> We'd git some large Gorillas and we'd use them for police,
> Then git a Hippopotamus for Justice of the Peace. . . .[60]

The very fact of "aping" or mimicking high European culture is also lampooned: "And then have Wagner sung by parrots every night."[61] This shows that the play is ultimately held together by a meta-narrative in which mimicry of whites and of other blacks—of high European culture and "authentic" African roots—is secondary to the complex yet absurd politics of masquerade itself.

The Beggar Maid Becomes a Queen: Desexing the Dark Continent

Not only are the law and the police, the Talented Tenth and black charlatans unmasked by the masking and multilayered mimicry that is *In Dahomey*. The complexity of the black woman's relationship to both white gender norms and the norms of black patriarchy is also addressed by the play. It uses the issue of gender to isolate and interrupt the overwhelmingly male articulations of Africa, race, and nation while simultaneously working against the racism implicit within white standards of womanhood and female sexuality. To work against both these assumptions, which fundamentally denied the possibility of black female participation, required that black women—black middle-class women in particular—reject and disprove them by directly engaging them. This was, of course, done via mimicry and countermimicry. For example, to reject and disprove the assumption that black women could not be "true" women because of their race, black women performed according to the existing definitions of "true" womanhood and thus mastered that persona. To master this form was in a sense to undo the notion that the form was natural, thereby biologically impossible for black women. However, to introduce into this performance of the white fiction of womanhood desires specific to pan-Africanism and racial assimilation added complex layers of difference behind that mask of the true.

Yet there was more to this performance of "true" womanhood on the other side of the gender and racial line. Engaged by black women, this performance simultaneously rejected and disproved the patriarchal notion that racial political representation was the exclusive preserve of black males; it emphasized that many black women engaged those universalized political roles as well, however problematic they may have been. Wearing the mask of the impossible, they made the impossible possible. In doing so, black women succeeded in something akin to the achievement of Bert Williams's double minstrelsy: they did not, as most have argued, make clear the truth of race and gender; instead they masked themselves and thereby revealed that the assumed standards of truth and authority were themselves masks, deployed to maintain various systems of hierarchical differentiation. Those standards could also be engaged by way of a poetics and politics of masking in order to expand the perceived notions of black womanhood and black female political participation and complicity. However, this gender-specific struggle for their own right to masking is also critiqued by the play for its implication in the general contradictions that beset a suddenly globalized anti-racist discourse of race. Without access to an actual performance of *In Dahomey*, much of its attempt to insert gender into its multiple theoretical and political engagements is lost to contemporary readers and it is only possible to speculate on its visual and aural impact on its multiple audiences and on both men and women. We do know, however, that throughout the performance of the song "Leader of the Colored Aristocracy" most of the male statements are doubled and echoed by a female response that both mimics and criticizes the male voice. Despite its stridency and its urgency about its participation and inclusion, that voice uncritically shares the larger political intent of the male statements by explicitly inserting the presence of the female voice into that intention.

George Walker's proclamation "To be the leader of the color'd aristocracy, is my ambition" is, for example, constantly doubled by the echo "is her ambition."[62] The statement "I have a yearning" for power and nobility is also echoed and doubled by "She has a yearning." Even the claim that "from the high-ton'd aristocratic white folks how to lead / I have been learning" is followed by "She has been learning."[63] This depicts a level of black female complicity in tandem with a distinctly black feminist demand to be included in this gesture of black national and diasporic power and control. This gesture is contained by the essentialist-nationalist language of race which signifies and prioritizes African Americans who in this play literally, figuratively, and politically "represent"—and thereby erase—continental Africans. Veritably all the statements clarifying the ambition for power in the song are echoed and doubled by the interjection of the female pronoun. In this doubling the play simultaneously links the African American woman's struggle for equality to its critique of the African American elite. It thus goes further, suggesting that the obsession with authority, legitimacy, power, and domination is not limited to African American males. The politics of gender inclusion is here described as a politics of exploitative complicity in tandem with a politics of black female assertion.

It is therefore necessary to situate *In Dahomey* in relationship to the turn-of-the-century political situation of African American women. As Hazel Carby documents in *Reconstructing Womanhood*, the struggles of African American women against both white supremacy and black patriarchy began to crystallize at the turn of the century and so could not be ignored by this significant performance—particularly not with as powerful and as popular a performer as Ada Overton Walker involved. Because much of this struggle was located in the black middle class, one must remember Cedric Robinson's argument that this class was simultaneously contending with the contradictions of race and imperialism, class and historical dispersal. In short, it was wrestling with its own powerlessness at home and its symbolic and cultural power abroad. As the African American elite began to define and establish itself politically through and against the presence of African American working-class culture, it had to contend with its own rise to global significance as the most powerful group of blacks in the colonial and neo-colonial world. It is this cultural and political significance that motivates the blackface performances that begin to spring up all over the African diaspora. However awkwardly, these performances engage, mock, and pay homage to African Americans via a blackface performance which was often deemed to be authentically African American as opposed to white. So the noble struggle to transform and be included within the activist Talented Tenth also made black middle-class women prey to these same global contradictions and to the peculiar arrogance of a culture whose local oppression masked its global impact. In this the play is once again uncannily prescient. It depicts a discursive tug of war between an aspirant African American male hegemony and an interruptive yet coincident African American female critique of that hegemony which ultimately works to maintain that hegemony on cultural if not sexual grounds.

None of this is to suggest that the play does not validate and dramatize the black woman's self-inclusion into these emergent black, global discourses of resistance and power. This is clearly the play's primary interest as far as the issue of race and gender is concerned. "She is the leader of the colored aristocracy" is repeated through the end of the song, which concludes with this persona, which was surely Ada Overton Walker—really the first professional black female choreographer in America—openly debating onstage with the male voice whose authority she contests. This national voice becomes suddenly paternal and explicitly patriarchal in preparing her for marriage:

> To get in high society I've always had an ambition,
> And since I've got the brass, now we
> Are sure to have position
> A royal prince my little girl shall wed,
> For since the days of lords and dukes have sped,
> It takes a prince to put you at the head
> Of the best society. . . .[64]

Suddenly faced with actual global, cultural, and political power in Dahomey as well as in the United States, this national voice needs to consolidate and institutionalize its power and property in much the way any bourgeoisie must—via a marriage. In this the black female body is a figure of the type of exchange usually reserved for white women but here a sign of black, patriarchal bourgeois enfranchisement with more than a faint whiff of aristocratic pretension. It is interesting that this national voice even has a daughter, since it would have been much truer to the spirit of this mimicry of a traditional narrative for it to be focused on a son, a prince and heir. This would have enabled the "Colored Aristocracy" to imagine itself unproblematically transplanted to Africa with its lineage intact. The specter of a wife could then have been something manageable on the farther margins of the plot. Perhaps even a native "Dahomeyan Queen" could have made this set of well-worn clichés work for its audience.

With the use of the daughter, the patriarchal national voice is forced to find a suitable "prince" in order to place her "at the head / Of the best society," since her sex is precisely what prevents her from directly ascending to that position. It is unlikely, considering the general logic of the play, that such a prince could be found in the Dahomey colony, where only backward and primitive natives were available. He would have to be imported. So the daughter is a liability where a son would have maintained the line and the power without need of marriage. This choice of a daughter, however, is very much a part of the play's attempt to also address the changing tensions of gender and sexuality in African American culture and politics. The very dependence on the conventional "marriage plot" no doubt reflected an awareness on the part of the writers that the audience included more than a few females and that that segment of its audience wanted its own issues contended with on Broadway. In *In Dahomey* this female voice is resistant, contentious, and determined to navigate her own way through the thicket of meanings that constitutes the Dahomey of black signifying. It is not a national voice but a specific one that aspires to inclusion in that national sounding despite (or while being blind to) its problematic global resonance. The traditional desire to secure one's own socioeconomic position by securing in turn the patriarchal line is resisted by the "she" of the performance, who would rather engage a more equitable sharing of power. She would also rather explore the notion of romantic love, which more often than not is a mere synonym for individual choice, sexual independence, or a refusal to accept the hereditary status quo. She sings:

> Surely you're only mocking
> Such levity is simply shocking.
> Your prince for me would be too far above. . . .[65]

She does, however, unquestionably accept that marriage itself is necessary and that her only power lies within that acceptance. With the tacit acknowledgment that she must marry, the African American woman's struggle against both white racism and intra-racial patriarchy is here curiously figured through a discourse of romantic choice: *whom* she chooses to marry. This fairly standard ending in which the daughter of the nouveaux riche is married off to a high-born son is placed by the play in context of the history of black female struggles to be included in the dominant ideology of "true" womanhood and domesticity that defined (white) womanhood up to and beyond the Civil War. Because the song's obsession with domesticity is shared by the black female voice while at the same time critiquing the black male obsession with social rank and nobility, the tensions of race, gender, and domesticity in the play need to be explored directly. As Carby details, the white ideology of "true" womanhood required that white women adhere to a strict code of domesticity, childbearing, and child rearing. Most importantly, they were to be wives, gleefully submitting to social and sexual control by men. For the "true" woman, chastity was a prized quality and social commodity, second only to a "natural" gift for performance. Indeed, this ideology was one that implicitly valued performance. This latter point can be gleaned from Carby's assertion that "the parameters of the ideological discourse of true womanhood were bound by a shared social understanding that external physical appearance reflected internal qualities of character and therefore provided an easily discernible indicator of the function of a female of the human species."[66] In other words, the cult of "true" womanhood (or the cult of domesticity) was responsive to visual, performative codes read as an authentic, essentialized gender identity. Chastity looked a certain way; as did virtue, as did patience, as did submission. In imagining the possibilities of resistance to these expectations, one is reminded of the Jamaican womanist Carolyn Cooper's creative collision of Caribbean "indigenous feminism" with Luce Irigaray's polemics when she writes of "the ultimate subterfuge: to evade domesticity in the very act of seeming to embrace it."[67] However, there is no room in this tantalizing description of a black feminist "Anansi tactics" for the tragic weight of the comic mask as represented by Bert Williams's ever-dour visage. His was a tragic weight produced by a relentless countersignifyin(g), an evasion forever trapped in the act of reactively performing that which one is purportedly evading. This is the tragic weight that comes from acknowledging that often the only thing separating resistance from conformity is irony.

Since the ideology of "true" womanhood as visually constructed as well as produced by oral and gestural codes, one could easily imagine—à la Marjorie Garber, Judith Butler, and the perspectives they have ushered in—the intrinsic politics and limitations of masking at work for women within this otherwise constricting ideology. "True" women acted a certain way and looked a certain way. Black women, still reeling from the harsh and vicious sexual stereotypes of slavery and the ascendant maleness of black twentieth-century political discourse, had to work much harder to not simply become "true" women but to perform as such, to occupy the mask that white women wore. "True" African American women adhered to even stricter performance codes that worked both with and against the conventional racist representations of black women which emerged partly from minstrelsy. The dominant context of masking and performance was already defined by the blackface tradition and the stereotypes of black women were institutionalized there by popular repetition. For African American women this performance of the "true" was maddeningly multiple, especially considering the specific concern for "chastity" that emerged in response to both the ideologies of plantation slavery and the subsequent performance of black womanhood on the minstrel stage: "They had to define a discourse of black womanhood which would not only address their exclusion from the ideology of true womanhood but, as a consequence of this exclusion, would also rescue their bodies from a persistent association with illicit sexuality."[68] Certainly white men had been performing in blackface as African American women since the middle of the nineteenth century; and by the time of the "boom" in black blackface, African American men had been performing as African American women, promoting the comic and sexual stereotypes that were established by the white tradition. Ada Overton Walker's presence in the Williams and Walker shows was calculated to work against the history of these kinds of representations and within the bourgeois context of "true" womanhood. Thanks to Annemarie Bean, we know that just at the point where minstrelsy was mutating into vaudeville—the era dominated by the Williams and Walker shows—there were African American women performers who specialized in performing as African American males.[69] Bean describes a politics of "double inversion" at work in these gendered "racechanges," a term she borrows from Susan Gubar. This helpful but problematic description is well worth quoting at length:

> These performances by the African American minstrels inverted (and, in the case of the women, double inverted) the notions set up by white minstrelsy: that the African American male body was deformed, overdetermined, and emasculated and that the African American female body was highly sexualized and whorish. When performed by African American female minstrels, gender impersonation doubly inverted the representations of blackness rendered by white minstrelsy. White minstrelsy stereotyped African American women as comic and/or whorish; African American male impersonators chose to perform their female selves through maleness, thereby eradicating any connection with the stereotypes previously generated. African American male impersonator's double inversion of color and gender directly tapped into the anxieties that the dominant culture had about African American women and men. By changing the nature of those characterizations, black minstrelsy, in effect, negated their "coloring" and asserted themselves as a race with first, a proud history, and second an exciting present. African American performing artists could impressively participate, in numbers higher than the percentage of blacks in the general population, and electrify their audiences with new notions of what a black man or woman performer was capable of on stage.[70]

Bean's discussion here rests on the basic foundationalism of racial and gender essentialism, which is what supports the quasi-nationalism of her sense of black resistance. It assumes that there is, to paraphrase Judith Butler, a racial and sexual coherence or identity prior to its social construction and sees in black minstrelsy the reclamation of that a priori coherence. In the passage there is a clear distinction between "real" African American men and the "false" women they performed, just as there is a clear distinction between "real" white men and the "false" stereotypes they exploited, and so forth. The act of "negating" one's coloring here functions as an even more melodramatic reversal of Rogin's "wiping off" gesture wherein the "real" self exaggerated the contrastive space between the mask and flesh. Rather than burrowing deeper into representation, as Bert Williams did, or layering black skin with black mask, black sex with black sex, a "true" black self emerges from Bean's study unscathed to take a triumphalist bow. Gender functions in the same way, for Bean: by reclaiming the black female mask, a "truer"—that is, prediscursive—representation of black women could be expressed with and against minstrelsy.

At this point, it may be helpful to use In Dahomey with and against Bean's discussion. Since the play did function within a relatively self-aware metacritique of mimicry, minstrelsy, and masking, it is worth quoting from the brilliant song "On Emancipation Day," penned by Paul Laurence Dunbar himself for In Dahomey. Though not explicitly about gender and sexuality, this song complements Bean's description of a performance context dominated by the ritualized and theatricalized performance of the other. It also ups the ante, since this is a context where the "real" is itself always already a performance and is already doubled in advance of any self-conscious masking:

> On Emancipation day,
> All you white fo'ks clear de way . . .
> Coons dress'd up lak Masqueraders,
> Porters arm'd lak rude invaders
> When dey hear dem ragtime tunes
> White fo'ks try to pass fo' coons on Emancipation day.[71]

The play here establishes itself as being rooted in a constant denaturing of identity and a relentless set of performance exchanges which delegitimize any claim to authority on the part of any one narrative or political position. However comical, its foundation is an anti-foundationalism that revels in the interaction and interchange of roles, histories, fantasies, and desires. For example, "Coons" dressed up like Masqueraders only emphasize how the "Coon" is itself already a political fiction, a mask, a double which then performs not as another thing or person but as generalized "Masqueraders."

Remember, Bert Williams spent years studying and perfecting the "realness" of the coon with his partner George Walker: he even studied under the great European pantomimist Pietro to achieve the secret of authentic representation. "Porters" are here in uniform, in costume, and now arm themselves like "rude invaders." These black porters are parodies of not just colonists but African American colonists suddenly cast in the role of imperial forces of subjugation. This particular transformation is no doubt as comical as the gorilla becoming a police officer or the hippopotamus becoming a justice of the peace as in the song "On Broadway in Dahomey Bye and Bye." One can be sure that the absurdity of these exchanges and role reversals is made tragic by the absurdity of the racism that suggests that racial and cultural identities were in fact fixed and that black porters could not become invaders or that blacks could not become other than they were constructed by white racial fantasy—or that black women could not become "True" women.

In this explicitly carnivalesque vision of freedom, only "white fo'ks" seem naked, unreal, pathetically authentic, and utterly without exchange value. Keep in mind that this relentless self-othering is described in the song as occurring as a sign of "Emancipation." This is where white folks must "clear de way," suggesting a celebratory politics to these role reversals and a sense of freedom that has come from layers of racial artifice, not from authenticity. Emancipation is here reversed in that it comes not from "wiping off" artifice and not from "negating one's coloring," since one's coloring is the primary mask; it comes from the ability to freely choose and wear masks. Emancipation day indeed, which is to say that "white fo'ks" and males can no longer be the sole performers of otherness and must now be played and ridden by the masks they had once denigrated. Mimesis becomes identified as a two-way phenomenon, and that is the closest to "emancipation" the play can imagine. The hierarchies change here when white folks don't perform as Negroes simply to emphasize their whiteness. They now seek entry into a new political dispensation which requires that they "pass fo' coons."

It must be remembered that despite the play's lack of grounding in racial essentialism, In Dahomey, along with the entire oeuvre of Williams and Walker, was explicitly meant as an anti-racist performance—not an anti-race performance. As such race was accepted as a biological fact, though this fact was constantly made flexible and manipulable through the performance of multiple intra-racial differences. The work attained its primary critique of racism through the destabilizing of identity or authority; through this primary critique, it achieved a multi-faceted self-critique of the political ramifications of African American nationalism, patriarchy, and self-representation. Judith Butler's notion of "the feminine as a site of subversive multiplicity" can be used here to explore a use of race as a site of subversive and internal polyphony.[72] Because of In Dahomey's quibbling with mimicry and its own mockery of mimesis, because there are already so many layers at work beneath even the black woman's deployment of the minstrel mask, for Bean to call this process a "double inversion" is as problematic and limiting as the privileging of Du Bois's double-consciousness in a context no longer defined by the binary logic of African American racial discourse.

The latter has been previously discussed. But it bears repeating that since a West Indian was the aesthetic core of the performance and performed not only a white stereotype but also the stereotype of an African American, something far more trigonometric than simple "doubling" is at work. Since African Americans in In Dahomey performed as Africans who were represented as "different" despite operating within a dominant racial logic of essentialized "sameness," then something far more, dare we say, *fractal* was going on at the start of the era of modernism. Gender and its contradictions only serve to show just how many layers, doubles, and doubled doubles were at work on this particular minstrel stage. In Dahomey and the general work of Bert Williams served to complicate and assault the romantic nationalist notion that blacks constituted a singular culture, as represented by Bean's phrase "a race with first, a proud history, and second an exciting present." Nor was it a singular class, nor did it speak in a singular dialect, nor was its history singular or even singularly proud despite all the now institutionalized quasi-nationalist clichés of racial uplift. The implications for these racial and gendered contradictions in the context of contemporary African American feminism has, by the way, yet to be fully engaged. This is particularly the case as it involves the texts and contexts of Caribbean and African women. Although contemporary feminism has been willing to fragment "gender" with the politics of "race," it is still not the case that the category of race—as in "black women"—has been sufficiently fragmented by "culture," history, and the varieties of gender relationships endemic to the non-American black world.

The diasporic cross-cultural interruption signified by Bert Williams's presence is as important as the cross-gender interrogation signified by the words and the work of Ada Overton Walker. As an African American woman, she played the explicitly gendered other to Bert Williams's implicit and tacitly foreign otherness. In an important attempt to resuscitate the reputation and significance of this African American pioneer, David Krasner writes:

> At a time when black women were compelled to rein in their expectations and bridle their imaginations, Aida (sometimes spelled Ada) Walker did the opposite. During her career she made her presence felt in several ways: she was an accomplished cakewalker, teaching the cakewalk to elite, white society; she established herself as the highest paid and most popular female actress, singer, and dancer of the Williams and Walker vaudeville company; she choreographed all of the Williams and Walker shows, including *In Dahomey* (1902–1905), *Abyssinia* (1905–1907), and *Bandana Land* (1907–1909); and she was considered one of the brightest stars on the vaudeville stage. Despite the overwhelming presence of the male stars in her company . . . she managed to gain recognition as a consummate performer during the first decade of the twentieth century.[73]

Put in more political terms, Ada Overton Walker served consistently to reiterate that the "Negro" did not constitute a singular gender and that the interruptive voice of the modernist black woman shared also in the ambivalences and ambiguities of the emergent discourses of African diaspora. The desire for African American middle-class women to define themselves as befitting "true" womanhood despite the contradictions of class and imperialism was of major significance to the kind of gender performance at work in *In Dahomey*. This was where Ada Overton Walker came in. Beyond her innovations in choreography and dance, she ensured that the specific struggles of African American women were also included within the aesthetic and political space of black modernist minstrelsy. She was a tireless advocate for African American women in the theater. Like Bert Williams and her husband George Walker, she wrote and published many essays, including "Colored Men and Women on the Stage" for the *Colored American Magazine* in 1905 and "Opportunities the Stage Offers Intelligent and Talented Women" in the *New York Age* in 1908. Not only was she the primary engine behind the cakewalk and other "Negro dances" favored by their audiences in America and in England, she also performed modern dances as well as her own innovative and quasi-Africentric "Ethiopian" dances.

Overton Walker was so well-regarded a performer that when her husband fell ill while performing *Bandana Land* in 1909 she took over his role and successfully performed alongside Bert Williams as her husband. It would take another book to fully explore the meanings set free and the meanings silenced by that particular encounter of black masquerade differences. Largely because of her presence, black women in the Williams and Walker shows were always chaste, proper, and explicitly racially representative. Their performances were in line with the bourgeois, neo-Victorian ideals of the African American middle class and were perhaps an evocation of the "ancient African chastity" that Du Bois would feel so nostalgic for and proclaim as lost in *The Souls of Black Folk*.[74] It was also probably as a result of her presence that the issue of marriage was often featured in these performances rather than the libidinal excesses typical of later all-black Broadway shows, where black women had less direct authority over the performance itself. One of the modern dances that Overton Walker performed solo was *Salome*, made infamous by Isadora Duncan. She challenged the notion that only white women could perform this sexually controversial dance, but "she had to suppress the erotic component of her dancing" for reasons of the very tensions of race, class, and gender that have been discussed thus far.[75] These were tensions that not only equated race and the primitive but also placed race in direct opposition to a bourgeois civility that articulated and deployed itself along gender lines. As Krasner puts it:

> As a result, her choreography, although notable for its grace, was also known for its propriety. Walker had to be especially careful not to offend black audiences, while she simultaneously refused to succumb entirely to prudery. She affected the bourgeois norms of good taste, which meant she submitted her costume to a regime of concealment and restraint. Yet she also wore exotic and provocative costumes frequently attributed to modern white dancers. As a well-known member of the Harlem community, Walker was likely to be under considerable pressure to conform to a middle-class society caught up in social propriety and racial uplift, while simultaneously she felt compelled to join her fellow white female dancers by presenting her version of "Salomania."[76]

Considering the history and the associations of this particular dance, one wonders why she would even choose to attempt it. The very choice of a dance as risqué as Salome was obviously a powerful statement not only against primitivism and the white sexualization of the black woman but with and against a racial uplift that was cast in distinctly male terms. Overall she may have "affected" the norms of "true" womanhood but by choosing this particularly overdetermined dance she also directly challenged the Victorian, anti-erotic prudery of racial uplift. The "concealment and restraint" at work in her performance was deployed in relationship to both white audiences and the black bourgeoisie, but also in relationship to the oft-described "male gaze" and those black and white women who also policed the borders of "true" womanhood. A black Salome then becomes a *naked mask*, a performance which begs for and invites the "male gaze," the black bourgeois nationalist gaze, the emergent feminist gaze and taunts all of them to confront each other in the self-controlled appearance and disappearance of this black woman's body onstage. To choose this dance and to render it both chaste and sensual, anti-racist yet black was an open expression of her multiply tongued discursive flexibility which was able to de-link race from excessive sexual license while claiming sexuality as the possible site of black female empowerment: "Aida Walker not only endured the idea of primitivism in America; she continued to choreograph within an American cultural framework replete with racial codes. Walker negotiated a minefield of representations while simultaneously developing a unique choreography."[77] This kind of dancing through a "minefield" also placed Overton Walker at the beginning of a modernism that would be obsessed by and would fetishize the body and the performance of black women from Josephine Baker to Florence Mills.

With the politics and significance of Ada Overton Walker contextualized, it is now possible to return to and conclude with the back and forth debate that occurs in the song "Leader of the Colored Aristocracy," that between the patriarchal voice of the black nationalist bourgeoisie and its feminized, internal other. As it continues in performance the song becomes increasingly focused on the gender debate, seeming to leave behind its sarcasm and mockery of black bourgeois values and its criticism of the internal dynamics of racial uplift. These multiple issues, however, are merely masked by the song as it begins to contain them in the now primary language of race and gender. The song develops into something of quite high seriousness, and the comic genre in which it began mutates into something grandiloquently humanistic and rings suddenly anthemlike. At the same time the gender debate actually begins to accommodate and simultaneously represent a powerful critique of the patriarchal voice and all that it stands in for. Class elitism, materialism, and an exploitative nationalism become explicitly subsumed by the response to the voice of the father, which emerged from the daughter's claim on her own romantic and sexual agency.

The father goes on to describe what it takes to achieve "High Society":

> A lot of gold
> Lay'd by in gilt edged stocks
> A few town lots,
> Let's say a dozen blocks. . . .[78]

He of course assumes—as does she—that direct access to these things is only available to a "royal prince" and to a woman only through marriage. But it is when he reaches the end of this description of cash, capital, and real estate that the song cunningly reveals the racial politics of cash, capital, and real estate:

> A high-toned house that builded up on rocks,
> Then you're in society.[79]

The "high-toned" house is obviously a dig at the obsession with whiteness—"light skinned" or high yellow—and its symbolic or exchange value. The lyrics mockingly characterize this obsession with skin tone as being at the heart of a racial uplift configured in patriarchal and middle-class terms. Despite being "builded" up on rocks, which is where the wise man constructs his home according to the old hymn, the wisdom of such a value system is questioned by the song itself before she even speaks out against it directly. The father then begins to describe more of what he intends for his daughter:

> . . . think of a house on some big avenue
> And a prince who would spend all his time wooing you. . . .[80]

Keep in mind that this black ascent to royalty and power is made possible through the recolonization of Africa and through the subjection of its natives to an African American bourgeoisie. As before, her humble rebuttal begins thus:

> Surely you're only mocking
> Such levity is simply shocking.
> Your prince for me would be too far above . . .[81]

Her criticism and rejection quickly begin to grow, not in vehemence or intensity but in scale, scope, and vision. For example, her perception of domesticity, "true" womanhood, and "love" begins to engulf the politics of racism and classism:

> Love looks not at estate
> Oh No!
> 'Twere folly one should think it so

The beggar maid becomes a queen
Who through her lover's eyes is seen.
We care not for the world of fools
Love dignifies the soul it rules.
The pomp of kings the pride of state
Are nought when love o'er-takes the great.[82]

The song abandons the individualistic and self-centered notion of romantic love and goes even further than the discourse of race and nation that has already been identified as structured by the language of patriarchy and symbolic whiteness. Her definition of "love" and "choice" enable her to make much broader claims about class and power as she attempts a leveling of intra-racial social categories through the language of gender and love. She calls for a greater politics of love which transcends the "pomp of kings" (black, white, male, or otherwise) and the "pride of state" (Dahomey, Harlem, or the United States). She imagines a love that refuses socioeconomic, racial, and sexual hierarchies entirely and levels the playing field of history and culture. Rather than imagining this transcendent love through some apolitical gesture of liberal history-lessness or through a then more dangerous language of miscegenation, this leveling is here a product of masking. Aware of the multiple layers of performance at work in a context where minstrelsy was the primary space of popular racial discourse, she suggests that since interactions are only performances, identities largely masked, then any one thing can function as any other thing where identities are unfixed, even though essences were held to be static. The black and female struggle at the time, after all, was for more access to social, cultural, and political freedom, which is to say, access to greater social, cultural, and political roles and identities despite a common acceptance of biological determinations.

In other words, in In Dahomey identities are unfixed, not essences, since both race and gender were accepted by even the most radical and progressive black thinkers as rooted in biology. The space of masking and performance was a space in which social, political, cultural, and historical *roles* were denatured. Even the lowliest black man or woman could potentially be anything he or she desired by performing it convincingly:

The humble cot becomes a throne
Whose dwelling place love makes his own
So all man's heart and being sing
Love is the King! Love is the King! Love is the King![83]

Idealistic to be sure, but powerful as a statement emanating from the Broadway stage just when black cultural positions were ossifying into the essentialist nationalism that would come to characterize much African American modernism as well as the pan-Africanism of the Garvey movement. Powerful in a time when the socioeconomic fragmentation of the black community throughout the diaspora forced the most culturally powerful blacks into a mode of benevolent racial dictatorship. And not least of all, powerful in a time when white racism depended on essentialist fixity and identitarian rigidity for its irrational logic of social segregation. This logic was constantly threatened by the bogey of black excellence in spaces previously unimaginable, such as Broadway.

From "evah darkey is a king" to every "beggar maid becomes a queen," the language of masquerade, minstrelsy, and transformation is a progressive one employed to critique the obsession with fixing power that is alive in the would-be "colored aristocracy" but primarily in a world of institutionalized racism and the radical social policing of the color line. Again, the leveling is also meant obviously to go far beyond gender in its implications, despite the fact that the "beggar maid"/queen transformation is still dependent on "her lover's eyes" to fix her on either side of the mask. But as idealistic and as sentimental as it sounds to the contemporary ear, this song does feature a woman's assertion of her right to choose a husband being transformed into a transcendental plea for intra-racial equality. That this was present in the first all-black Broadway spectacle and deemed as significant as the exploration of history, class, and the internal contradictions of black diaspora makes it even more remarkable.

CHAPTER 6 Claude McKay's Calypso

Only Bert Williams could occupy the iconic and symbolic space in Federico García Lorca's poem quoted in the epigraph at the beginning of this book. His persona was that "great despairing king" tragically dethroned but silently singing with "his multitude," presiding over a "masqueraded Harlem."[1] This particular moment and this particular cultural stage were so loud in their epic tragedy and their penchant for grandiose performativity that their echoed "rumor" attracted blacks from throughout the African diaspora: "From the left, from the right, from the South, and from the North."[2] In the words of the West Indian journalist and militant W. A. Domingo:

> Almost unobserved, America plays her usual role in the meeting, mixing and welding of the colored peoples of the earth. A dusky tribe of destiny seekers, these brown and black and yellow folk, eyes filled with visions of an alien heritage—palm-fringed seashores, murmuring streams, luxuriant hills and vales—have made an epical march from the four corners of the earth to the Port of New York and America. They bring the gift of the black tropics to America and to their kinsmen.[3]

Harlem was Lorca's "cleft," a version of Wilson Harris's "womb of space" which signals a fissure in the multiple narratives of colonialism and slavery where distinct histories and historical products engage and catalyze each other in the shadows of America's self-denying imperial ascendance. In this, Harlem and its renaissance were home, and the tropics and Africa their margins. As home Harlem was less a place of origin than an inevitable imperial destiny, a stage whereon the anxieties of history and the modernist shock of catalyzed newness were performed. Minstrelsy functioned in that modernist cleft, as "the first emanation of a pervasive and purely American mass culture" which could not help but absorb within it the catalytic possibilities of black-on-black culture contact.[4]

It was in part the presence of wildly popular black performers like Bert Williams, Ada Overton Walker, and George Walker, as well as the "jazz age" they helped usher in, that Harlem was so often described in its time and in ours as something of a carnival. This is why it is so strange that even today the Bakhtinian discourses of the carnivalesque are still slow to engage and be appropriated by Afro-diasporic experiences of carnival. Certainly the equation between carnival and the carnivalesque is fairly idiomatic in contemporary discourse. Yet the significant differences are yet to be taken seriously, since the Bakhtinian carnivalesque and the Afro-Caribbean "carnival complex" are simply assumed to signify each other unproblematically, when in truth they have more to offer each other in their differences. For example, the intricacies of color, class, and hybridity that are central to carnival in the Caribbean are nowhere present in Bakhtin's reading of the politics of the folk—a folk that he does often reduce to a simplistic and romantic stereotype. These intricacies could complicate and advance the understanding of not only multiple and multidirectional social contradictions but also how the state responds to these contradictions and the forms and rituals that are produced by and through them. The fact that the carnivalesque can function as a sophisticated form of containment in which the state ritualizes otherness, difference, and "performance" in order to sustain hierarchies—well, that too is to be learned from the Caribbean and its neocolonial histories. Much is to be gained in reading Bakhtin within and against the racial tensions and cultural histories of specific Afro-Caribbean folk forms rather than simply plugging the latter into the metastructures of the former. This would be as problematic as a reading of minstrelsy from the outside in, without an understanding of the layers of masking and disappearance behind the burnt cork.

Patti Capel Swartz explores the broader sense of the carnivalesque in her re-examination of the Harlem Renaissance, "Masks and Masquerade: The Iconography of the Harlem Renaissance." In discussing descriptions of Harlem from artists as diverse as Arna Bontemps and Ossie Davis, she writes: "The iconography of the Harlem Renaissance is akin to that of the masque or carnival—of perceptions and reversals, of expectations about the performer, and of a reversal of societal positions in that the normally marginalized person or group gains control."[5] For Caribbean writers and musicians in Harlem, this scenario empowered their West Indian diasporic vision—after all, Capel Swartz's words accurately describe the racial and political fluidities of West Indian culture and history itself. Although she suggests that the very epistemological and political sense of carnival, of something potentially subversive in the air, exists in a variety of Harlem Renaissance texts, she does also strangely trace back the "idea of the mask, the masque, and the masquerade" to Bakhtin's notion of carnival, as if to suggest that the writers and artists of that era were not aware of their own explicit traditions of masking, street theater, parades, subversive performativity, and, in the case of West Indians, carnival itself, which was sublimated and incorporated into the culture of art of the host community.[6]

"No Nationality": Claude McKay and the Poetics of Carnival

It is perhaps an awareness of this lack of a full exploration of the connections between the Afro-Caribbean /African American carnival complexes and Bakhtin that inspires another scholar, Robert A. Russ, in " 'There's No Place Like Home': The Carnival of Black Life in Claude McKay's *Home to Harlem*." This essay appropriately appears in a collection entitled *Harlem Renaissance Re-examined* edited by Russ with Victor A. Kramer. By now re-appraisals and re-examinations of the Harlem Renaissance have become quite a cottage industry, as African American literature has moved to the center of literary academic discourse and as historical validation has become commodified and canonized as the dominant gesture of black literary study. Russ's and Kramer's collection would have done better to re-examine the previous re-examinations, such as Cary Wintz's recent exhaustive series, though it must be lauded for even mentioning Bert Williams, as does Nellie Y. McKay in her contribution, " 'What Were They Saying?': Black Women Playwrights of the Harlem Renaissance." Sadly, even this brief reference only continues the enigma of that black masquerader, since it wrongly states that Williams starred in the 1921 premiere of *Shuffle Along*. The error can be understood in that it suggests a perhaps overzealous attempt to link this important pioneer of Harlem's glory to what is arguably the performance that heralds the arrival of the Harlem Renaissance itself—again, a result of the politics of validation that has transformed black literary and cultural study into one long and relentless series of affirmations.

By the time of this play Williams was a physically ailing member of the previous generation, a living legend who was fully acknowledged as being largely responsible for its very possibility. By its premiere, Williams was more concerned with the rise of Charles Gilpin, the African American actor who performed the lead role in the original production of Eugene O'Neill's *The Emperor Jones*. The role of Brutus Jones was initially rejected by Paul Robeson, who finally consented to play it in 1924 and rode it to stardom. Williams, who had worked long and hard in the world of comic representation, had long hoped that his success would finally allow him access to a serious dramatic role. The selection of Gilpin, a minor actor, was perhaps the final blow in a career trapped behind the black mask of a tragic longing for respectability. In his autobiography *A Long Way from Home*, Claude McKay celebrates *Shuffle Along*, the comedy that, more than *The Emperor Jones*, signaled the emergence of black renaissance. He writes, "There had been nothing comparable to it since the Williams and Walker Negro shows."[7] And as if to locate a common aesthetic and politics in this postminstrel tradition, he argues, "Negroes have traditionally been represented on the stage as a clowning race. But I felt that if Negroes can lift clowning to artistry, they can thumb their noses at superior people who rate them as a clowning race."[8] McKay's interest in blackface minstrelsy figures importantly in his autobiography, where he consistently suggests that minstrelsy—like primitivism—was a black critique of Western culture and its racist, imperialist structures. For example, he poeticizes the radical, subversive, and politically intrusive nature of the minstrel figure in language traditionally reserved for the trickster and goes so far as to position that figure as the central aesthetic and political challenge to Western modernity:

> Poor, painful black face, intruding into the holy places of the whites. How like a specter you haunt the pale devils! Always at their elbow, always darkly peering through the window, giving them no rest, no peace. How they burn up their energies trying to keep you out! How apologetic and uneasy they are—yes, even the best of them, poor devils—when you force an entrance, Blackface, facetiously, incorrigibly, smiling or disturbingly composed. Shock

them out of their complacency, Blackface; make them uncomfortable; make them unhappy! Give them no peace, no rest. How can they bear your presence, Blackface, great, unappeasable ghost of Western civilization![9]

Rather than describing minstrelsy as something within the control and purview of white spectatorship—and despite his use of minstrelsy to mock Garvey and his political failures—McKay depicts it here as something that whites attempt to keep out, some ghost of racial history and colonial guilt come angrily knocking on the window of assimilation.

As a "black face" becomes transmuted into blackface in his paragraph, as a description becomes a persona, it becomes clear that for McKay minstrelsy was no longer a product of white desire or projected racist fantasies but instead a projection—an aggressive reprojection—of a black desire for entry, for enfranchisement, for revenge. However, this "ghost" is "unappeasable." Because it is a mask it will always function as a problem, a question, a sign of lack that must always haunt the epistemological regimes of the West. Obviously, this take on the black mask as a sign of the kind of black radicalism that the Jamaican poet was known for could not have emerged from a reading of white minstrelsy. And it probably couldn't be derived easily from McKay's first exposure to blackface while he was still in Jamaica. This interpretation of blackface is without question informed and produced by an intimacy with the nationalist minstrelsy of black performers like Williams and Walker for whom the black mask was a strategy employed for the sake of radically altering the status quo.

At the end of Home to Harlem McKay advocates a politics of diversion and doubling which he finds at work in black masquerade, one that exists despite the blindness of racist stereotyping and connects even more powerfully minstrelsy and black primitivism: "Haunting rhythm, mingling of naïve wistfulness and charming gayety, now sheering over into mad riotous joy, now, like a jungle mask, strange, unfamiliar, disturbing, now plunging headlong into the far, dim depths of profundity and rising out as suddenly with a simple, childish grin. And the white visitors laugh. They see the grin only."[10] These are much more subtle and sophisticated views of minstrelsy and cross-racial masquerade than the one he presents in his autobiographical My Green Hills of Jamaica. That work is much more Catholic apologia than the kind of scandalous autobiography readers would have expected considering his reputation. In it McKay describes a Jamaican view of African American minstrelsy and its racial meanings: "Our general opinion of American Negroes was that they were clowns more or less. All those that we saw in Kingston on the street were the happy-go-lucky clowning types who sang 'coon' songs for the white men and they seemed to like it . . . . so we had an entirely wrong impression of the American Negro."[11] One wonders if the difference between these views of minstrelsy has anything to do with the differences in where and how McKay positions himself—first, in America as a young upstart hoping to articulate a "New Negro" perspective via his reading of blackface, and then later as an older embittered figure, hostile to those who would claim his work during his penurious exile.

Given the strong orthodox swing at the end of his life, one must take with a grain of salt this conclusion, which belies McKay's own work and the work of Bert Williams: "Our Negroes even though they were very poor would not sing clowning songs for white men and allow themselves to be kicked around by them."[12] The presence of locally produced minstrel theater in Jamaica after the arrival of American-styled shows also belies McKay's trademark over-romanticizing of "our Negroes." This statement suggests that some of the tensions at work in his relationship with his "Afro-Yank rivals" during the Harlem Renaissance may have left him embittered and resentful and caused him to distance himself from the kinds of masks at work in his own fiction.[13] Even though he admits a "wrong impression" of African Americans—which is to say, he had misrecognized the "coon" mask as flesh—he still ends this discussion with a strong statement about the indomitable strength and vitality of the Jamaican "folk" which simultaneously implies a constitutional weakness in the culture of African Americans. Valuable here, though, is McKay's sense of a crucial difference between West Indian and African American folk cultures, both of which he celebrated as authentically "African" and the privileged site of the primitive, comic spirit that was the heritage of the entire diaspora and the antidote to the pious sanctimony of the African American Talented Tenth. Yet he refused to collapse them into each other and spent his entire life as a prose writer exploring the overlaps, the contradictions, the tensions, and the glorious moments of cross-cultural synthesis between variant black folk traditions.

Home to Harlem, of course, is at the center of Russ's essay, and minstrelsy and carnival are at the center of McKay's work despite these near-final words from My Green Hills of Jamaica, which, as before, belie the comic minstrelsy at work in his own fiction. But despite being based on a Caribbean writer whose relationship to black folk culture has rarely been questioned, and despite being based on a novel that features so much explicit conversation about intra-racial, cross-cultural tensions and differences, Russ's view is predictably more Bakhtin than calypso. What limits his reading and that of so many others from Alain Locke to the present is the racially limited and culturally narrow reading of the "folk" alongside a real inability to explore the Afro-Caribbean "carnival complex" for its own indigenous discourses of cross-cultural signifyin(g) and verbal/representational play. Also predictably, in using Bakhtin's crucial dialectic between "official" and "unofficial" culture, Russ is able to acknowledge McKay's cultural distinctiveness as a West Indian in Harlem but subsume this difference into the traditional bichromatism of the "white culture"/"black culture" binary which parallels and privileges the former dialectic and the nation within which it is articulated. Despite being aware of the fact that in the novel McKay is "less concerned with propagandistic messages and more with the interaction between people and cultures," Russ like most others spends precious little time exploring just how different those various black cultures in *Home to Harlem* are meant to be seen and just how contentious and exciting a Harlem constituted by such radical internal differences really was.[14] For him Bakhtinian polyphony is ultimately binary and is helpful in exploring the dialogic tensions between black and white cultures and in the service of "making possible a sense of community and a feeling of solidarity among Black people."[15]

A close reading and thorough understanding of Bakhtin would show that true polyphony and true dialogism never rest within the borders of even a beleaguered and oppressed community and its expressive traditions. True polyphony creates an ever-shifting sense of community by radically destabilizing discursive solidarity or identitarian gestures. In short, the carnivalesque as a force of subversion favors no specific community, just as Anansi cannot be claimed by any specific ideology as s/he is the undoing of both ideology and specificity. True polyphony features what could be called a dialogized heteroglossia, which occurs not only between speakers but also within each speaker. It occurs not only between "official" and "unofficial" registers but within them as well. This was Harlem, where both centripetal and centrifugal forces of language and culture, history, and power collided and remade America. Russ, however, goes on to assert that "although McKay draws not on the European folk festival of carnival, but on the folk culture—language, stories, behavior, attitudes, and traditions—of Jamaican people, African-American people, and others of African descent, the spirit of the folk culture as imagined is quite consistent, regardless of its origin."[16] True, McKay does not draw from European folk traditions to root his carnivalesque play and politics, and true, he does draw directly from a fairly broad set of diverse black folk traditions as well as his omnivorous consumption of Western literature and philosophy. However, "black" for McKay was never utterly consistent in that it was always much more than "African American," just as "folk" was always much more than simply rooted in the geosymbolic notion of the American South and just as "dialect" was one of multiple cultural possibilities within the English language.

Russ goes as far as to discuss whether McKay did or did not read Bakhtin in order for his work to be appropriately described as carnivalesque. This is an unnecessary move, almost as if one would expect Wilson Harris or the Trinidadian novelist Earl Lovelace to need Bakhtin before articulating the most sophisticated poetics of carnival yet imagined. Indeed, it is in his 1986 essay "Carnival Theatre: A Personal View," written to commemorate the legendary Notting Hill Carnival in England, that Harris admits to having only recently discovered the work of Mikhail Bakhtin—this a full three years after his epochal The Womb of Space.[17] Like Harris or Lovelace, McKay worked in a cultural context where carnivalesque representations and strategies were inevitable by virtue of a number of factors. First among these factors was the omnipresence of masking and masking traditions available to him as a Caribbean writer but also as a writer obsessed with "unofficial" black urban culture where masking, subterfuge, costuming, and sexual play and performance was/is common. Also, there was that broad sense of Harlem as a relentless celebration of color, difference, and subversive sexual and social possibilities. This sense informs the rush and energy of so many Harlem Renaissance texts, from Langston Hughes to Rudolf Fisher, from Bessie Smith to Aaron Douglass to Sam Manning and Marcus Garvey: all of them were aware that something greater than themselves was afoot in the broader cultural climate of Harlem.

In his review of Shuffle Along, published the year before Home to Harlem was published, McKay describes the new urban vision of race:

> The Negro must get the warmth, color and laughter out of his blood, else the white man will sneer at him and treat him with contumely. Happily the Negro retains his joy of living in the teeth of such criticism; and in Harlem, along Fifth and Lenox avenues, in Marcus Garvey's Hall with its extravagant paraphernalia, in his churches and cabarets, he expresses himself with a zest that is yet to be depicted by a true artist.[18]

That his view of the carnival of black diversity would make a sort of equivalence between the political "paraphernalia" of Garvey, the thriving black churches, and the cabarets is a gesture mixing high and low registers of culture that would make Bakhtin proud. McKay put his finger on the pulse and sound of the energies of Harlem early on and intended to be that "true artist" with the publication of his first novel. But then his radical mixing of high and low registers in his fiction led to his being dismissed by the more conservative black intelligentsia as a purveyor of pornography. It is interesting to note that one of the few things that W. E. B. Du Bois and Marcus Garvey both publicly agreed on was how much they both hated *Home to Harlem*. Much of the novel is merely a haze of impressions, colors, sounds, rumors, and wildly ornate descriptions of wildly ornate characters: it is often dizzying simply because McKay is attempting to replicate the experience of being at a carnival, or in a parade, or in the midst of a perpetual celebration where differences, masks, and unsanctioned combinations of opposites emerge and disappear against a rapidly moving, kaleidoscopic background.

So although he employed the South as icon and the African American vernacular in *Home to Harlem* and in *Banjo*, it was as much a masquerade and a marketing strategy as it was a pan-African gesture. Using traditional and stereotypical African American symbols was for him a trickster's hustle because it was obviously the dominant cultural myth behind the Harlem Renaissance and the primary reference point for his readers. These were the readers who he had long learned were much less interested in his particular dialect poetry in a time when the African American dialect was a contested yet central literary, musical, and theatrical language. Despite Edward Kamau Brathwaite's horrible claim that McKay "forsook his nation language" in order to be "universal," McKay's work actually examines that vertiginous state of being produced by the infinite possibilities of sound and cultural power within one language.[19] This is "plural masking," where the colonial subject is perpetually suspended in a performance which is diasporic because in it there is no landfall. Rather than achieve the "universal" of Standard English, McKay shifted back and forth, in and out of dialect masks—including both a British-inflected and Americanized Standard English alongside the African American and Afro-Caribbean dialects. He was exactly what Deleuze and Guattari champion in their manifesto of "minor literatures" and linguistic deterritorialization: "a nomad and an immigrant and a gypsy in relation to his own language."[20]

A generation earlier, Bert Williams was faced with a similar knowledge. He knew there was much less work for one who would aestheticize his West Indian vernacular than for one who had mastered the recognizable sound of race as America began its quick climb to global sovereignty and as the African American vernacular began to travel the world along with those ever-spreading technologies of mimesis such as minstrelsy and the phonograph. Like Williams, McKay drew directly from African American minstrelsy in his fiction in order to represent "Negro" archetypes. Good examples of this are the figure of "Jake" in *Home to Harlem* and the character "Banjo" in its eponymous sequel, who begins the novel by celebrating the fact that "the American darky is the performing fool of the world today. He's demanded everywhere."[21] Both these characters are noble savages drawn directly from plantation stereotypes and are stock figures from American racial fantasies. Much like the work of peers such as Zora Neale Hurston, Carl Van Vechten, and Langston Hughes, McKay's primitivism in *Home to Harlem* depended on the classic early-twentieth-century-American equation between "authentic" African sensibilities and the folk culture of the South. Yet in both of these novels, McKay expands the frame of reference of these minstrel figures and their plantation patrimony and makes them into transnational icons forced into conversation and collision with blacks from all over the colonial world.

In addition to wearing the mask of the "authentic" African American, McKay employed the various masking traditions of the Caribbean as they came to bear on the black minstrelsy of Caribbean minstrel performers like Bert Williams and even lesser-known figures such as calypsonians like the Guyanese vaudevillian Phil Madison and the legendary Sam Manning, whose destiny was tied intimately to Amy Ashwood Garvey and, in a small way, to pan-Africanism. These calypsonians, like many others, were directly influenced by Bert Williams, whose success no doubt partly signified the success of a West Indian in a time where racism and anti-immigrant sentiments threatened to fracture the struggling black Harlem community. This was a moment when black immigrants felt most urgently the tensions between and among American culture, African American culture, "home" islands, and the shifting class and culture relationships produced by inexorable micropolitical encounters. Calypso was the primary folk sounding of this generation of Anglophone West Indian immigrants and made its mark within the intraracial, cross-cultural signifying structures of *Home to Harlem*.

Although the bulk of recorded calypsos from this period were recorded in the 1930s, it is important to note that the folk form of *kaiso* and its quick evolution into calypso had already become incredibly popular in Trinidad by the turn of the century. As discussed in chapter 4, most of the early songs were recorded in New York by migrant calypsonians shipped by entrepreneur

Edouardo Sa Gomes to New York to perform in local Caribbean venues while recording. The 1912 calypsos of Lovey's Band are recognized as the first to be recorded in New York; but the West Indian vogue in Harlem in the early 1920s inspired the greatest number of these recordings. Migrant musicians were joined by immigrant Caribbean performers then resident in Harlem and by African American jazz musicians moonlighting in New York recording studios. Caribbean musicians involved included the legendary composer Lionel Belasco, the St. Vincentian pianist Walter Merrick, the violinist Cyril Monrose, and the guitarist Gerald Clark, who led one of the most popular West Indian ensembles in New York until the 1930s. Although most of this music was recorded primarily to be shipped back to Trinidad for carnival, much of it was not only available in New York but written with the New York Caribbean community in mind. Because of this change in focus, which entailed a mixing of the music with ragtime and jazz, much of this music has been decried for its lack of Trinidadian authenticity. However, it is historically charitable to hear these "weak" and diluted calypsos as the beginning of a hybrid Afro-Caribbean / African American sound and culture in modernist New York. This hybridizing of sound and culture enabled Sam Manning, Bill Rogers, Wilmoth Houdini, and others to become successful as calypsonians in America, as local extensions of the carnival complex.

Where jazz and blues were specific to the African American context of migration, racism, and the forbidding challenges of democracy, calypso was also the sound of the changing imperial power structures in the Caribbean which brought many West Indians to Harlem after having been displaced in their own land by the American empire. The difficulties of assimilation and double assimilation in the host nation were necessarily balanced with an awareness of and concern for the difficulties at home. Calypso was poised to speak on multiple levels, addressing issues of a black community in transit. "No Nationality," an early calypso from the great Atilla the Hun, who is also one of the form's early historians, provides a strong sense of the modernist Caribbean political and cultural climate:

> Long ago I was a real Trinidadian
> I used to boast of my native land
> But now to go near to Cumoto I am afraid
> And at Teteron Bay I'm forbidden to bathe
> So don't bother with me and nationality
> For that's all abound in hypocrisy . . .
> Long ago you who remember know

To any part of Trinidad you could go
To Arima, Sangre Grande, or Tamboo Laytay
Siparia to Los Iros Bay
But today if below Carenage you venture
You'll find yourself in a prohibited area
The Yankee sentry will shoot you and then declare
You had no right in America. . . .[22]

Neocolonialism and its peculiar effects are defined, critiqued, and explored in calypsos going back to the early decades of the twentieth century. The lyrics of Attila's calypso document how one's "real Trinidadian" identity and social position become usurped and erased by an America that has imported and imposed itself on the island. The song's ambivalence about America is balanced by a wit that is itself a burden to the calypsonian. Here the "real" becomes a sign of nostalgia, as the native land disappears right beneath the singer's feet. This local America supplants native ground and guards its own transplanted borders with weapons and an unassailable economy driven by Caribbean oil deposits and the hemispheric reach of the Monroe Doctrine. The only resistance available is the vernacular. Ironically, this language is produced by even more historical violence than the guns of Yankee sprawl, for example, the formative presence of multiple empires in a short space of time: the French, the British, and now the Yankee.

That calypso was already a recorded form by the time of Attila's song also reveals that the hemispheric presence of America owed to mimetic technologies such as the phonograph and radio, forms on which minstrelsy had already made an impact in the early globalization of the "black" vernacular. Hence the ambivalence of the calypsonian as the message of his resistance is contained by the medium of its expression and dissemination. America's ambient presence is enough here to not only spur migration but more importantly to instigate a basic rejection of the arbitrariness and hypocrisy of national identity itself, especially when the borders and native landscape are subject to the whims of larger geopolitical and cultural forces. Again, the islands themselves had already been back and forth in ownership and in cultural influence:

In the British Gent we put our trust
But they never consider us
In those days Hitler was on top and things were bad
What did they care about Trinidad

For fifty old destroyers so it is said
They sold those valuable bases over our head
And today we don't know who are masters in this land
If it's the English or the American . . .
The Yankees launched a real social invasion
They did as they pleased in my native land
They had a lot of money and spent lavishly
And they broke down the pillars of our aristocracy
I must confess they helped us financially
But they played hell with our morality
They took all our girls and had a glorious time
And left us blue-eyed babies to mind. . . .[23]

Even though it was written in the early 1930s, this classic song helps to fully
situate the work of Claude McKay and Bert Williams in the migratory poetics
of Caribbean carnival which existed within the migratory politics of American
imperialism and within the emergence of a black cultural and political renaissance. The song manifests tensions and concerns that had been alive from
the turn of the century and that had been sung in the tents of carnival since
the end of the previous century. The global presence of the Yankees and the
internal homelessness of the "native" are here, as are the shifting political
and cultural affiliations of imperial competition. Also present is the mas-
culinized sense of the loss of cultural power, sexualized via the language of
rape and jealousy, alongside the compromising nature of capitalism which
would lead to neocolonialism ("I must confess they helped us financially").
And last but certainly not least, we are presented with the attempt to perfect a
new vernacular folk sound. This is a crucial part of the cultural template from
which Claude McKay and other calypsonians constructed a black migrant
poetics in which Harlem became increasingly present as a construct also of
the West Indian imagination.

McKay could never quite let go of his romanticized nostalgia for the Caribbean, which he balanced alongside his equally romanticized and intensely
sexualized wanderlust. He attempted to maintain "real Jamaican" status and
the attendant longings of the immigrant with his own fascination for the geopolitical contradictions of the modernist world as described by Attila. It is perfectly logical that he would have mediated these tensions via the West Indian
immigrant community, where both could be maintained: memory and desire,
authenticity and transformation, home and elsewhere. In fact, where *Home to
Harlem* would emphasize its African American-ness by means of Jake's experi-

ence in the demimonde, *Banjo* and *Gingertown* emphasize McKay's great interest in diasporic subcultures and black immigrant communities. The Caribbean immigrant community is the space wherein calypso was as vital a form as jazz and which was more important to the Anglophone Caribbean immigrants as an aural sign of "elsewhere" and as a direct conduit to the language and the concerns of their embattled island homes. This remains unchanged today with reggae/dancehall, calypso, soca, and many other Caribbean forms in the Anglophone, Francophone, and Spanish-speaking Caribbean.

It is interesting, then, that so much is known about McKay's dealings with the Greenwich Village left, with Frank Harris, Max Eastman, *The Liberator*, and that entire downtown scene of reckless bohemians. And there is abundant information about McKay's tense yet fruitful relationship with African American intellectuals, artists, and "real" people. Yet there is no information, save precious hints in his writings, of his relationship to the immigrant West Indian community in Harlem. It is known that his 1940 monograph *Harlem: Negro Metropolis* paid attention to the cultural diversity of the Harlem community. It is known also that he had intended to write a book, to be called "The Tropics in New York," that would specify the micropolitical concerns of black immigrant Harlem. In his biography of McKay, Wayne F. Cooper writes:

> Early in 1942, McKay applied again for a Rosenwald Fund grant, this time to do a study of West Indian immigrants in New York City. "My purpose," he explained, "is to write a book about them which is to be entitled, 'The Tropics in New York.'" Natives of the Caribbean, he estimated, constituted about one-third of Harlem's population and numbered about 100,000. He wished to explain their "native backgrounds" and "the customs and activities of the various island groups" in order to understand better "their contributions to the social, political and religious life of Harlem, showing them in their churches and clubs and in business. Also their particular forms of amusement, marriage customs and distinctive style of cuisine." McKay also planned to give some attention to the small groups from various parts of Africa who had settled in Harlem and other parts of New York. They would, he emphasized, all be studied as individual groups "(instead of persons) in their relationship and associations with the native American group of Negroes."[24]

Alongside his known tensions with African Americans—or African American intellectuals—it is easy to accept that like many black immigrants, ill at ease in their new home, McKay strained against the tension of double assimilation and sought to maintain a connection not just to the past but to the newer, migrant folk forms of the Caribbean. The influence of forms such as carnival and calypso preceded him to New York. Where Eric Walrond's much more brilliant and experimental fiction could find no primary audience on account of its unapologetically non-American and radically polyphonous, multi-accented blackness, McKay would mask those centrifugal influences in the dominant, more accessible language of "jazz age" poetics and African American minstrelsy. As he writes in A Long Way from Home, "I desired to achieve something new, something in the spirit and accent of America."[25]

Claude McKay's Picong

It only takes a quick listen to the early New York–recorded calypsos of the late teens and twenties to realize that McKay's trademark nostalgia for his island home, his obsession with color, class, and sex, his fluctuating dialect poetics—his "code switching," as linguists would call it—has a precedent. Also, his migrancy and his rampant celebration of a poly-dialectical life are informed by that music which was widely available to and popular within the immigrant West Indian community in Harlem. Although recorded in 1934, Bill Rogers's "West Indian Weed Woman" echoes the sentiments and the very narrative of McKay's "The Tropics in New York," which appeared in 1922's Harlem Shadows. The poem longingly describes

> Bananas ripe and green, and ginger-root,
> Cocoa in pods and alligator pears,
> And tangerines and mangoes and grape fruit,
> Fit for the highest prize at parish fairs.[26]

The poet employs these particular fruits as signs of island origin, as indigenous products deracinated by an American imperial sprawl that feeds on displacement and migration. These fruits are products of a capitalist world system which has the effect of producing both "the exotic" by displacement and the sweet pain generated by a modernism that fetishized and commodified nostalgia as the language of desire. McKay's language is lush and heart-felt but also powerful in its attempt to use Standard English to convey a longing for a space outside and anterior to the world made by Standard English.

The Guyanese vaudevillian Bill Rogers would do much the same thing in his calypso, going even further into the vernacular and digging deeper into cultural specificity than McKay ever could—even in his dialect poetry, which ironically suffers from an exilic longing similar to that in the work McKay produced in actual exile. Placing the song next to McKay's poem shows the continuities between them and suggests that rather than the former giving birth to the latter, both drew directly from themes, tropes, and gestures at work in the calypsos of the time. In keeping with the poetics and politics of masking in the carnival complex, Rogers's "real" name was Augustus Hinds: Bill Rogers was his stage name, just as Claude McKay used the pseudonym Eli Edwards so as not to compromise his job as a waiter and just as Bert Williams kept his "real" name a secret until his death. "West Indian Weed Woman" concerns an encounter with a West Indian market woman on the streets of New York. It is an extremely long, rapid-fire blazon of weeds, bushes, herbs, and fruits, of which but a few will be mentioned here. It is performed in such a way as to combine both talking and singing at a high speed and suggests an interesting precursor to the "sing-jaying" or deejay style of Jamaican reggae, Trinidadian calypso, and, of course, African American hip hop. Indeed, the crossovers between calypso and hip hop, calypso and reggae, are pathetically underexplored—but, of course, this talk or singing style was precisely the style pioneered and made famous by Bert Williams onstage and on record. The song goes:

> She had cassava mumma, cooocoo piaba
> Jacob's ladder and piti guano
> Fingle bush, Job's tear, pite payi
> A jumbie bottle and white cleary
> Bile bush, wild cane, duck weed, anise seed
> Wara bitters and wild gray root
> She even had down to a certain bush
> Barbajans does call "puss-in-boot."[27]

This song not only depends on the insider knowledge of the Caribbean immigrant community and its folk traditions; it produces a sense of the Anglophone Caribbean community's own sense of cultural exclusivism there in the midst of an African American exceptionalism. These herbs, weeds, bushes, and roots are, after all, products of Trinidad that more than likely had escaped the commodification of mainstream industry because they were so specific, so rural, and so obscure. To have arrived on the streets of New York is to have been brought there not by "produce imperialism" but by the organic hands of black, typically female migrant labor. The cultural exclusivism is accomplished primarily by a firm refusal to translate and make the song accessible to non-Caribbean listeners. But it does more than simply emphasize the African American/West Indian divide in Harlem and in the English language: it fragments it further by translating something even into the microspecific vernacular of the Barbadian community. This small moment of translation is an important gesture of cross-cultural community building in which fragmentation requires poly-dialectal facility as a prerequisite to sharing space, race, and sound.

Although the golden age of calypso in New York began just before World War II and extended through the war period, it is the recorded songs that tend to define that age. However, songs such as "West Indian Weed Woman" and "No Nationality" were being sung and performed in Harlem from much earlier on in the century. Claude McKay would most certainly have had access to this music and its signifying systems. He in fact refers to "the 'Calypso' songs of today" while lovingly describing Jamaican field songs in his ethnographic My Green Hills of Jamaica.[28] Right after this passing reference to calypso, he spends a number of paragraphs cataloguing "yams, boiled plantains, cocoas, plenty of fish, chunks of meat" and "splendid coffee trees, cocoa trees, yams and congo peas" and so forth; an entire litany of exile that evokes his own "The Tropics in New York" and "West Indian Weed Woman."[29] A much more powerful connection between Claude McKay and the calypso form exists in Home to Harlem, which includes a calypso. Right after a blues song about "Dixie" is performed, in which the singer laments the absence of a "brown gal," the novelist tells us this:

A red-brown West Indian among them volunteered to sing a Port-of-Spain song. It immortalized the drowning of a young black sailor. It was made up by the bawdy colored girls of the port, with whom the deceased had been a favorite, and became very popular among the stevedores and sailors of the island.

"Ring the bell again,
Ring the bell again,
Ring the bell again,
But the sharks won't puke him up.
Oh, ring the bell again . . .
"Empty is you' room,
Empty is you' room
Empty is you' room,

But you find one in the sea.
Oh, empty is you' room . . .
"Ring the bell again,
Ring the bell again,
Ring the bell again,
But we know who feel the pain.
Oh, ring the bell again."

The song was curious, like so many Negro songs of its kind, for the strange strengthening of its wistful melody by a happy rhythm that was suitable for dancing.[30]

The placement of each song suggests a transcultural conversation in two vernaculars, a call and response where culturally specific and historically distinct genres respond to each other and attempt to sound either a cross-temporal space of racial community or a dissonant space of transnational distinctiveness. From "Dixie" in the American South to Port-of-Spain in the Caribbean, one could not be more blatantly symbolic. From jazz in New Orleans to calypso in Port-of-Spain: that is both the geography and psycho-geography of the Harlem Renaissance according to this novel and this writer. And in a novel that more often than not explores the conflictual differences between and among black cultures in Harlem, this is a moment where McKay roots and routes the two then new musical forms in a shared and trans-national racial sensibility produced out of metonymy and catalysis. This sensibility stretches the borders of the "national sounding" sought by Houston Baker in his take on Harlem's poetics and politics. Calypso sounds within this oral/aural vernacular space to both fracture and reshape the contours of black national community. As seen in McKay's take on Harlem's sound, black community is multi-accented and poly-dialectal, existing in the space between and among cultural differences.

McKay knew that the dialectic of "official"/"unofficial" in Bakhtin's "two-world condition" equally and simultaneously applied to West Indian immi-grants in Harlem in relation to the African American community. It was the "Afro Yanks" who provided their most intimate and daily experience of other-ness as well as a shared sense of political possibility. This curious form of otherness was and is distinct from the racial discourse of the time be-cause it was structured by that dominant notion of—and expectation of—racial sameness which more than often was generated by the African Ameri-can social world. An anecdote from his autobiography presents an example of how McKay wore black internal differences as masks which enabled multiple signifying. Because racial sameness was the dominant logic of perception and categorization, he was able to manipulate it via his choice of voice much in the way Bert Williams would. While working as a waiter on a train in 1918, he found himself arrested by police officers during a layover in Pittsburgh. These officers were rounding up the detritus of black northern migration: vagrants, draft dodgers, and the unemployed who dared maintain a presence on the street. McKay faced a judge who had been handing out stiff sentences:

> To my surprise, as soon as I had finished, the judge asked me if I were born in Jamaica. I said "Yes, Sir," and he commented: "Nice place. I was there a couple of seasons ago." And, ignoring my case and the audience, the judge began telling me of his trip to Jamaica and how he enjoyed it, the climate, the landscape, and the natives. He mentioned some of the beauty spots and I named those I knew. "I wish I were there instead of here," he said. "I wish I were there too," I echoed him.[31]

And what a powerful echo that was, a mimic gesture which suggests similarity to the ear of the judge but which is pregnant with more difference than can be catalogued or mapped. It is not just that his vernacular and cultural differences are here recognized and singled out by a figure that so well represents white American power—a white American power for whom the Caribbean had already become a prominent site of the pleasure industry called tourism. This figure hears McKay's black distinctiveness: his sound as cultural difference separates him from the African Americans who are then punished for the visual difference of their race. His voice becomes in this case enough for whites to select West Indians as a prized, often idealized group of blacks who then set off the problems of African Americans in bold contrast. It in fact allows white racism to then assume that the problems of African Americans are not related to race at all but to their aberrant "culture," which is also a sentiment often shared by black immigrants from Africa and the Caribbean (or even African American elites from as far back as Du Bois in facing the black urban poor).

McKay's response highlights this complicity with white racism while at the same time shows his awareness of linguistic and vernacular masking in the polyglot black Harlem community. It is a response that would have made LoBagola proud and is reminiscent of Bert Williams's one moment of vernacular quasi-authenticity on the Broadway stage. McKay continues:

Very willingly the judge obliged me and dictated a statement to a clerk, which
he signed. As he handed me the slip, he smiled and said: "You see, I could
place you by your accent." I flashed back a smile of thanks at him and
resolved henceforth to cultivate more my native accent.[32]

"Cultivate" that sound which was "native." *Wear a fez*. This choice makes
sense only if there was either a fear of the accent being lost to the dialects of
America or a previous decision to suppress it in order to function in a climate
of some hostility to it. Clearly in the latter case it was not white America that
was hostile to it: for them it was an exotic sign of either touristic service and
lilting island difference, or of some model intra-minority status. The lesson
learned was that McKay would then perform himself in such a way as to make
it impossible for him to be misrecognized (or misheard) as the hated racial
other despite being very clearly a poet of racial consciousness and no small
degree of militancy. This is no contradiction because it is the other side of
Bert Williams's mask: the inability to speak one's own dialect because the
visual mask of racial sameness was so overwhelming. Eric Walrond would
describe the outcome of this latter scenario via a mysterious "friend" named
"Williams." In his magnificent "Vignettes of the Dusk," Walrond writes:

> Williams is a Jamaican. But he is thoro[ugh]ly, spiritually, euph[em]isti-
> cally American. Some dusky folks, mistaking him for a native, so perfect is
> his philological assimilation—I am referring to those Afro-Africans who
> speak of West Indians as "monkey chasers"—come to him and say, "You
> know, Bill, dem monkey wimmin is de dummest—"
> But Williams, who owns a lovely home in Jersey, and has a pretty wife, a
> jewel of one of the best colored families of Baltimore, is not a citizen. And he
> doesn't intend to be one. He has been here twenty years. "America is all
> right," he'd say, "but I ain't taking no chances!"[33]

One can't help but wonder if this anonymous "Williams" bears any resemblance to the famed comedian of whom Walrond once said:

> To us, to whom he meant so much as an ambassador across the border of
> color, his memory will grow richer and more glorious as time goes on. For
> Bert Williams blazed the trail to Broadway for the Negro actor. It was he who
> made it possible for shows like "Shuffle Along," "The Plantation Revue,"
> "Liza" and "Strut Miss Lizzie" to go on Broadway. Not only that, but serious
> dramas of a tragic-superstitious nature which require a great deal of emo-
> tional acting, like "Taboo" and "The Emperor Jones," of which Charles

Gilpin, a contemporary of Williams, was star—plays of this sort Bert Williams was directly responsible for bringing to Broadway.[34]

From a West Indian writer who specialized in West Indian topics during the early part of the twentieth century and who explored the gaps, frictions, and syncretic beauty of multicultural black Harlem, what stands out here is Walrond's use of "us" and "ambassador." Certainly the first Williams has voluntarily disappeared into an African American mask, one which, given his marriage into the Afro-Yank elite, signifies a socioeconomic arrival in a culture where such an arrival will always be limited. As depicted here this disappearance is a form of mimicry, kleptoparasitic in its purest form. Still "Williams" maintains a very clear sense of his own Caribbean otherness, which allows him to function and perform as "black" but with an escape clause: a space between performance and authenticity in which the black diaspora is itself employed as cultural praxis.

The second Williams as an "ambassador" maintained that same cultural loophole in order to cross not only racial divides but intra-racial ones. He was a West Indian ambassador in an immigrant Harlem where "black" was always culturally contested despite being the only available language of anti-racist struggle. Unlike the first "Williams" he publicly performed his disappearance, using invisibility to signify the death of one empire (the British) and the spectacular birth of another (the American). So as he was celebrated by "black" Harlem and white Broadway, his secret meanings were simultaneously West Indian and "Nobody." As he perfected the "real Negro" by rendering it artful and therefore artificial, the unrepresentable black otherness that enabled that performance—the cultural excess—was inaudible but remained. Therefore his very presence as an African American icon was at least a triple-entendre. The same must be said of Claude McKay, whose resistance to racial homogeneity inspired a novel within which distinct black cultures are in an aggressive competition for cultural and linguistic space. As the member of a minority within a minority, he could only be heard as a "black" writer and had to submerge his criticisms and mockery of that sub-hegemonic host community in a language that simultaneously supported and celebrated the politics of race.

The mockery and these criticisms emerge by way of what in the language of calypso is called *picong*, a form of signifyin(g) unique to the Trinidadian carnival complex. *Picong* is a form of calypso, which depends on ritual abuse, playful competition, and an aggressive yet highly subtle wit. It is a Caribbean variant of "the dozens" in the African American context and is very much at work in *Home to Harlem* as an intercultural gesture of both difference and intimacy and an assault against the very binaries of American cultural politics. W. A. Domingo describes the setting of black intercultural Harlem in such a way as to clear the space within which these back and forth rituals of signifying were being played. For the immigrant West Indians Harlem was significant:

> Here they have their first contact with each other, with large numbers of American Negroes, and with the American brand of race prejudice. Divided by tradition, culture, historical background and group perspective, these diverse peoples are gradually hammered into a loose unit by the impersonal force of congested residential segregation.[35]

What is crucial here is Domingo's description of "double assimilation" as a process of being "hammered into a loose unit." This image of the hammer is particularly resonant for West Indians. Its microparticular meanings could not have been employed by African American writers and thinkers in quite this way. Though united in a struggle against binary racial coding and its racist implications, they could not have imagined the pain and pressure that "race welding" presented to foreign blacks. Also, they could not imagine themselves having any cultural power analogous to the white American cultural norms that presented assimilation as an impossible necessity forged through violence.

Walrond's use of the insulting term "monkey chaser" in the passage above is also of great importance to *Home to Harlem*. Although a term of some abuse, it can be read as a cross-cultural form of "playing the dozens" just as McKay and other West Indian writers would mock and jibe at the ways and attitudes of the African American community through their own forms of *picong*. Rudolph Fisher, the African American physician, novelist, and short story writer, isolates this term in his wonderful examination of colliding black migrations in Harlem during its renaissance. His story "City of Refuge" in the *New Negro* anthology and his fascinating story "Ringtail"—the title itself a direct reference to the pejorative "monkey chaser"—are detailed explorations of West Indian/African American differences in terms of language, style, cultural affiliation, and political sensibilities. A brief example of Fisher's participation in this intercultural and transatlantic conversation that was Harlem can be found in "Ringtail." Fisher's main character, the pompous Cyril Sebastian Best, exploits intra-racial cultural difference in order to navigate the African American–dominated streets of Harlem. In this following cultural/psychological profile, readers are made privy to the kinds of internal performance at work in these micropolitical encounters between two distinct cultural groups who share the mask of racial commonality in a city that offered refuge for all manner of black migrants:

> There were British West Indians in Harlem who would have told Cyril Sebastian Best flatly to his face that they despised him—that he would not have dared even to address them in the islands; who frequently reproved their American friends for judging all West Indians by the Cyril Sebastian Best standard. There were others who, simply because he was a British West Indian, gathered him to their bosoms in that regardless warmth with which the outsider ever welcomes his like.
>
> Among these latter, the more numerous, Cyril accordingly expanded. His self-esteem, his craftiness, his contentiousness, his acquisitiveness, all became virtues. To him self-improvement meant nothing but increasing these virtues, certainly not eliminating or modifying any of them. He became fond of denying that he was colored, insisting that he was "a British subject," hence, by implication, unquestionably superior to any merely American Negro. And when two years of contact convinced him that the American Negro was characteristically neither self-esteemed nor crafty nor contentious nor acquisitive, in short—quite virtueless, his conscious superiority became downright contempt.[36]

Fisher should be celebrated for being one of the few African American writers of his time to take seriously the differences and tensions between the various black cultural groups who were engaging and encountering each other in modernist New York. His understanding of the differences between island culture/class/color relationships and those found and manipulated in the United States is extraordinary as one witnesses the shifting affiliations and self-definitions at work in the African American apprehension of Cyril Sebastian Best. This is also given some attention by Domingo in his "Gift of the Black Tropics." In response to the "undiscriminating attitude on the part of native Negroes, as well as the friction generated from contact between the two groups," what has been created is "an artificial and defensive unity among the islands which reveals itself in an instinctive closing of their ranks when attacked by outsiders."[37] Certainly the national flexibility of a character like Best becomes merely a way to create even sharper borders between him and the African American community; yet the sense of difference and the pressure generated by that difference is strong enough to sustain those intra-racial borders and generate a war of black exceptionalisms played out in vernacular tones. Fisher, however, isn't so simplistic as to describe a singular West Indian view. He provides subtle yet telling differences within that community while at the same time mocking "monkey-chaser" Cyril Sebastian Best's mockery of "the American Negro."

Fisher also questions and critiques the African American use of the term "monkey chaser," suggesting that in its utterance African Americans perpetuate the oppressive power structure that makes assimilation and equality impossible. In "City of Refuge" the main character, King Solomon Gillis, who, fresh from the South, has never before encountered a West Indian, asks this of streetwise hustler Mouse Uggam:

> "What make you keep callin' him monkey-chaser?"
> "West Indian. That's another thing. Any time y' can knife a monk, do it. They's too damn many of 'em here. They're an achin' pain."
> "Jess de way white folks feels 'bout niggers."
> "Damn that. How 'bout it? Y' want the job?"[38]

The question is unanswered, quickly forgotten and left to dangle in the reader's mind despite Mouse Uggam's seeming disinterest in its implications. That the question is here articulated by a character who Fisher represents as a naïve, untutored black bumpkin suggests that for Fisher the hostilities and tensions between the groups is not only an urban phenomenon but a recent one. King Solomon Gillis need not be a card-carrying "New Negro" in order to note the eerie parallel between racism and black American ethnocentrism.

McKay's *Home to Harlem* is the flip side of the cross-cultural game of "the dozens" that can be found in Fisher's work. In this novel "monkey chasers" and signifying monkeys dance with and around each other, though without the psychological depth and historical nuance of a story as brief as "Ringtail." That this novel was the first black best-seller and that it also features cross-cultural/intra-racial tensions and conversations should bring to mind the historical significance of *In Dahomey* as the first of its type, which also had buried within it the cross-cultural and intra-racial problematizing of race. But where Fisher's work details the problems of African Americans and Afro-Caribbeans in what Locke called that "great race welding," it isn't aware of the politics of double assimilation, which is primarily what motivates the rejectionist gestures of Cyril Sebastian Best and Claude McKay. As seen in the earlier passages from *A Long Way from Home*, McKay felt that Walrond's "philological assimilation" was to be resisted while simultaneously fighting against racism. Both gestures were essential and both were ineluctably radical. McKay knew how important the politics of this "plural masking" was to black immigrants for whom assimilation was at least a double process and for whom race was still the primary engine with which to build a new intraracial, cross-cultural community.

As Winston James puts it in his A Fierce Hatred of Injustice, even from his earliest years McKay himself "lived on the borders, intersections and within the interstices of many worlds."[39] James roots McKay's penchant for fragments, margins, and intersections in his Jamaican experience, so as to banish the problematic notion that it is the American experience of race that is most valuable about his work and sensibilities. This reading of McKay's Jamaican experience and his dialect poetry importantly argues that the continuities between the pre-immigrant and post-immigrant experiences are at least as significant as the writer's adventures in America, Europe, the Soviet Union, and North Africa. As noted earlier, it is true that even his Jamaican dialect poetry is marked by the kind of nostalgia or exilic longing that would characterize the work he produced after migrating and roaming from country to country. Many commentators have also celebrated McKay's position within the cracks and on the edges of so many social and cultural worlds. They have done so in such a way as to privilege his time away from "home"—from his globetrotting to his obsession with the "seamier" side of American urban life (which James would connect to McKay's time as a police officer in Kingston); from his intellectual curiosity (honed by his eclectic childhood reading) to his political inconsistencies (from the diversity of opinions available to him in Jamaica) to his bisexuality. Regrettably, there is no mention of this in James's otherwise fulfilling interrogation.

Despite discussing his sexuality, Wayne Cooper also limits this arena of McKay's life by labeling him homosexual, thereby simplifying McKay's quite complex desires, as critics are ever wont to do. In Caribbean Waves, one of the more recent books on Claude McKay, Heather Hathaway is content to label him a misogynist for his animalistic description of some female characters—without, it seems, an awareness of the poetics and politics of McKay's ideology of primitivism, which operates alongside his complex sexual identification. McKay, it must be said, did maintain the mask of heterosexuality and in fact exaggerated it in his fiction much in the way calypsonians (or contemporary reggae deejays or rappers) hyperbolically celebrated their heterosexuality in song and dance. Indeed, his stressing of heterosexuality was in tandem with his exploitation of the minstrel stereotype: as a mask for not only racial and cultural complexity but also a sexual ambiguity which had no language of expression in the poetics of its time. After all, there is no evidence that McKay was ashamed of or tormented by his sexual explorations. All in all, the internal and linguistic borders he crossed were perhaps greater and more plentiful than the mundane geopolitical or psychosocial lines of the modernist world order. He also celebrated his own borderlessness. Entering North Africa, where he "for the first time in [his] life felt singularly free of color-consciousness," he told a messenger from the British Consulate: "I said I was born in the West Indies and lived in the United States and that I was an American, even though I was a British subject, but I preferred to think of myself as an internationalist."[40] He then defined an "internationalist" as a "bad nationalist."[41] A stanza from "No Nationality" speaks very much to his statelessness, but with much more anxiety than the utopian spirit of this McKay (as opposed to the one present in "The Tropics in New York"):

> I really don't know if I'm an American
> Though I know bloody well I'm no Englishman
> And that is why I tell the boys don't bother with me
> Cause I ain't got no nationality.[42]

McKay, however, was more faithful to his West Indian distinctiveness than have been many of his critics and readers. In thinking through this aspect of McKay's literary reception, P. S. Chaudhan writes: "Unable, or unwilling, to read McKay as a writer from Jamaica, then a British colony, and hence as one with a mindset entirely different from that of the Harlemite, many critics have landed themselves in a puzzle."[43] Heather Hathaway echoes this concern in *Caribbean Waves*. In response to this "puzzle," she situates McKay as well as Paule Marshall in multiple locations—Caribbean and African American, which is clearly an invaluable gesture in its destabilizing of a comfortable "blackness" which is often a mask for the diasporic reach of an African American exceptionalism. However, the competitive gestures and power imbalances implicit in these multiple locations are not fully explored in her analysis. One gets the raw fact of multiple situatedness as key to a diasporic sprawl and to textual interpretation, while the constitutive and productive tensions of micropolitical encounters are never fully unearthed. Hathaway's work on McKay is telling in that her attempt at multiple-situatedness locates an "ethics of inclusion" in *Home to Harlem*, for example, in which the male characters forge a transnational racial solidarity in the harsh, lynching-mad world of early-twentieth-century America.[44] But by not taking seriously the book's intense focus on fragmenting the transnational black social world by means of an exploration and exploitation of intra-racial tensions, antagonisms, and cross-cultural opacities (not to mention its assault on the sexual prudery of racial uplift by way of McKay's primitivism), she ultimately returns McKay if not to the Americanized category of "Negro" (or to African American literature), then to the equally Americanized binarism of an unaccentuated "black" via a romantic discourse of solidarity. This in effect manages to suture both the contexts she initially attempts to keep apart: the larger and more dominant African American and the smaller yet greatly significant West Indian.

But as to the alleged puzzle of McKay's location, through the language of *picong* or cross-cultural signifying there really is no puzzle, or at least the puzzle *as such* reveals the limitations of the critical intelligence landlocked within its racial orthodoxies. Critics have simply read him through the lens of race as a problematic way to solve this complexity—much like playing checkers on a chessboard. The Jamaican poet's race militancy was also a curious and puzzling thing, adding to his complexity. In the inimitable words of Harold Cruse in his Caribbophobic *The Crisis of the Negro Intellectual*, "West Indians are never so 'revolutionary' as when they are away from the islands."[45] This much was true of McKay, whose commitment to communism had always been questioned since his focus on race and his deeply romantic sensibilities never quite washed with the hard-liners of the white left and the orthodoxies of Caribbean militants like W. A. Domingo, Grace Campbell, and others in the African Blood Brotherhood. As chronicled in Winston James's *Holding Aloft the Banner of Ethiopia*, the Brotherhood was the first black communist organization in the United States and primarily comprised West Indian immigrants.

The marginal and fragmented social, cultural, and political space that McKay occupied can be perceived in such a way as to maintain the integrity of racial struggle but open up the accented spaces of internal difference. His was the space of the calypsonian who dwells within the social and racial contradictions of a colonial society and who sings with a necessarily forked, split, and multiple tongue; his crossroads are significantly more transnational and diasporic than those of the blues singer who, despite deep pre-Christian and West African connections, stands somewhere between a very American North and South. Where other black writers of his generation attempted to suture the spaces between these multiple worlds, McKay attempted to transform those fissures and clefts into poetry, or, more accurately, into fiction, since it is in his fiction that the calypsonian in him is allowed to speak. His poetry was always masked—sonnets, dialect, *Negro*, where his fiction was, as Bakhtin would have appreciated, the space where intra-racial dialogism and polyphony could be sounded, heard, read. Here he used black masks to make these sounds that work with and against an emergent, landlocked black nationalism. He used carnival as a method of expressing and exploring a world made new by imperialism, slavery, migration, and black-on-black cultural contact. As McKay writes in *Home to Harlem*, the novel was his attempt to sound "the warm accent" of the city's "composite voice."[46] Every word of this sounding was laced with intervernacular signifying and *picong*.

Perhaps most centrally in regard to his carnivalesque poetics, McKay explicitly attempted to use *Home to Harlem* to depict multiple forms of black languages and cultures and histories—true internal multiplicity, the "composite voice"—against not only a monologic whiteness but also against a sub-hegemonic African American "blackness." Like *In Dahomey*, this barely plotted novel is *about* intra-racial diversity, as is evident in its famous obsession with the colors, tones, and various shades of black skin. It is also *about* transnational black polyphony, as evident in even this random scene from the first half of the novel:

> A yell startled the cabaret. A girl had slapped another's face and replied to her victim's cry of pain with, "If you no like it you can lump it!"
>
> "You low an' dutty bobbin-bitch!"
>
> "Bitch is bobbin in you' sistah's coffin."
>
> They were West Indian girls.
>
> "I'll mek mah breddah beat you' bottom foh you."
>
> "Gash it and stop you' jawing."
>
> They were interrupted by another West Indian girl, who wore a pink-flowered muslin frock and a wide jipi-jappa hat from which charmingly hung two long ends of broad pea-green ribbon.
>
> "It's a shame. Can't you act like decent English people?" she said. Gently she began pushing away the assaulted girl, who burst into tears.
>
> "She come boxing me up ovah a dutty black 'Merican coon."
>
> "Mek a quick move or I'll box you bumbole ovah de moon," her assailant cried after her. . . .
>
> "The monkey-chasers am scrapping," Zeddy commented.
>
> "In a language all their own," said Jake.
>
> "They are wild womens, buddy, and it's a wild language they're using, too," remarked a young West Indian behind Jake.[47]

Later on in the novel we are told that the West Indian expletive "bumbole" has been adopted by Jake as his own private appropriation of this seemingly alien and much more primitive—therefore more complex and vital, in McKay's thinking—language.[48] The differences between vernaculars are so emphasized in the book that they stand out as one of the text's most important meta-narratives. Jake's acknowledgment of the distinctiveness of the West Indian vernacular is a part of McKay's desire for it to be acknowledged by his readers. In *Harlem Shadows*, his first book of poetry published in the United States, he went as far as to classify the two black vernaculars in terms of difficulty and cultural authenticity: "The speech of my childhood and youth . . . was the Jamaica dialect . . . which still preserves a few words of African origin, and which is more difficult of understanding than the American Negro dialect."[49]

In keeping with the politics of *picong*, this suggests that a hierarchy of vernaculars exists in *Home to Harlem*. For example, by deeming this language even wilder and more primitive than the African American vernacular, McKay was covertly signifying against the fetish for the African American vernacular that defined the literature and music of the Harlem Renaissance. One must remember that he was originally the most important and innovative writer of the Caribbean vernacular but had to function in a literary and cultural climate where that language was marginalized by the great interest in African American vernacular expression as it emerged partly through minstrelsy. That language was also initially marginalized by McKay's own desire to achieve an archaic form of that vernacular called British Standard English through his commitment to the sonnet form. Perhaps it was there that he spoke in the tongue of his British colonial heritage, where in his early fiction he spoke in the composite dialects of America. But for the arch-primitivist of the renaissance movement, any group of blacks that could be described as being "wilder" and more primitive than another was therefore closer to Africa and obviously superior.

The scene quoted above, like others in the novel which feature "wild" West Indians, focuses on black Caribbean women. For McKay they had always signified a more potent and dangerous sexuality, which presumably emanated from some unsullied, precolonial ancestral essence; after all, McKay was a great admirer of D. H. Lawrence and does use bizarre lines like this one in *Home to Harlem*: "The wild, shrieking mad woman that is sex seemed jeering at him."[50] A character like "Latnah" from *Banjo* will take this set of associations along with vague notions of racial hybridity and cultural cosmopolitanism to their most pornographic pseudo-philosophical conclusion. To McKay's credit, in his great attempt at carnivalesque cultural and political reversal he rejects and mocks the "pure," "unsullied," and unbearably noble stereotype of the black woman held by black elite discourse and culture from the Harlem Renaissance to the current moment. "True" womanhood is as much his target as it was Ada Overton Walker's and Bessie Smith's. However, McKay replaces it with an image that was eerily close—well, identical—to the white American racist stereotype. He does this despite his commitment to the revolutionary potential of open, cross-racial, and homosexual sexuality; and this despite producing a novel in which the vast majority of the women are not only aggressive sexual agents (as opposed to the prim and proper women of staid black bourgeois cultural production) but are also economically empowered in such a way as to keep perpetually unemployed and economically variable "sweetmen" floating around for their own pleasure.

But even in this, the space between the "wilder" West Indian woman and the African American woman is subtly broadened through his almost invisible countersignifying of cultural superiority. The aforementioned scene is ironic in its use of the term "English," which signifies two things: first, a non–African American colonial mentality where Great Britain dominates the pole of respectability; and second, a value system that is revealed as being so indebted to colonialism that it hearkens back to that earlier form of domination simply to reject the politics of the new home that is Harlem: "It's a shame. Can't you act like decent English people?" Although McKay was never known for his subtlety (excepting perhaps in his own narrative of sexuality), this is no accident of representation but a dense form of ironic, self-referential masking that was necessary in order to maintain race while struggling against its cultural and sexual limitations. But, to be fair to the overall design of Home to Harlem, McKay refused to articulate a preference for one black vernacular over another and in fact mastered and sympathized with the one which was not his own. Recall that the main character Jake "was very American in spirit and shared a little of that comfortable Yankee contempt for poor foreigners. And as an American Negro he looked askew at foreign niggers. Africa was jungle, and Africans bush niggers, cannibals. And West Indians were monkey-chasers."[51] As if it weren't already obvious, the archetypal "Negro-ness" of Jake is here emphasized and tied to the global contradictions of race, nation, and diaspora. Where Cedric Robinson would link the African American middle class specifically to these contradictions, McKay here includes poor and working-class Negroes who may not benefit from the "wages of whiteness," in David Roediger's words, but do benefit from a national sense of African American identity no matter how fragile and contradictory this identity may be. The novel even begins with Jake's anti-Arabism and goes on to show how despite his travels throughout the world, his knowledge of other black cultural spaces and histories—Africa and the Caribbean, to be precise—is tragically lacking upon his return. His parochialism is made clear after we are told that "bumbole" is his new favorite word, and just as he meets the character Ray for the first time.

It is important to note that their first conversation includes an interchange in which they both speak French. Both of them have traveled and have had access to a world of racial, cultural, and linguistic differences. Jake had learned the language while fighting in France in World War I. For Ray:

> "C'est ma langue maternelle."
>
> "Hm!" Jake made a face and scratched his head. "Comprendre pas, chappie. Tell me in straight United States."
>
> "French is my native language. I—"
>
> "Don't crap me," Jake interrupted. "Ain'tchu—ain'tchu one of us, too?"
>
> "Of course I'm Negro," the waiter said, "but I was born in Hayti and the language down there is French."
>
> "Hayti . . . Hayti," repeated Jake. "Tha's where now? Tha's—"
>
> "An island in the Caribbean—near the Panama Canal."[52]

Much of the novel is written from Jake's perspective, which is culturally landlocked despite his international travel and multiple cross-cultural encounters in Europe and beyond. It is hard to imagine that a character like Jake, who has traveled extensively, would have never even heard of Haiti. One wonders if McKay is merely stressing and overstating a point about Jake as representative of a certain sort of black thinking or a certain stereotyped African American persona. The American structure of race has stayed with this everyman from station to station, port to port, and has remained static— and all blacks encountered are assumed to be merely "one of us." In the novel, this parochial perspective only begins to change with the introduction of the angst-ridden Caribbean intellectual Ray, who teaches Jake primarily about the African diaspora and all its differences. By the end of that first conversation, Jake's perspective significantly widens and deepens:

> Jake sat like a big eager boy and learned many facts about Hayti before the train reached Pittsburgh. He learned that the universal spirit of the French

Revolution had reached and lifted up the slaves far away in that remote island; that Black Hayti's independence was more dramatic and picturesque than the United States' independence and that it was a strange, almost unimaginable eruption of the beautiful ideas of the "Liberte, Egalite, Fraternite" of Mankind, that shook the foundations of that romantic era.[53]

Here again, even in what might be read simply as a proto C. L. R. Jamesian reading of pan-African struggle—in which the French Revolution itself was the source of an authentic "African" revolt—one witnesses a cross-cultural moment of signifying as Ray compares the freedom struggles of Caribbean Haiti to the struggles of American independence. The former was "more dramatic and picturesque" than the latter, a comparison meant to chip away at the sacredness of America's own creation myth, which is key to its exceptionalism. Ray tells Jake about "the old destroyed cultures of West Africa" but refuses the romanticized precolonial bias of Afrocentrism by balancing those past glories with "their vestiges . . . black kings who struggled stoutly for the independence of their kingdoms" and "the little Republic of Liberia, founded by American Negroes."[54] In the face of this information Jake "felt like a boy who stands with the map of the world in colors before him, and feels the wonder of the world around him."[55] Because Jake's is the dominant perspective of the novel, all its assertions of West Indian inferiority or superiority must be refracted against the limitations and transformations of this uber-African American who so grows as to lose his narrow cultural perspective. That he is taught history, the world, and the black diaspora by a West Indian is no accident; it is central to McKay's argument to have Jake's sense of "us" be transformed and globalized by Ray.

It must be noted that *Home to Harlem* was written in a context of heightened anti–West Indianism in the black Harlem community, even though the text is usually read as a New Negro (or rather, "authentic") version of Carl Van Vechten's *Nigger Heaven*. It was published just months after Marcus Garvey's deportation, with the "Garvey Must Go" hostility still rampant in the streets. As represented by McKay, Jake's anti–West Indianism and parochialism must be read and heard as being "triply-voiced." This type of sounding is a less Americo-centric version of Houston Baker, who in a very important gesture assaults the racial parochialism of his own binary nationalist poetics by speaking of Caliban's "triple" discursive play. McKay's voice resonates on these multiple cultural frequencies if the text is situated within the context of the anti–West Indianism of the time and against McKay's known tensions with African American intellectuals. Also evident in his narrative is the West

Indian discomfort with a form of assimilation that was rarely ever named or identified as such: intra-racial, that black mask behind which both Walrond's "Williams" and Bert Williams felt trapped. Ray himself feels trapped by this form of intra-racial assimilation, despite being explicitly hostile to racial assimilation. This is clear in his discussion of his transition from proud Haitian—before the military and cultural presence of American imperialism—to a minstrel stereotype in black Harlem:

> He remembered when little Hayti was foundering uncontrolled, how proud he was to be the son of a free nation. He used to feel condescendingly sorry for those poor African natives; superior to ten millions of suppressed Yankee "coons." Now he was just one of them and he hated them for being one of them.[56]

He has become a "coon," forced into this mask by virtue of migration and colonization—and to become a "coon," in his thinking, is to become an African American. This returns to mind McKay's own admission that the first African Americans he had ever seen while still in Jamaica were (or seemed to be) "coons." However, Ray has not actually lost his racial equality here, but his cultural privilege. This results from the logic of intra-racial assimilation, which forces him into a loathsome sameness, a commonality formed by a shared lack of power.

This moment in the novel is remarkably candid. One can imagine the years of pain pressed into this passage by a writer who saw in Ray what this writer sees in Bert Williams: a vision of diasporic paralysis where the historical contradictions and cultural differences in a world made by colonialism and slavery become too much to maintain by a relentless and unending masking. They become too much for a mind forced to accept the binary logic of race despite having been reared by something much more fluid though only arguably less restrictive. One is reminded of "No Nationality"'s rejection of national boundaries when reading Ray's "home thoughts":

> These men claimed kinship with him. They were black like him. Man and nature had put them in the same race. He ought to love them and feel them (if they felt anything). He ought to if he had a shred of social morality in him. They were all chain-ganged together and he was counted as one link. Yet he loathed every soul in that great barrack-room except Jake. Race . . . Why should he have and love a race?
>
> Races and nations were things like skunks, whose smells poisoned the air of life.[57]

What is important here is that this questioning of the category of race and this discomfort with the notion of nation only exists for Ray and McKay in a context of black-on-black interaction and cross-cultural tension. Both men share a penchant for idealizing their island homes and use nostalgia to wipe clean the racial and socioeconomic contradictions of those homes; however, it is the presence of the intra-racial black other and the specter of a sameness without distinctions which fills Ray with such hatred and casts him into a terrifying carnival of self-loathing.

And despite his great insight and learning, his sensitivity to the cultures of the African diaspora, it is ironically to Jake, the African American stereotype, that Ray turns for stability. Here McKay's own body/mind binarism wins out over his African American/Afro-Caribbean signifying. Jake as primitive, however parochial, embodies a life-spirit that is unmatched by the effete intellectualism of Ray, however Caribbean and however diasporic. Ray in fact leaves Harlem by the end of the novel, and it is with Jake that McKay's final sentiments rest. So, if it is not sufficiently obvious: *Home to Harlem* is told from the perspective of an African American who hates West Indian and other diaspora blacks; but it is written by a West Indian writer who is wary of American blacks and whose manipulation of the African American vernacular is interesting considering that it is the Jamaican vernacular he was known for. From deep within the "jungle" of African American vernacular signifyin(g)—in the throat of Bre'r Rabbit—we see the complex web of the "ginnal" Caribbean trickster—Anansi the Spider. It is a sign of McKay's success at passing as an African American writer that this text has so often been seen as the representation of an African American or black modern voice.

Home to Harlem features a kind of vernacular signifying which questions the assumptions present in the Du Boisian formula of double-consciousness and present in even Henry Louis Gates's postmodern vernacular reading of Du Bois in *The Signifying Monkey*. This latter text is linked to Du Bois primarily because both texts employ African origins to claim a linguistic/aesthetic doubleness that is American while assuming a one-to-one relationship among all those black signifying communities, aligning them against dominant white and colonial meanings by way of a "parallel discursive universe" that is "outside the Western tradition."[58] After all, it is no great step from double-consciousness to an Afro-Bakhtinian reading of the "double-voiced" text. To speak of West Indians in this context is to ask about the nature of the "double," of Esu-Elegbara as a foundational principle when two of the god's children compete in a common cultural/semantic field. *Home to Harlem* was written in order to explore the logic of the interaction. This reading of Home to Harlem and the transnational migrant poetics of McKay therefore argues that the trope of carnival does not need to be rooted in a reading of Bakhtin as it was always already at work in McKay's poetics, which he always claimed to be rooted in black—that is, Caribbean and African American—folk and urban cultures.

McKay must be lauded for being perhaps the only black modernist of the Harlem generation to devote much time and effort to representing West Africans in his fiction. Rudolf Fisher's The Conjure Man Dies is another important text which includes a West African as a central figure of both ancestral presence and—curiously—of its palpable absence. Along with West Indians (Anglophone and Francophone) and African Americans, West Africans are present and significant in both Home to Harlem and its sequel Banjo, which might be one reason why McKay's fiction was so influential for the West African and Francophone Caribbean writers, poets, and artists who made up the movement of French Negritude. In fact, the discourses and cultural figures central to Negritude are mentioned, discussed, mocked, and evaluated in Banjo, thereby shifting the locus of black modernism from its American nascence to its Francophone diasporic continuance. A focus on these "other" Negroes was crucial to the diasporic focus of the texts' signifying and even more crucial to an emergent pan-Africanism that was increasingly centered on the local concerns of blacks in America, if not the West. Non-American blacks allowed McKay, Walrond, and even Rudolph Fisher to carnivalize early-twentieth-century African American and Afro-Caribbean discourses of racial exceptionalism and to relentlessly expand the frontiers of the racial "us."

Coda: A Rumor of Presence

The climate of infinite reversals and possibilities, the rush of danger and the heady scent of multiple freedoms: sexual, political, aesthetic, and social. No Harlem-era writer went further into this than Claude McKay, who threw himself body and mind into the thrilling carnival of black modernist urbanity. His struggle was to balance cultural difference with the political necessity of race, while exploring the various social, sexual, and cultural possibilities open to the black artist in the first century of freedom. The carnivalesque mode of representation empowered him in his struggle and enabled his relentless sounding of multiple black vernaculars as a sign of modern black sensibilities. But there was much more to his use of the carnivalesque, coming as it did from the mind of a writer whose "head was a circus where everything went circling round and round," as we are told of the character Banjo.[59] Through this mode of representation, Home to Harlem suspended and upended not only the norms of racist, white American culture but also the emergent transnational cultural authority of African Americans in the African diaspora. And judging from its effect on Garvey, it also sent shivers of dis-ease into the ranks of the immigrant West Indian petite bourgeoisie.

The novel's microspecific concerns for the multiple colors, shades, and textures of black skin reversed and fragmented the simplistic black and white logic of American racism and threatened all ideologies based on that same logic. Indeed, McKay's obsession with the infinite variations and gradations of color was seen by some critics as reflecting a West Indian perspective on race, one out of place in the United States.[60] This is exactly what Du Bois accused Garvey of: importing the intra-racial antagonisms of Jamaica to an America where "Negroes recognize no color line in or out of the race, and they will in the end punish the man who attempts to establish it."[61] Perhaps the problem with this assertion is that it is so focused on rejecting color lines that it neglects the all too real cultural lines that emerge in a generalized African American community (and Garvey was severely punished—in his time and often still in ours—by a Black Atlantic criticism that continues to banish him). The carnivalesque also allowed McKay to reverse the staid Victorianism of the Talented Tenth by frankly and pornographically depicting a social world where women not only sought and enjoyed sex but were often the only economically empowered characters in a world of rampant black male migrancy and unemployment. This sexual explicitness was and is read by the Afro-American elite as well as by Marcus Garvey and no doubt even black working-class orthodoxies as a deeply problematic political move, since black female sexuality had always signified the "purity" and the integrity of the patriarchal image of the race. Because chastity and domesticity was deemed a prerequisite for assimilation, freedom, or equality in the United States, McKay's exploration of "free love" among the urban folk was more than simply sensationalism. It was a political protest that was unrecognizable as such in its time. As Wayne Cooper puts it: "To those who believed in decorum and restraint and also to those whose first concern was always to project black grievances onto the national stage, Home to Harlem seemed a betrayal of racial trust and solidarity."[62]

McKay's text is loud and unruly and offensive, full of ritual abuse, largely to disrupt the smooth flow of African American exceptionalism so as to participate in the construction of a community that was simultaneously black and otherwise; a community where sexuality and color were celebrated, not amputated by an insecure elite; a community whose sense of "Africa" or "the Caribbean" or black difference was not mythic and romanticized but ultimately dependent on the street-level interactions of distinct black peoples— in and out of bed. Where as a modernist McKay could afford to make his case into a crusade, Bert Williams had to remain silent, emitting his vernacular difference only once on the Broadway stage. However, if one rereads *Home to Harlem* carefully, aware of the secret histories and subtle masquerades explored in this book, it should become glaringly obvious that Bert Williams also occupies the central iconic and symbolic space of this novel. So in this turn to Claude McKay—the most conspicuous of all modernist Afro-cosmopolitan border crossers—one must turn in closing to his most significant novel for the reappearance of a powerfully silent and historically overlooked meta-conversation about black minstrelsy, double assimilation, and a form of signifying that has effectively disappeared from history.

This conversation is about the man who integrated Broadway, about the persona who, like Esu-Elegbara, allows McKay to speak with and against an African American modernism that was tightening its own aesthetic and discursive borders during a moment where West Indians found themselves "home" in a Harlem which often doubly rejected them as black and as immigrants and which they in turn doubly rejected as Yankee and American. With Bert Williams at the back of his throat (a potent sign of the anansi continuum visible in Brathwaite's work), McKay's soundings attempt a vernacular re-imagining of race in a climate of severe racial terror and lynching. Bert Williams makes a guest appearance in *Home to Harlem*, first as a "rumor," then as a nameless absence who performs in silence; a figure that although not quite Bert Williams, evokes him as something in between myth and icon, memory and dream: a liminal possibility. Although the novel was published a few years after his death, it documents the first few years of the twenties, where his presence and his influence were still very much felt. In its depiction of the panoply of black life and the impact of West Indian cultural presence, the novel could hardly have neglected him. Also, *Home to Harlem* was attuned to a generational changing of the guard as "New Negroes" claimed cultural center stage from their elders and dared to recklessly redefine themselves and their own possibilities. Bert Williams was a necessary reference point for an older Harlem culture that had established the roots of the city's then current vogue. Of course, he had also become a sign of that which the New Negroes themselves would come to loathe and fear—the minstrel. However, as we have seen, McKay's relationship to blackface was ever complicated by his awareness of linguistic, cultural, and sexual masks.

The reader first hears Williams's name uttered by the hard-drinking, lusty Miss Curdy, who boasts, "In my sporting days I knew Bert Williams and Walker and Adah Overton . . . and all that upstage race gang."[63] This passage suggests that Bert Williams is a figure from the past, from a golden time. It also makes clear that his politics was not the politics of black minstrelsy as we have come to accept (a self-hating collaboration with the ideologies of white supremacy) but instead was in fact race-conscious despite its evident elitism. Much later in the novel, his name is dropped by the very fashionable Madame Mulberry, who "gossiped reminiscently of Bert Williams, George Walker and Aida Overton Walker, Anita Patti Brown and Cole and Johnson."[64] Once again, Bert Williams *was*; and considering the time in which the novel is set—and written—any reader would have clearly known that Williams had passed away fairly recently. However, in a section that also mentions "James Reese Europe, the famous master of jazz," it is "rumored that Bert Williams might drop in after midnight. Madame Mulberry was certain he would."[65] Inconsistent, perhaps—mythic, absolutely.

In the build-up to the possible (or impossible) appearance of the dead-but-not-quite-absent performer, the reader is then presented with a setting that can only be described as carnivalesque. More specifically, it is a setting so much like a Caribbean carnival tent that its language should be savored and its details contemplated:

> The owner of the cabaret knew that Negro people, like his people, love the pageantry of life, the expensive, the fine, the striking, the showy, the trumpet, the blare—sumptuous settings and luxurious surroundings. And so he had assembled his guests under an enchanting-blue ceiling of brilliant chandeliers and a dome of artificial roses bowered among green leaves. Great mirrors reflected the variegated colors and poses. Shaded, multi-colored sidelights glowed softly along the golden walls.
>
> It was a scene of blazing color. Soft, barbaric, burning, savage, clashing, planless colors—all rioting together in wonderful harmony. There is no human sight so rich as an assembly of Negroes ranging from lacquer black through brown to cream, decked out in their ceremonial finery. Negroes are like trees. They wear all colors naturally.[66]

Bakhtin is helpful here, but clearly unnecessary to our understanding of McKay's view of race, Harlem, masquerade, and ultimately of his own novel, which is also described here. Although not the final scene of the novel, this scene is its emotional crescendo, its final orgasmic burst of color before the almost "planless" text meanders and finally loses energy and the reader's interest. The description of multiple types and colors of black people "rioting together in wonderful harmony" is simply stunning for its time as a representation of a transatlantic, quasi-Afrocentric *bacchanal* where violence is sublimated in the language of individual performance and play. This was, after all, a time of major race riots and a general white fear of vengeful, rampaging blacks now free to exact historical retribution in rising tides. But this passage is only the first half of the crescendo. It only prepares the reader for the sudden appearance of a performer who is never named but whose presence stills the crowd and creates an utterly unique moment in the narrative. The section must be quoted at length because, although Bert Williams is never named directly, the silence surrounding his absence is not only enough to strongly suggest him: it is entirely appropriate considering his world-famous persona of "Nobody":

> The dancing stopped. . . . A brief interval and a dwarfish, shiny black man wearing a red-brown suit, with kinks straightened and severely plastered down in the Afro-American manner, walked into the center of the floor and began singing. He had a massive mouth, which he opened wide, and a profoundly big and quite good voice came out of it.
>
> > "I'm so doggone fed up, I don't know what to do.
> > Can't find a pal that's constant, can't find a gal that's true.
> > But I ain't gwine to worry 'cause mah buddy was a ham;
> > Ain't giwine to cut mah throat 'cause mah gal ain't worf a damn.
> > Ise got the blues all ovah, the coal-black biting blues,
> > Like a prowling tom-cat that's got the low-down mews.
> >
> > "I'm gwine to lay me in a good supply a gin,
> > Foh gunning is a crime, but drinking ain't no sin.
> > I won't do a crazy deed 'cause of a two-faced pal,
> > Ain't gwineta break mah heart ovah a no-'count gal
> > Ise got the blues all ovah, the coal-black biting blues,
> > Like a prowling tom-cat that's got the low-down
> > mews."
>
> There was something of the melancholy charm of Tchaikovsky in the melody. The black singer made much of the triumphant note of strength that reigned over the sad motive. When he sang, "I ain't gwine to cut mah

throat," "Ain't gwine to break mah heart," his face became grim and full of will as a bull-dog's.

He conquered his audience and at the finish he was greeted with warm applause and a shower of silver coins ringing on the tiled pavement. An enthusiastic white man waved a dollar note at the singer and, to show that Negroes could do just as good or better, Maunie Whitewing's sleek escort imitated the gesture with a two-dollar note. That started off the singer again.

"Ain't gwine to cut mah throat . . .
Ain't gwine to break mah heart . . ."

"That zigaboo is a singing fool," remarked Jake.[67]

Bert Williams? Well, for one thing, Williams could never be described as "dwarfish," though while in character he never stood up straight, perfecting the self-humiliating hunch that black men were supposed to maintain in the presence of whites. But Claude McKay never met Bert Williams and there is no record of him having ever seen the comedian perform, though it is entirely possible and perhaps likely. "Dwarfish" says much more about Williams's persona and his memory than his actual physique or material presence. The phrase "kinks straightened and severely plastered down in the Afro-American manner" is telling, though, since it comes from a West Indian writer and from a novel that details the differences in style, language, and attitude between African Americans and Afro-Caribbeans in Harlem. The "Afro-American manner" emphasizes that this performer has perfected the symbolic and stereotypical style-codes of the American Negro, which, because it is culturally specified, no longer stands as a universal representation of "the Negro." Because this "shiny black man" is described as being in the moment of performance, the figure cut onstage is the image of a mask in motion, of categories in crisis—it no longer functions as even a sign of any sort of "Negro," hence McKay's statement fifteen pages later about the blindness of white spectatorship: "They see the grin only." They hear only through the "massive mouth" of an age-old mask cleverly wrought so as to often blind the performer's own community. McKay's concern is primarily with that rootless space of negotiation, negation, and reversal that exists behind the mask. What is silent and invisible in his view are the layers of meanings that exist prior to the grin itself and prior to the gestures of comic self-annihilation.

Bert Williams? Well, the performance of this nameless comedian is directly based on the shtick that Bert Williams invented, perfected, and canonized. There is no mention of the performer in *Home to Harlem* wearing burnt cork, yet it is no doubt a performance that exists deep within the traditions and conventions of minstrelsy. But one should be permitted to imagine this event as occurring at one of those after-parties, juke joints, shebeens, or—as they once called them in Caribbean London—blues dances or *blues*. These "underworld" black cultural institutions are where celebrated black performers momentarily leave their white success and perform "hardcore" or "down home style" or just freely without the pressure of "crossover" in an intimate all- or primarily black session. Even without mention of a mask, the "massive mouth" and the sad expression and the context convey the image and the icon of the black minstrel Bert Williams, even if it is not or could not actually be Williams. After all, the reader is consistently told that Bert Williams both was and is a presence and that he would be appearing at this very party that Jake is now attending. The song performed here could literally be one of the dozens that Bert Williams recorded over his career, up to February 24, 1922, when he recorded "Not Lately" for Columbia. Again, 1922 was the year in which Claude McKay's *Harlem Shadows* was published. The very next day Williams collapsed onstage in blackface while starring in *Under the Bamboo Tree*. The following month he was dead of pneumonia.

McKay's reading of this mysterious performance in *Home to Harlem* is based on a reading of the minstrel mask that is overdetermined by the presence of Bert Williams both in early-twentieth-century Harlem and in the novel itself. In discussing the performance McKay acknowledges its determination, strength, and grace, fully aware that it can be and has easily been eclipsed by the racism of white viewers or the emergent self-consciousness of African American bourgeois nationalism. It would take McKay's generation to begin daring to tease, celebrate, and problematize the historical fissures between black communities in Harlem. In order to fashion a sense of community not built on intra-racial, cultural hierarchies, or the bichromatic longings of white power and African American resistance, it is more than appropriate to read *Home to Harlem* as in part homage to Bert Williams. In this performance that signals the end of the novel, we are witness to something that could not have happened in Williams's lifetime. From underneath the dour and tragic mask-beneath-a-mask, by way of McKay's kaleidoscopic refraction of its plural meanings, it is now possible to imagine if not hear the wry sound of a certain Caribbean spider.

NOTES

Introduction

1 Allen G. Debus, "Bert Williams on Stage."

1. *Black Minstrel, Black Modernism*

1 Bert Williams, "Comic Side of Trouble," 61.
2 Eric Ledell Smith, *Bert Williams*, 147.
3 James Weldon Johnson, *Black Manhattan*, 109.
4 Allen Woll, *Black Musical Theatre*, xiii.
5 Ethan Mordden, *Broadway Babies*, 30.
6 Ann Douglas, *Terrible Honesty*, 77.
7 Williams, "Comic Side of Trouble," 60.
8 Ibid.
9 Ibid., 33.
10 George Walker, "The Negro on the American Stage," 247.
11 Smith, *Bert Williams*, 107.
12 Ibid., 167.
13 Blanche Ferguson, "Black Skin, Black Mask," 16.

14 Booker T. Washington, "Bert Williams," 316.

15 Nick Tosches, *Where Dead Voices Gather*, 176.

16 Walker, "Negro on the American Stage," 247.

17 Ibid., 245.

18 Williams, "Comic Side of Trouble," 60.

19 Mabel Rowland, ed., *Bert Williams—Son of Laughter*, 44.

20 Ann Charters, *Nobody*, 19.

21 Smith, *Bert Williams*, 102.

22 Zora Neale Hurston, "Characteristics of Negro Expression," 24.

23 Johnson, *Black Manhattan*, 89.

24 Walker, "Negro on the American Stage," 248.

25 Ellison, *Shadow and Act*, 47.

26 Michael Rogin, *Blackface, White Noise*, 14.

27 Walker, "Negro on the American Stage," 248.

28 Smith, *Bert Williams*, 101.

29 Alain Locke, ed., *The New Negro*, 4.

30 Frantz Fanon, *Black Skin, White Masks*, 14.

31 Alison Donnell and Sarah Lawson Welsh, eds., *The Routledge Reader in Caribbean Literature*, 85.

32 Wilson Harris, *Selected Essays of Wilson Harris*, 184.

33 Smith, *Bert Williams*, 132.

34 Wilson Harris, "Carnival Theatre: A Personal View," in *Masquerading*, 42.

35 Fanon, *Black Skin, White Masks*, 8.

36 Smith, *Bert Williams*, 82.

37 George Lamming, *Pleasures of Exile*, 166.

38 Douglas, *Terrible Honesty*, 75.

39 Ibid., 76.

40 Smith, *Bert Williams*, 89.

41 Ibid., 78.

42 Ibid., 117.

43 Charters, *Nobody*, 18.

44 Rogin, *Blackface, White Noise*, 43.

45 Smith, *Bert Williams*, 132.

46 Douglas, *Terrible Honesty*, 328.

47 Mordden, *Broadway Babies*, 30.

48 Eric Lott, *Love and Theft*, 25.

49 Ibid., 234.

50 Marjorie Garber, *Vested Interests*, 66.

51 Richard D. E. Burton, *Afro-Creole*, 59.

52 W. E. B. Du Bois, "The Contribution of the Negro to American Life and Culture," in *Writings by W. E. B. Du Bois in Periodicals*, 150.

53 Louis J. Parascandola, ed., *"Winds Can Wake Up the Dead,"* 65.

54 Ibid., 64.

55 Harold Cruse, *Crisis of the Negro Intellectual*, 121.

56 Charters, *Nobody*, 128.

57 Ibid.

58 Gilles Deleuze and Felix Guattari, *Kafka*, 9–10.

59 Wilson Harris, *Womb of Space*, 147.

2. *Migrations of a Mask*

  1 Washington, "Bert Williams," 389–90.

  2 Locke, *New Negro*, 7.

  3 Washington, *Papers*, 391.

  4 Charters, *Nobody*, 134.

  5 Ibid.

  6 Frank C. Taylor and Gerald Cook. *Alberta Hunter*, 33–34.

  7 Charters, *Nobody*, 17.

  8 Ibid., 19.

  9 Ibid., 139.

 10 Deleuze and Guattari, *Kafka*, 19.

 11 Ibid., 18.

 12 Harris, *Womb of Space*, 110.

 13 Rowland, *Bert Williams—Son of Laughter*, 112.

 14 Janet Brown, "The 'Coon-Singer' and the 'Coon-Song,' " 5.

 15 Williams, "Comic Side of Trouble," 33.

 16 Jessie Fauset, "Symbolism of Bert Williams," 255.

 17 Jessie Fauset, "The Gift of Laughter," 163–64.

 18 Fauset, "Symbolism of Bert Williams," 256.

 19 J. A. Rogers, *World's Great Men of Color*, vol. 2, 373.

 20 Rowland, *Bert Williams—Son of Laughter*, 9.

 21 Channing Pollack, "Harvest of My Years," quoted in Smith, *Bert Williams*, 157.

 22 Williams, "Comic Side of Trouble," 60.

 23 Rowland, *Bert Williams—Son of Laughter*, 13–14.

 24 Locke, *New Negro*, 14.

 25 W. E. B. Du Bois, *Souls of Black Folk*, 45–46.

 26 Claude McKay, *Long Way from Home*, 350.

 27 J. E. Casely Hayford, *Ethiopia Unbound*, 163.

 28 Ibid., 180.

 29 Ibid., 182.

 30 Gerald Early, ed., *Lure and Loathing*, xix.

 31 Paul Gilroy, *The Black Atlantic*, 120.

 32 Locke, *New Negro*, 14.

 33 Ibid., 15.

34 Du Bois, *Writings by W. E. B. Du Bois in Periodicals*, 173.

35 Woll, *Black Musical Theatre*, 32.

36 Locke, *New Negro*, 5.

37 Ibid., 3.

38 Ibid., 4.

39 Ibid., 3, 47.

40 Ibid., 48.

41 Johnson, *Black Manhattan*, 42.

42 Ibid., 4.

43 Du Bois, *Souls of Black Folk*, 223.

44 Johnson, *Black Manhattan*, 35–36.

45 Locke, *New Negro*, 164.

46 Johnson, *Black Manhattan*, 35.

47 Charters, *Nobody*, 38.

48 Houston A. Baker Jr., *Modernism and the Harlem Renaissance*, 39.

49 Du Bois, *Souls of Black Folk*, 45. Italics added.

50 Ibid.

51 Michael Taussig, *Mimesis and Alterity*, 237.

52 Locke, *New Negro*, 22.

53 Ibid., 38.

54 Baker, *Modernism and the Harlem Renaissance*, 37.

55 Ibid., 15.

56 Ibid., 25.

57 Ibid., 27.

58 Washington, "Bert Williams," 391.

59 Baker, *Modernism and the Harlem Renaissance*, 33.

60 Smith, *Bert Williams*, 18.

61 Williams, "Comic Side of Trouble," 58, 60.

62 Baker, *Modernism and the Harlem Renaissance*, 17.

63 Fanon, *Black Skin, White Masks*, 14.

64 Nathan Irvin Huggins, ed., *Voices from the Harlem Renaissance*, 264.

65 Ibid., 251.

66 Rogin, *Blackface, White Noise*, 49.

67 Michael North, *The Dialect of Modernism*.

68 Washington, "Bert Williams," 389.

69 Ibid., 391.

70 Rowland, *Bert Williams—Son of Laughter*, 217–18.

71 Smith, *Bert Williams*, 110.

72 Washington, *Papers*, 388.

73 Ibid., 391.

74 Ibid., 389.

75 Ibid., 388.

76 Smith, *Bert Williams*, 146.

77 William J. Mahar, "Ethiopian Skits and Sketches," 180.

78 Ellison, *Shadow and Act*, 48.

79 Harris, "Carnival Theatre," in *Selected Essays of Wilson Harris*, 40.

80 Ellison, *Shadow and Act*, 53.

81 Ibid., 47–48.

82 Smith, *Bert Williams*, 146.

83 Ibid.

84 Homi Bhabha, *The Location of Culture*, 85.

85 Ellison, *Shadow and Act*, 55.

86 Ibid.

3. *Black-on-Black Cross-Culturality*

1 Ralph Ellison, "On Bird, Bird-Watching, and Jazz," in *Shadow and Act*.

 2 Annabelle Melzer, *Latest Rage the Big Drum*, 70.

 3 Baker, *Modernism and the Harlem Renaissance*, 50.

 4 Ibid.

 5 Ibid., 51.

 6 Du Bois, *Souls of Black Folk*, 45.

 7 Tony Martin, ed., *African Fundamentalism*.

 8 W. E. B. Du Bois, "The Hands of Ethiopia," in *Writings*, 948.

 9 Marcus Garvey, *The Philosophy and Opinions of Marcus Garvey*, 310.

10 Ibid., 311.

11 Du Bois, *Writings by W. E. B. Du Bois in Periodicals*, 173.

12 Garvey, *Philosophy*, 310.

13 Robert Hill, "Making Noise," 198.

14 George Schuyler, *Black Empire*, 274.

15 Claude McKay, *Harlem*, 152.

16 Ibid., 143.

17 Schuyler, *Black Empire*, 274.

18 McKay, *Harlem*, 132.

19 Parascandola, "Winds Can Wake Up the Dead," 123.

20 Ibid., 110.

21 Amy Jacques Garvey, *Garvey and Garveyism*, 79–80.

22 Garvey, *Philosophy*, 311.

23 Robert Hill, "Making Noise," 184.

24 Ibid., 185.

25 Ibid., 198.

26 Scott McLemee, ed., *C. L. R. James on the "Negro Question,"* 115.

27 Du Bois, *Writings by W. E. B. Du Bois in Periodicals*, 174.

28 Du Bois, *Writings*, 1167.

29 Ibid., 1168.

30 Ibid., 992.

31 Winston James, *Holding Aloft the Banner of Ethiopia*, 98.

32 Du Bois, *Writings by W. E. B. Du Bois in Periodicals*, 175.

33 Edouard Glissant, *Caribbean Discourse*, 24.

34 Ibid., 26.

35 W. A. Domingo, "Gift of the Black Tropics," 344.

36 Irma Watkins-Owens, *Blood Relations*, 81.

37 Ibid., 29.

38 McKay, *Harlem*, 135.

39 Locke, *New Negro*, 348.

40 Robert Hill, "Making Noise," 199.

41 Bill Brown, *The Material Unconscious*, 212.

42 Ibid.

43 Eric J. Sundquist, *To Wake the Nations*, 291.

44 Rogin, *Blackface, White Noise*, 4.

45 Ibid., 56.

46 Ibid., 43–44.

47 Huggins, *Voices from the Harlem Renaissance*, 309.

48 Ibid., 308.

49 Heather Hathaway, *Caribbean Waves*, 4.

50 Aubrey Bonnett, "West Indians in the United States of America," 157.

51 Ibid., 158.

52 Ibid., 156.

53 Ibid., 153.

54 Mikhail Bakhtin, *The Dialogic Imagination*, 185–86.

55 Locke, *New Negro*, 3.

56 Thorstein Veblen, *The Theory of the Leisure Class*.

57 Henry Louis Gates Jr., *Figures in Black*, 20.

58 Henry Louis Gates Jr., *Signifying Monkey*, 55.

59 Teshome H. Gabriel, "Toward a Critical Theory of Third World Films" and "Third Cinema as Guardian of Popular Memory"; Bhabha, "The Commitment to Theory," in *The Location of Culture*.

60 Darlene Clark Hine, "In the Kingdom of Culture," 338.

61 Gates, *Figures in Black*, 51.

62 Ibid., 42.

63 Ibid., 20.

64 Ibid., 5.

65 Rogin, *Blackface, White Noise*, 43.

66 Parascandola, "Winds Can Wake Up the Dead," 65.

67 Ibid.

68 Edward Kamau Brathwaite, *History of the Voice*, 81.

69 Patrick Taylor, *The Narrative of Liberation*, 146.

4. The Global Economy of Minstrelsy

1 Locke, *New Negro*, 7.

2 Sidney W. Mintz and Richard Price, *The Birth of African-American Culture*, 18.

3 Paul Edwards, ed., *Equiano's Travels*, xii.

4 Olaudah Equiano, *The Interesting Narrative*, 237.

5 Ibid., 238

6 Ibid., 5.

7 Ibid.

8 Brent Hayes Edwards, *The Practice of Diaspora*, 99.

9 Many of Van Der Zee's photos are reproduced in *Harlem on My Mind*, ed. Allon Schoener.

10 McKay, *Harlem*, 168.

11 Ibid., 169.

12 Ibid.

13 Ibid.

14 Ibid.

15 Bernth Lindfors, ed., *Africans on Stage*.

16 Ibid., 259.

17 Charters, *Nobody*, 76.

18 Bernth Lindfors, "Ethnological Show Business," 215.

19 Ibid., 216.

20 Ibid.

21 Ibid.

22 Anne McClintock, "Soft-Soaping Empire: Commodity Racism and Imperial Advertising," in *Imperial Leather*, 207–31; Curtis Hinsley, "The World as Marketplace," 344–65.

23 Lindfors, "Ethnological Show Business," 216.

24 Ibid.

25 Ibid., ix.

26 Ibid., 217.

27 David Killingray and Willie Henderson, "Bata Kindai Amgoza Ibn LoBagola," 259.

28 Lindfors, "Ethnological Show Business," 217.

29 Ibid., 258.

30 Makonnen, *Pan-Africanism from Within*, 62.

31 Ellison, *Invisible Man*, 488.

32 Ibid., 487.

33 Ibid., 484.

34 Ibid., 499.

35 Ibid., 498–99.

36 Killingray and Henderson, "Bata Kindai Amgoza Ibn LoBagola," 236.

37 Locke, *New Negro*, 342.

38 Parascandola, *"Winds Can Wake Up the Dead,"* 92.

39 Douglas, *Terrible Honesty*, 457.

40 Parascandola, *"Winds Can Wake Up the Dead,"* 118.

41 Ibid., 281.

42 Ibid.

43 Rosemary Garland Thomson, ed., *Freakery*, 207.

44 Bill Brown, *The Material Unconscious*.

45 LoBagola, *An African Savage's Own Story*, 17.

46 Ibid., 45.

47 Ibid., 48.

48 Ibid., 47.

49 Ibid.

50 Equiano, *The Interesting Narrative*, 1.

51 Ibid., 37.

52 Ibid., 34.

53 Ibid., 82.

54 Du Bois, *Souls of Black Folk*, 224.

55 LoBagola, *An African Savage's Own Story*, 49.

56 Ibid.

57 Ibid., 228.

58 Ibid., 240.

59 Ibid., 242–43.

60 Ibid., 240.

61 Ibid., 242.

62 Killingray and Henderson, "Bata Kindai Amgoza Ibn LoBagola," 231.

63 Ibid.

64 Hinsley, "The World as Marketplace," 359.

65 Shane Peacock, "Africa Meets the Great Farini," 93.

66 Ibid., 94.

67 Ibid., 89.

68 Killingray and Henderson, "Bata Kindai Amgoza Ibn LoBagola," 240.

69 LoBagola, *An African Savage's Own Story*, 238.

70 Ibid., 237.

71 Ibid., 258.

72 Ibid., 239.

73 Ibid., 238.

74 Ibid., 79.

75 Ibid., 85.

76 Ibid., 59.

77 Ibid., 235.

78 Ibid., introduction, 9.

79 Ibid.

80 Ibid., 12.

81 Ibid., 13.

82 Killingray and Henderson, "Bata Kindai Amgoza Ibn LoBagola," 253.

83 Ibid., 255–56.

84 Smith, *Bert Williams*, 4.

85 Garber, *Vested Interests*, 67.

86 Veit Erlmann, " 'Spectatorial Lust,' " 121.

87 Edmund John Collins, "Jazz Feedback," 181.

88 Tosches, *Where Dead Voices Gather*, 35.

89 Collins, "Jazz Feedback," 180.

90 Ibid.

91 Ibid., 183.

92 Donald R. Hill, *Calypso Callaloo*, 157.

93 Hollis Liverpool, "Chalkdust," 267.

94 Baker, *Modernism and the Harlem Renaissance*, 18.

95 Liverpool, "Chalkdust," 411.

96 Ibid.

97 Glissant, *Caribbean Discourse*, 242.

98 Reinard W. Sander, ed., *From Trinidad*, 7.

99 Ibid., 28.

100 Hazel V. Carby, *Cultures in Babylon*, 135–45.

101 C. L. R. James, *Beyond a Boundary*, 25–26.

102 Derek Walcott, *What the Twilight Says*, 34–35.

103 Sander, *From Trinidad*, 31.

104 Walcott, *What the Twilight Says*, 8.

105 Raymond Quevedo [Attila the Hun], *Atilla's Kaiso*, 53.

106 Gordon Rohlehr, *Calypso and Society*, 393.

107 Donald R. Hill, *Calypso Callaloo*, 157.

108 Ibid.

109 Watkins-Owens, *Blood Relations*, 155.

110 Roaring Lion, *Calypso*, 77.

111 Ibid., 26.

112 Ibid., 27.

113 Ibid., 28.

114 Rohlehr, *Calypso and Society*, 101–2.

115 Ibid., 79.

116 Watkins-Owens, *Blood Relations*, 155.

117 Ibid.

118 Errol Hill, *Jamaican Stage*, 103.

119 Ibid., 268.

120 Robert Hill, "Dread History."

121 Errol Hill, *Jamaican Stage*, 268.

122 Ibid., 269.

123 Thomas Carlyle and John Stuart Mill, *"The Nigger Question"* and *"The Negro Question."*

5. In Dahomey

1 Peacock, "Africa Meets the Great Farini," 363.
2 Hazel Carby, *Reconstructing Womanhood*, 5.
3 Ibid.
4 Lindfors, *Africans on Stage*, 142.
5 Sundquist, *To Wake the Nations*, 292.
6 Lindfors, *Africans on Stage*, 142.
7 Ibid.
8 Ibid., 135–36.
9 Carby, *Reconstructing Womanhood*, 5.
10 Charters, *Nobody*, 25.
11 Lindfors, *Africans on Stage*, 135.
12 Ibid., 136.
13 Robert W. Rydell, "Darkest Africa," 135.
14 Sally Duensing, "Artifacts and Artifictions."
15 Rydell, "Darkest Africa," 144.
16 Walker, "Negro on the American Stage," 247.
17 Ibid., 247–48.
18 Smith, *Bert Williams*, 51.
19 Ibid., 50.
20 Ibid., 62.
21 Ibid., 53.
22 Ibid., 69.
23 Charters, *Nobody*, 69–70.
24 Smith, *Bert Williams*, 15.
25 Williams, "Comic Side of Trouble," 33.
26 Ibid.
27 Ibid.
28 Charters, *Nobody*, 105.
29 Smith, *Bert Williams*, 51.
30 Rowland, *Bert Williams—Son of Laughter*, 45.
31 Charters, *Nobody*, 69.
32 Sundquist, *To Wake the Nations*, 291.
33 Smith, *Bert Williams*, 54.
34 Sundquist, *To Wake the Nations*, 580.
35 Steven Watson, *The Harlem Renaissance*, 98.
36 Smith, *Bert Williams*, 45.
37 Leonard E. Barrett, *The Rastafarians*, 96.
38 Smith, *Bert Williams*, 59.
39 Ibid., 51.
40 Maud Cuney Hare, *Negro Musicians and Their Music*, 160.

41 Walker, "Negro on the American Stage," 248.

42 Sundquist, *To Wake the Nations*, 292.

43 Charters, *Nobody*, 74–76.

44 Smith, *Bert Williams*, 55.

45 Ibid.

46 Jesse A. Shipp, Paul Laurence Dunbar, and Will Marion Cook, "Leader of the Colored Aristocracy," in *In Dahomey*.

47 Cedric J. Robinson, "W. E. B. Du Bois and Black Sovereignty," 145–46.

48 Ibid., 145.

49 Du Bois, "Hands of Ethiopia," in *Writings*, 948.

50 Robinson, "W. E. B. Du Bois," 151–52.

51 Shipp, Dunbar, and Cook, "Leader of the Colored Aristocracy."

52 Shipp, Dunbar, and Cook, "My Dahomean Queen," in *In Dahomey*, 18–19.

53 Garvey, *Philosophy*, 68; Du Bois, "Hands of Ethiopia," in *Writings*, 947.

54 Shipp, Dunbar, and Cook, "On Broadway in Dahomey Bye and Bye," in *In Dahomey*, 43–44.

55 Ibid., 50.

56 Ibid., 44.

57 Ibid., 44–45.

58 Ibid., 46.

59 Woll, *Black Musical Theatre*, 38.

60 Shipp, Dunbar, and Cook, "On Broadway in Dahomey Bye and Bye," 47–48.

61 Ibid., 49.

62 Shipp, Dunbar, and Cook, "Leader of the Colored Aristocracy," 49.

63 Ibid.

64 Ibid.

65 Ibid.

66 Carby, *Reconstructing Womanhood*, 25.

67 Carolyn Cooper, *Noises in the Blood*, 66.

68 Carby, *Reconstructing Womanhood*, 32.

69 Annemarie Bean, James V. Hatch, and Brooks McNamara, eds., *Inside the Minstrel Mask*, 182.

70 Ibid., 181.

71 Shipp, Dunbar, and Cook, "On Emancipation Day," in *In Dahomey*, 102–3.

72 Judith Butler, *Gender Trouble*, 19.

73 David Krassner, "Black Salome," 199.

74 Du Bois, *Souls of Black Folk*, 50.

75 Krassner, "Black Salome," 199.

76 Ibid.

77 Ibid., 198.

78 Shipp, Dunbar, and Cook, "Leader of the Colored Aristocracy."

79 Ibid.

80 Ibid.
81 Ibid.
82 Ibid.
83 Ibid.

6. Claude McKay's Calypso

1   Federico García Lorca, "The King of Harlem," Selected Poems of Federico García Lorca, 123, 115, 123.
2   Ibid., 121.
3   Domingo, "Gift of the Black Tropics," 341.
4   Tosches, Where Dead Voices Gather, 11.
5   Patti Capel Swartz, "Masks and Masquerade," 376.
6   Ibid.
7   McKay, Long Way from Home, 142.
8   Ibid., 141.
9   Ibid., 145.
10 Claude McKay, Home to Harlem, 337.
11 Claude McKay, My Green Hills of Jamaica, 80.
12 Ibid.
13 McKay, Home to Harlem, 290.
14 Robert A. Russ, " 'There's No Place Like Home," 355.
15 Ibid., 357.
16 Ibid., 356.
17 Harris, "Carnival Theatre," in Selected Essays of Wilson Harris, 42.
18 McKay, Home to Harlem, xii.
19 Brathwaite, History of the Voice, 20.
20 Deleuze and Guattari, Kafka, 19.
21 Claude McKay, Banjo, 14.
22 Quevedo, "No Nationality," 140.
23 Ibid., 140–41.
24 Wayne F. Cooper, Claude McKay, 349–50.
25 McKay, Long Way from Home, 4.
26 Claude McKay, Selected Poems of Claude McKay, 31.
27 A. Hinds, "West Indian Weed Woman."
28 McKay, My Green Hills of Jamaica, 19.
29 Ibid.
30 McKay, Home to Harlem, 291–92.
31 McKay, Long Way from Home, 8.
32 Ibid., 9.
33 Parascandola, "Winds Can Wake Up the Dead," 92.
34 Ibid., 65.

35 Domingo, "Gift of the Black Tropics," 341–42.

36 Rudolph Fisher, Joy and Pain, 26.

37 Domingo, "Gift of the Black Tropics," 343.

38 Fisher, Joy and Pain, 64.

39 Winston James, A Fierce Hatred of Injustice, 51.

40 McKay, Long Way from Home, 300.

41 Ibid.

42 Quevedo, Atilla's Kaiso, 141.

43 Cary D. Wintz, ed., Black Culture and the Harlem Renaissance, 45.

44 Hathaway, Caribbean Waves, 60.

45 Cruse, Crisis of the Negro Intellectual, 47.

46 McKay, Home to Harlem, 267.

47 Ibid., 96–97.

48 Ibid., 130.

49 Claude McKay, Harlem Shadows, xix.

50 McKay, Home to Harlem, 328.

51 Ibid., 134.

52 Ibid., 130–31.

53 Ibid., 131.

54 Ibid., 135.

55 Ibid., 134.

56 Ibid., 155.

57 Ibid., 154–55.

58 Gates, Signifying Monkey, xxii.

59 McKay, Banjo, 14.

60 Cooper, Claude McKay, 258.

61 Du Bois, "Marcus Garvey," in Writings, 977.

62 Cooper, Claude McKay, 242.

63 McKay, Home to Harlem, 67.

64 Ibid., 318.

65 Ibid., 319.

66 Ibid., 319–20.

67 Ibid., 322–23.

BIBLIOGRAPHY

Archer-Straw, Petrine. *Negrophilia: Avant-Garde Paris and Black Culture in the 1920s*. New York: Thames and Hudson, 2000.

Baker, Houston A. Jr. *Modernism and the Harlem Renaissance*. Chicago: University of Chicago Press, 1987.

Bakhtin, Mikhail. *The Dialogic Imagination*. Edited by Michael Holquist. Translated by Caryl Emerson and Michael Holquist. Austin: University of Texas Press, 1981.

Barnum, P. T. *Struggles and Triumphs*. Edited by Carl Bode. New York: Penguin Classics, 1981.

Barrett, Leonard E. Sr. *The Rastafarians: Sounds of Cultural Dissonance*. Boston: Beacon, 1977.

Bean, Annemarie. "Black Minstrelsy and Double Inversion." In *African American Performance and Theatre History: A Critical Reader*, edited by Harry J. Elam Jr. and David Krasner. New York: Oxford University Press, 2001.

Bean, Annemarie, James V. Hatch, and Brooks McNamara, eds. *Inside the Minstrel Mask: Readings in Nineteenth-Century Blackface Minstrelsy*. Hanover, N.H.: Wesleyan University Press, 1996.

Bhabha, Homi. *The Location of Culture*. London: Routledge, 1994.

Bogle, Donald. *Toms, Coons, Mulattoes, Mammies, and Bucks: An Interpretive History of Blacks in American Films*. New York: Continuum, 1989.

Bonnett, Aubrey. "West Indians in the United States of America: Some Theoretical and Practical Considerations." In *Emerging Perspectives on the Black Diaspora*, edited by Aubrey Bonnett and G. Llewellyn Watson. Lanham, Md.: University Press of America, 1990.

Bradbury, Malcolm, and James McFarlane, eds. *Modernism: A Guide to European Literature, 1890–1930*. London: Penguin, 1976.

Brathwaite, Edward Kamau. *History of the Voice: The Development of Nation Language in Anglophone Caribbean Poetry*. London: New Beacon, 1984.

Brown, Bill. *The Material Unconscious: American Amusement, Stephen Crane, and the Economies of Play*. Cambridge, Mass.: Harvard University Press, 1996.

Brown, Janet. "The 'Coon-Singer' and the 'Coon-Song': A Case Study of the Performer-Character Relationship." *Journal of American Culture* 7, nos. 1–2 (Spring–Summer 1984): 1–8.

Burton, Richard D. E. *Afro-Creole: Power, Opposition, and Play in the Caribbean*. Ithaca, N.Y.: Cornell University Press, 1997.

Butler, Judith. *Gender Trouble: Feminism and the Subversion of Identity*. New York: Routledge, Chapman, and Hall, 1990.

Calypso Pioneers: 1912–1937. Produced by Dick Spottswood and Donald Hill. Rounder Records, 1989.

Carby, Hazel V. *Cultures in Babylon: Black Britain and African America*. London: Verso, 1999.

——. *Reconstructing Womanhood: The Emergence of the Afro-American Woman Novelist*. New York: Oxford University Press, 1987.

Caretta, Vincent, ed. *Unchained Voices: An Anthology of Black Authors in the English-Speaking World of the Eighteenth Century*. Lexington: University Press of Kentucky, 1996.

Carlyle, Thomas, and John Stuart Mill. *"The Nigger Question" and "The Negro Question."* Edited by Eugene R. August. New York: Meredith, 1971.

Casely Hayford, J. E. *Ethiopia Unbound: Studies in Race Emancipation*. London: Africana Modern Library #8 / Frank Cass, 1969.

Charters, Ann. *Nobody: The Story of Bert Williams*. London: Macmillan, 1970.

Chaudhan, P. S. "Rereading Claude McKay." In *The Harlem Renaissance 1920–1940: Analysis and Assessment, 1980–1994*, edited by Cary D. Wintz. New York: Garland, 1996.

Clarke, John Henrik, with Amy Jacques Garvey, eds. *Marcus Garvey and the Vision of Africa*. New York: Vintage, 1974.

Collins, Edmund John. "Jazz Feedback to Africa." *American Music* 5 (Summer 1987): 177–92.

Cooper, Carolyn. *Noises in the Blood: Orality, Gender, and the "Vulgar" Body of Jamaican Popular Culture*. Durham, N.C.: Duke University Press, 1995.

Cooper, Wayne F. *Claude McKay: Rebel Sojourner in the Harlem Renaissance*. New York: Schocken, 1987.

——. *The Passion of Claude McKay: Selected Poetry and Prose, 1912–1948*. New York: Schocken, 1973.

Cowley, John. *Carnival, Canboulay, and Calypso: Traditions in the Making*. Cambridge: Cambridge University Press, 1996.

Cripps, Thomas. *Slow Fade to Black: The Negro in American Film, 1900–1942*. New York: Oxford University Press, 1977.

Crowley, Tony. *Standard English and the Politics of the English Language*. Urbana: University of Illinois Press, 1989.

Cruse, Harold. *The Crisis of the Negro Intellectual: A Historical Analysis of the Failure of Black Leadership*. New York: Quill, 1984.

Dash, J. Michael. *The Other America: Caribbean Literature in a New World Context*. Charlottesville: University Press of Virginia, 1998.

Davis, Angela. *Blues Legacies and Black Feminism*. New York: Pantheon, 1998.

Debus, Allen G. "Bert Williams on Stage: Ziegfeld and Beyond." Pamphlet. *Bert Williams: The Middle Years, 1910–1918*. Archeophone Records 5003, 2002.

Debus, Allen G., and Richard Martin. "The Incomparable Bert Williams: The Williams and Walker Years." Pamphlet. *Bert Williams: The Early Years, 1901–1909*. Archeophone Records 5004, 2004.

Deleuze, Gilles, and Félix Guattari. *Kafka: Toward a Minor Literature*. Edited by Dana Polan. Minneapolis: University of Minnesota Press, 1986.

Domingo, W. A. "Gift of the Black Tropics." In *The New Negro: Voices of the Harlem Renaissance*. New York: Atheneum, 1992.

Donnell, Alison, and Sarah Lawson Welsh, eds. *The Routledge Reader in Caribbean Literature*. London: Routledge, 1996.

Douglas, Ann. *Terrible Honesty: Mongrel Manhattan in the 1920s*. New York: Farrar, Straus and Giroux, 1995.

Du Bois, W. E. B. *The Souls of Black Folk*. New York: Signet Classics, 1982.

——. *Writings*. New York: Literary Classics of the United States, 1986.

——. *Writings by W. E. B. Du Bois in Periodicals Edited by Others, Volume 2, 1910–1934*. Edited by Herbert Aptheker. Millwood, N.Y.: Kraus-Thomson, 1982.

Duensing, Sally. "Artifacts and Artifictions." In *Presence of Mind: Museums and the Spirit of Learning*, edited by Bonnie Pitman. Washington: American Association of Museums, 1999.

Early, Gerald, ed. *Lure and Loathing: Essays on Race, Identity, and the Ambivalence of Assimilation*. New York: Penguin, 1994.

Edmondson, Belinda. *Making Men: Gender, Literary Authority, and Women's Writing in Caribbean Narrative*. Durham, N.C.: Duke University Press, 1999.

Edwards, Brent Hayes. *The Practice of Diaspora: Literature, Translation, and the Rise of Black Internationalism*. Cambridge, Mass.: Harvard University Press, 2003.

Edwards, Paul, ed. *Equiano's Travels*. Oxford: Heinemann, 1967.

Ellison, Ralph. "Change the Joke and Slip the Yoke." In *Shadow and Act*. New York: Vintage, 1972.

——. *Invisible Man*. New York: Vintage, 1972.

——. *Shadow and Act*. New York: Vintage, 1972.

Equiano, Olaudah. *The Interesting Narrative and Other Writings*. Edited by Vincent Caretta. New York: Penguin, 1995.

Erlmann, Veit. " 'Spectatorial Lust.' " In *Africans on Stage: Studies in Ethnological Show Business*, edited by Bernth Lindfors. Bloomington: Indiana University Press, 1999.

Fanon, Frantz. *Black Skin, White Masks*. Translated by Charles Lam Markmann. New York: Grove, 1967.

Fauset, Jessie. "The Gift of Laughter." In *The New Negro: Voices of the Harlem Renaissance*, edited by Alain Locke. New York: Atheneum, 1992.

——. "The Symbolism of Bert Williams." In *The Crisis Reader*, edited by Sondra Kathryn Wilson. New York: Random House/Modern Library, 1999.

Ferguson, Blanche. "Black Skin, Black Mask: The Inconvenient Grace of Bert Williams." *American Visions: The Magazine of Afro-American Culture* 7, no. 3 (June–July 1992): 14–18.

Fisher, Rudolph. *Joy and Pain*. London: X Press, 1996.

Foner, Nancy, ed. *The New Immigrants in New York*. New York: Columbia University Press, 1987.

Gabriel, Teshome. "Toward a Critical Theory of Third World Films" and "Third Cinema as Guardian of Popular Memory: Towards a Third Aesthetics." In *Questions of a Third Cinema*, edited by Jim Pines and Paul Willemann. London: British Film Institute, 1989.

Garber, Marjorie. *Vested Interests: Cross-Dressing and Cultural Anxiety*. New York: Routledge, 1997.

García Lorca, Federico. *The Selected Poems of Federico García Lorca*. Edited by Francisco Garcia Lorca and Donald M. Allen. New York: New Directions, 1955.

Garvey, Amy Jacques. *Garvey and Garveyism*. New York: Collier/Macmillan, 1970.

Garvey, Marcus. *The Philosophy and Opinions of Marcus Garvey; or, Africa for the Africans*. Edited by Amy Jacques Garvey. Dover, Mass.: Majority, 1986.

Gates, Henry Louis, Jr. *Figures in Black: Words, Signs, and the "Racial" Self*. New York: Oxford University Press, 1987.

——. *The Signifying Monkey: A Theory of African-American Literary Criticism*. New York: Oxford University Press, 1988.

Gates, Henry Louis, Jr., and Nellie Y. McKay, eds. *The Norton Anthology of African American Literature*. New York: Norton, 1997.

Gikandi, Simon. *Writing in Limbo: Modernism and Caribbean Literature*. Ithaca, N.Y.: Cornell University Press, 1992.

Giles, James R. *Claude McKay*. Boston: Twayne, 1976.

Gilroy, Paul. *The Black Atlantic: Modernity and Double Consciousness*. Cambridge, Mass.: Harvard University Press, 1993.

Glissant, Edouard. *Caribbean Discourse: Selected Essays*. Charlottesville: University Press of Virginia, 1992.

Griffin, Farah Jasmine. *"Who Set You Flowin'?" The African American Migration Narrative*. New York: Oxford University Press, 1995.

Guattari, Félix, and Gilles Deleuze. *On the Line*. Translated by John Johnston. New York: Semiotext(e), 1983.

Hare, Maud Cuney. *Negro Musicians and Their Music*. New York: G. K. Hall, 1936.

Harlem on My Mind. Edited by Allon Schoener. New York: New Press, 1995.

Harris, Wilson. "Carnival Theatre: A Personal View." In *Masquerading: The Art of the Notting Hill Carnival*. Catalogue. London: Arts Council of Great Britain, 1986.

———. *Selected Essays of Wilson Harris: The Unfinished Genesis of the Imagination*. Edited by Andrew Bundy. London: Routledge, 1999.

———. *The Womb of Space: The Cross-Cultural Imagination*. London: Greenwood, 1983.

Hathaway, Heather. *Caribbean Waves: Relocating Claude McKay and Paule Marshall*. Bloomington: Indiana University Press, 1999.

Hill, Donald R. *Calypso Callaloo: Early Carnival Music in Trinidad*. Gainesville: University Press of Florida, 1993.

Hill, Errol. *The Jamaican Stage, 1655–1900: Profile of a Colonial Theatre*. Amherst: University of Massachusetts Press, 1992.

Hill, Robert. "Dread History: Leonard P. Howell and Millenarian Visions in Early Rastafarian Jamaica." *Epoche: Journal of the History of Religions at UCLA* 9 (1981): 30–71.

———. "Making Noise: Marcus Garvey Dada, August 1922." In *Picturing Us: African American Identity in Photography*, edited by Deborah Willis. New York: New Press, 1994.

Hinds, A. "West Indian Weed Woman." In *Calypso Pioneers: 1912–1937*, produced by Dick Spottswood and Donald Hill. Rounder Records, 1989.

Hine, Darlene Clark. "In the Kingdom of Culture." In *Lure and Loathing: Essays on Race, Identity, and the Ambivalence of Assimilation*, edited by Gerald Early, 337–51. New York: Penguin, 1994.

Hinsley, Curtis. "The World as Marketplace: Commodification of the Exotic at the World's Columbian Exposition, Chicago, 1893." In *Exhibiting Cultures: The Poetics and Politics of Museum Display*, edited by Ivan Karp and Steven D. Lavine, 344–65. Washington: Smithsonian Institution Press, 1991.

Holder, Calvin. "West Indian Immigrants in New York City 1900–1952: In Conflict with the Promised Land." In *Emerging Perspectives on the Black Diaspora*, edited by Aubrey Bonnett and G. Llewellyn Watson. Lanham, Md.: University Press of America, 1990.

Huggins, Nathan Irvin. *Harlem Renaissance*. New York: Oxford University Press, 1971.

———, ed. *Voices from the Harlem Renaissance*. New York: Oxford University Press, 1995.

Hughes, Langston. *The Big Sea*. New York: Hill and Wang, 1964.

Humphrey, Chris. *The Politics of Carnival: Festive Misrule in Medieval England*. Manchester: Manchester University Press, 2001.

Hurston, Zora Neale. "Characteristics of Negro Expression." In *Negro: An Anthology*, edited by Nancy Cunard. 1934. Reprint, New York: Frederick Ungar, 1970.

———. *The Sanctified Church*. New York: Marlowe, 1981.

Ikonné, Chidi. *From Du Bois to Van Vechten: The Early New Negro Literature, 1903–1926*. Westport, Conn.: Greenwood, 1981.

James, C. L. R. *Beyond a Boundary*. London: Stanley Paul, 1963.

James, Winston. *A Fierce Hatred of Injustice: Claude McKay's Jamaica and His Poetry of Rebellion*. London: Verso, 2000.

——. *Holding Aloft the Banner of Ethiopia: Caribbean Radicalism in Early Twentieth-Century America*. London: Verso, 1998.

Johnson, James Weldon. *Black Manhattan*. New York: Knopf, 1930.

Karp, Ivan, and Steven D. Lavine, eds. *Exhibiting Cultures: The Poetics and Politics of Museum Display*. Washington: Smithsonian Institution Press, 1991.

Killingray, David, and Willie Henderson. "Bata Kindai Amgoza Ibn LoBagola and the Making of An *African Savage's Own Story*." In *Africans on Stage: Studies in Ethnological Show Business*, edited by Bernth Lindfors, 228–65. Bloomington: Indiana University Press, 1999.

Kramer, Victor A., and Robert A. Russ, eds. *Harlem Renaissance Re-examined: A Revised and Expanded Edition*. New York: Whitson, 1997.

Krassner, David. "Black Salome: Exoticism, Dance and Racial Myths." In *African American Performance and Theatre History: A Critical Reader*, edited by Harry J. Elam Jr. and David Krassner. New York: Oxford University Press, 2001.

Lamming, George. *The Pleasures of Exile*. Ann Arbor: University of Michigan Press, 1960.

Lemelle, Sidney, and Robin D. G. Kelley, eds. *Imagining Home: Class, Culture, and Nationalism in the African Diaspora*. London: Verso, 1994.

Levering-Lewis, David. *When Harlem Was in Vogue*. New York: Oxford University Press, 1989.

Lhamon, W. T., Jr. *Raising Cain: Blackface Performance from Jim Crow to Hip Hop*. Cambridge, Mass.: Harvard University Press, 1998.

Lindfors, Bernth. "Ethnological Show Business: Footlighting the Dark Continent." In *Freakery: Cultural Spectacles of the Extraordinary Body*, edited by Rosemarie Garland Thomson. New York: New York University Press, 1996.

—— ed. *Africans on Stage: Studies in Ethnological Show Business*. Bloomington: Indiana University Press, 1999.

Liverpool, Hollis. "Chalkdust." *Rituals of Power and Rebellion: The Carnival Tradition in Trinidad and Tobago, 1763–1962*. Chicago: Research Associates School Times Publications/Frontline Distribution International, 2001.

LoBagola, Ibn. *An African Savage's Own Story*. London: Knopf, 1930.

Locke, Alain, ed. *The New Negro: Voices of the Harlem Renaissance*. New York: Atheneum, 1992.

Lott, Eric. *Blackface Minstrelsy and the American Working Class*. New York: Oxford University Press, 1993.

Lowney, John. "Haiti and Black Transnationalism: Remapping the Migrant Geography of *Home to Harlem*." *African American Review* 34, no. 3 (fall 2000): 413–29.

Mahar, William J. *Behind the Burnt Cork Mask: Early Blackface Minstrelsy and Antebellum American Popular Culture*. Urbana: University of Illinois Press, 1999.

——. "Ethiopian Skits and Sketches: Contents and Contexts of Blackface Minstrelsy,

1840–1890." In *Inside the Minstrel Mask*, edited by Annemarie Bean, James V. Hatch, and Brooks Mcnamara, 179–222. Hanover, N.H.: Wesleyan University Press, 1996.

Makonnen, Ras. *Pan-Africanism from Within*. Nairobi: Oxford University Press, 1973.

Martin, Tony, ed. *African Fundamentalism: A Literary and Cultural Anthology of Garvey's Harlem Renaissance*. Dover, Mass.: Majority, 1983.

———. *Literary Garveyism: Garvey, Black Arts, and the Harlem Renaissance*. Dover, Mass.: Majority, 1983.

———. *The Poetical Works of Marcus Garvey*. Dover, Mass.: Majority, 1983.

Masquerading: The Art of the Notting Hill Carnival. Exhibition catalog. London: Arts Council of Great Britain, 1986.

McClintock, Anne. *Imperial Leather: Race, Gender, and Sexuality in Colonial Contest*. New York: Routledge, 1995.

McKay, Claude. *Banjo*. New York: Harcourt Brace Jovanovich, 1929.

———. *Harlem: Negro Metropolis*. New York: Harcourt Brace Jovanovich, 1968.

———. *Harlem Shadows*. New York, Harcourt, 1922.

———. *Home to Harlem*. Boston: Northeastern University Press, 1987.

———. *A Long Way from Home*. San Diego: Harcourt Brace Jovanovich, 1970.

———. *My Green Hills of Jamaica*. Unpublished manuscript. Schomburg Center for Research in Black Culture. New York: New York Public Library.

———. *The Selected Poems of Claude McKay*. New York: Harcourt Brace Jovanovich, 1953.

McKay, Nellie Y. " 'What Were They Saying?' A Selected Overview of Black Women Playwrights of the Harlem Renaissance." In *Harlem Renaissance Re-examined: A Revised and Expanded Edition*, edited by Victor A. Kramer and Robert A. Russ. New York: Whitston, 1997.

McLemee, Scott, ed. *C. L. R. James on the "Negro Question."* Jackson: University Press of Mississippi, 1996.

Melzer, Annabelle. *Latest Rage the Big Drum: Dada and Surrealist Performance*. Ann Arbor, Mich.: UMI Research Press, 1980.

Mintz, Sidney W., and Richard Price. *The Birth of African-American Culture: An Anthropological Perspective*. Boston: Beacon, 1976.

Mordden, Ethan. *Broadway Babies: The People Who Made the American Musical*. New York: Oxford University Press, 1983.

Moses, Wilson Jeremiah. *The Wings of Ethiopia*. Ames: Iowa University Press, 1990.

North, Michael. *The Dialect of Modernism: Race, Language, and Twentieth-Century Literature*. New York: Oxford University Press, 1994.

Palmeer, Ransford W. *Pilgrims from the Sun: West Indian Migration to America*. New York: Twayne / Simon and Schuster, 1995.

Palmer, Ransford W. *U.S.-Caribbean Relations: Their Impact on Peoples and Culture*. Westport, Conn.: Praeger, 1998.

Parascandola, Louis J., ed. *"Winds Can Wake Up the Dead": An Eric Walrond Reader*. Detroit: Wayne State University Press, 1998.

Peacock, Shane. "Africa Meets the Great Farini." In *Africans on Stage: Studies in Ethnologi-*

cal Show Business, edited by Bernth Lindfors, 81–106. Bloomington: Indian University Press, 1999.

Petras, Elizabeth McLean. Jamaican Labor Migration: White Capital and Black Labor, 1850–1930. Boulder: Westview, 1988.

Quevedo, Raymond [Atilla the Hun]. Atilla's Kaiso: A Short History of Trinidad Calypso. St. Augustine: University of the West Indies Press, 1983.

Ramchand, Kenneth. The West Indian Novel and Its Background. New York: Barnes and Noble, 1970.

Rampersad, Arnold. The Art and Imagination of W. E. B. Du Bois. New York: Schocken, 1990.

Roaring Lion. Calypso: From France to Trinidad, 800 Years of History. Trinidad: General Printers of San Juan, 1988.

Robinson, Cedric J. "W. E. B. Du Bois and Black Sovereignty." In Imagining Home: Class, Culture, and Nationalism in the African Diaspora, edited by Sidney J. Lemelle and Ribin D. G. Kelley. London: Verso, 1994.

Rogers, J. A. World's Great Men of Color. Vol. 2. 1947. Reprint, New York: Touchstone, 1996.

Rogin, Michael. Blackface, White Noise: Jewish Immigrants in the Hollywood Melting Pot. Berkeley: University of California Press, 1996.

Rohlehr, Gordon. Calypso and Society in Pre-Independence Trinidad. Port of Spain, Trinidad: Gordon Rohlehr, 1990.

Rowland, Mabel, ed. Bert Williams—Son of Laughter. 1923. Reprint, New York: Negro Universities Press, 1969.

Russ, Robert A. " 'There's No Place Like Home': The Carnival of Black Life in Claude McKay's Home to Harlem." In Harlem Renaissance Re-examined: A Revised and Expanded Edition, edited by Victor A. Kramer and Robert A. Russ. New York: Whitston, 1997.

Rydell, Robert W. "Darkest Africa." In Africans on Stage: Studies in Ethnological Show Business, edited by Bernth Lindfors, 135–55. Bloomington: Indiana University Press, 1999.

Said, Edward. Culture and Imperialism. New York: Knopf, 1993.

——. Orientalism. New York: Vintage, 1979.

Sander, Reinhard W., ed. From Trinidad: An Anthology of Early West Indian Writing. New York: Africana, 1978.

Schuyler, George. Black Empire. Boston: Northeastern University Press, 1991.

Shipp, Jesse A., Paul Laurence Dunbar, and Will Marion Cook. In Dahomey: A Negro Musical Comedy. London: Keith, Prowse, 1902.

Smith, Eric Ledell. Bert Williams: A Biography of the Pioneer Black Comedian. Jefferson, N.C.: McFarland, 1992.

Spencer, Jon Michael. The New Negroes and Their Music. Knoxville: University of Tennessee Press, 1997.

Sundquist, Eric J. To Wake the Nations: Race in the Making of American Literature. Cambridge, Mass.: Harvard University Press, 1993.

Taussig, Michael. *Mimesis and Alterity: A Particular History of the Senses*. New York: Routledge, 1993.

Taylor, Frank C., and Gerald Cook. *Alberta Hunter: A Celebration in Blues*. New York: McGraw-Hill, 1987.

Taylor, Patrick. *The Narrative of Liberation: Perspectives on Afro-Caribbean Literature, Popular Culture, and Politics*. Ithaca, N.Y.: Cornell University Press, 1989.

Thomson, Rosemarie Garland, ed. *Freakery: Cultural Spectacles of the Extraordinary Body*. New York: New York University Press, 1996.

Tillery, Tyrone. *Claude McKay: A Black Poet's Struggle for Racial Identity*. Amherst: University of Massachusetts Press, 1992.

Toll, Robert C. *Blacking Up: The Minstrel Show in Nineteenth Century America*. New York: Oxford University Press, 1974.

Tosches, Nick. *Where Dead Voices Gather*. Boston: Little, Brown, 2001.

Turner, W. Burghardt, and Joyce Moore Turner, eds. *Richard B. Moore, Caribbean Militant in Harlem*. Bloomington: Indiana University Press, 1988.

Veblen, Thorstein. *Essays in Our Changing Order*. Edited by Leon Ardzrooni. New York: Viking, 1954.

——. *The Theory of the Leisure Class*. New York: Macmillan, 1899.

Vickerman, Milton. *Crosscurrents: West Indian Immigrants and Race*. New York: Oxford University Press, 1999.

Walcott, Derek. *What the Twilight Says: Essays*. New York: Farrar, Straus and Giroux, 1998.

Walker, George. "The Negro on the American Stage." *The Colored American Magazine* 11, no. 4 (October 1906): 243–48.

Warner, Keith. *Kaiso! The Trinidad Calypso*. Washington: Three Continents Press, 1985.

Warren, Kenneth W. "Appeals for Misrecognition: Theorizing the Diaspora." In *Cultures of United States Imperialism*, edited by Amy Kaplan and Donald E. Pease. Durham, N.C.: Duke University Press, 1993.

Washington, Booker T. "Bert Williams." *Booker T. Washington Papers, Volume 10, 1909–11*. Edited by Louis R. Harlan and Raymond W. Smock. Urbana: University of Illinois Press, 1981.

Watkins-Owens, Irma. *Blood Relations: Caribbean Immigrants and the Harlem Community, 1900–1930*. Bloomington: Indiana University Press, 1996.

Watson, Steven. *The Harlem Renaissance: Hub of African-American Culture, 1920–1930*. New York: Pantheon, 1995.

Weschler, Lawrence. *Mr. Wilson's Cabinet of Wonder*. New York: Vintage, 1995.

Williams, Bert. "The Comic Side of Trouble." *The American Magazine* 85 (January–June 1918): 33–61.

Williams, Raymond. *The Politics of Modernism: Against the New Conformists*. Edited by Tony Pinkney. London: Verso, 1989.

Wintz, Cary D. *Black Culture and the Harlem Renaissance*. Houston: Rice University Press, 1988.

Wittke, Carl. *Tambo and Bones: A History of the American Minstrel Stage*. Durham, N.C.: Duke University Press, 1930.

Woll, Allen. *Black Musical Theatre: From Coontown to Dreamgirls*. Baton Rouge: Louisiana State University Press, 1989.

Yard, Lionel M. *Biography of Amy Ashwood Garvey, 1897–1969*. New York: Associated Publishers, 1989.

INDEX

Abyssinia, 12, 38, 63, 166, 201

"Africa Meets the Great Farini," 134

African Blood Brotherhood, 93, 233

African Savage's Own Story, An, 128–134, 135–139

Africans on Stage, 121

Anglo-Zulo wars, 122, 134

Atilla the Hun (Raymond Quevedo), 153, 217–219

Atlantic Monthly, 66, 69

"Back to Africa," 86, 89, 90, 107, 156, 182

Baker, Houston, 12, 29, 61, 65, 68–72, 77–78, 82–84, 86, 106–107, 110, 149, 224, 238

Baker, Josephine, 4, 11, 38, 176, 203

Bakhtin, Mikhail, 14, 104–105, 111, 127, 208–209, 213–215, 224, 234, 241–244

Bandana Land, 63, 69, 201

Banjo, 215, 220, 235–236, 241

"Barbarian Status of Women," 106

Barnum, P. T., 89, 122–124, 134, 172

Batouala, 128–129

Beacon, 151–153

Bean, Anne-Marie, 197–198, 200

Bhabha, Homi, 80, 108

Birth of African American Culture, 115

Birth of a Nation, 2, 22

Blackface. *See* Minstrels

Blackface, White Noise, 39, 97, 100, 149

Black Manhattan, 18–19, 32, 64 n.42

Black Skin, White Masks, 34, 71

Blood Relations, 94

Bonnett, Aubrey W., 103–104

Book of American Negro Poetry, 63–64

Brathwaite, Edward Kamau, 112, 128, 215, 243

Brice, Fanny, 20, 97

Brown, Bill, 129
Burroughs, Edgar Rice, 82, 128, 131
Burton, Richard, 13, 41, 131, 160
Butler, Judith, 41, 113, 196, 198, 200

Cakewalk, 2, 201
Caliban, 107, 238
Calypso, 13, 36, 150–154, 157, 216–224,
    227, 234; and vaudeville, 155–156
Calypso and Society in Pre-Independence Trini-
    dad, 156
Calypso Callaloo, 147–148
Campbell, Grace, 9, 233
Cantor, Eddie, 2, 21, 35, 40, 81
Carby, Hazel, 151–152, 161–162, 191–196
Caretta, Vincent, 117–119
Caribbean Discourse, 92
Caribbean Waves, 94, 100, 231–233
Carnivalesque, 199, 208–209, 241–242,
    244
Charters, Ann, 29, 48–49, 100, 163, 167,
    173
Chicago's World Columbian Exposition,
    134, 161–163
"City of Refuge," 228, 230
Clark, Gerald, 77, 217
Clarke, Austin, 112
Cole, Bob, 26, 74
Colored American Magazine, 201, 167
"Comic Side of Trouble, The," 52, 168–
    169
Cook, Will Marion, 26–27, 70
Coolidge, Calvin, 186–187
Cooper, Wayne F., 220, 231, 242
Crisis, 43, 52
Crisis of the Negro Intellectual, 43, 233
Cruse, Harold, 43, 233

Dada, 89, 96
Deleuze, Gilles, 45, 51, 215
Domingo, W. A., 93, 95, 126, 207, 228–
    229, 233
Douglas, Ann, 36–37, 40

Douglass, Frederick, 162–165, 167
Du Bois, W. E. B., 3, 4, 6, 9, 12, 15, 31,
    34, 48, 56, 64, 71, 72, 92, 93, 99, 106,
    108, 119, 124, 126, 165, 171, 215; on
    color line, 173–174; and double-
    consciousness, 25, 37, 42–43, 58–60,
    66–69, 72, 75, 77, 109, 125, 132, 168–
    169, 200, 240; on Garvey, 61, 85, 89–
    91, 107, 242; on Williams, 74–75. See
    also The Souls of Black Folk
Dunbar, Paul Lawrence, 3, 12, 26–27,
    64–66, 68, 70, 81, 153, 198

Early, Gerald, 60
Edward VII, 2, 122, 166
Edwards, Paul, 117–118
Ellington, Duke, 38, 176
Ellison, Ralph, 12, 33, 77–79, 80–82,
    105, 122, 125, 138
Emperor Jones, 37, 184, 210
Equiano, Olaudah, 117–119, 124, 128–
    132, 137
Erlmann, Veit, 142–143
Esu-Elegbara, 20, 95, 105, 107, 109–110,
    116, 125, 240, 243
"Ethnological Show Business: Footlight-
    ing the Dark Continent," 122
Europe, James Reese, 27, 244n65
"Evah Darkey Is a King," 122, 168, 188,
    206

Fanon, Frantz, 34–36, 71
Fauset, Jessie, 12, 42, 52–56, 64, 69
Fierce Hatred of Injustice, A, 231
Fisher, Rudolf, 2, 5, 107, 228–230, 241

Garber, Marjorie, 41, 105, 113, 138–140,
    196
García Lorca, Federico, 207–208
Garvey, Amy Ashwood, 9, 156–157, 216
Garvey, Amy Jacques, 9, 88
Garvey, Marcus, 3, 8, 9, 10, 15, 21, 50, 61,
    69, 81, 93, 99, 102, 107, 119–121, 128,

157, 168, 173–174, 176–178, 186–189, 211, 214; leader of UNIA, 13, 85–87, 89–92, 126; and masquerade, 56–57, 85, 86–92, 95–96

Gates, Henry Louis, 12, 20, 86, 95, 104, 106–109, 110, 112–113, 240

"Gift of the Black Tropics," 93, 229

Gilroy, Paul, 60, 110

Glissant, Edouard, 36, 92–93, 150, 152

Gomes, Eduardo Sa, 154, 156, 217

Gordon, George William, 158–159

Griffith, D. W., 2, 22

Guattari, Félix, 45, 51, 215

Harlem: Negro Metropolis, 87, 120, 220

Harlem Shadows, 50, 86, 221, 235, 247

Harris, Wilson, 34–36, 39, 45, 51, 78, 80, 208, 214

Hathaway, Heather, 94, 100, 231–233

Hayford, J. E. Casely, 59–60

Hemingway, Ernest, 2, 20

Henderson, Willie, 124–125, 128, 133, 135, 138–139

Hey, Hey, 156

Hill, Donald, 92, 147–148, 154

Hill, Errol, 157–158

Hill, Robert, 89–90, 94–96, 112, 158

Hine, Darlene Clark, 108

Hinsley, Curtis M., 123, 134, 138

Hogan, Ernest, 65, 74–75, 81

Holding Aloft the Banner of Ethiopia, 94, 233

Home to Harlem, 5, 10, 13, 91, 103, 211–213, 215–216, 219, 223, 228, 230, 232, 234–242, 247

Hopkins, Pauline, 166–167

Houdini, Wilmoth, 9, 217

Huggins, Nathan, 72

Hughes, Langston, 38, 42, 63–64, 99–100, 128, 176, 214, 216

Hunter, Alberta, 28

Hurston, Zora Neal, 31, 63–64, 179, 216

In Dahomey, 2, 12–14, 29, 37, 57, 63, 66, 70, 81, 88, 99, 122–124, 135, 156, 161, 170–172, 181–184, 191–197. Songs: "Evah Darkey Is a King," 122, 168, 188, 206; "Jonah Man," 181; "Leader of the Colored Aristocracy," 126, 184–185, 187, 189–190, 192, 203–205; "My Castle on the Nile," 177–179; "My Dahomean Queen," 188; "My Little Zulu Babe," 177, 179; "On Broadway in Dahomey Bye and Bye," 177, 188–190; "On Emancipation Day," 126; "The Phrenologist Coon," 177

Invisible Man, 122, 125

Jamaican Stage, 1655–1900, 157

James, C. L. R., 34, 36, 90, 96, 151–152, 157

James, Winston, 91, 94, 231, 233

Johnson, James Weldon, 3, 18–19, 32, 63–65, 74, 128

Jolson, Al, 2, 81, 97

Julian, Hubert Fauntleroy, 127

Kersands, Billy, 69, 81

Killingray, David, 124–125, 128, 133, 135, 138–139

King Kong, 83

Krasner, David, 201–202

Lamming, George, 36, 51

"Leader of the Colored Aristocracy," 126, 184–185, 187, 189–190, 192, 203–205

Liberia, 13, 186, 188–190

Lindfors, Bernth, 121–122, 124

Liverpool, Hollis "Chalkdust," 148–149

LoBagola, Prince Bata Kindai Amgoza Ibn, 11, 128–139, 144–145

Locke, Alain, 3, 34, 47, 56, 58, 61–62, 64, 71, 77, 106, 114, 165, 171, 213, 230

Long Way From Home, A, 210, 221, 230

Lott, Eric, 36, 40–41, 101, 113, 123

Lyrics of Lowly Life, 65–66

Madison, Paul, 154–155, 216
Majar, William J., 77–78
"Making Noise: Marcus Garvey, Dada, August 1922," 89
Makonnen, Ras, 124, 137–138
Manning, Sam, 9, 154–157, 214, 216–217
Maran, René, 128–129
Marx, Karl, 164–165
Material Unconscious, 97
McClintock, Anne, 123, 142
McKay, Claude, 5, 10, 11, 13, 14, 36, 38, 60, 63–64, 73, 85–87, 89, 87, 91, 96, 99–100, 103, 107–108, 111–112, 120–121, 128, 211–212, 214–216, 219–221, 231; on African Americans, 59, 212, 214, 220; on blackface minstrelsy, 59, 210–212, 215–216; and gender politics, 235–236; *Gingertown*, 220; and *picong*, 227–228, 233–235; sexuality of, 231–232; "The Tropics in New York," 220–221, 223, 232. See also *Home to Harlem*
McKay, Nellie, 209
Mimicry, 69, 76, 82–83, 89, 191; "all-aesthetic," 84–85, 97; deceptive and protective, 96, 105–106, 116–117; klepto-parasitic, 84, 86, 90, 104, 227; phan-eric, 84–85, 97
Minstrels: in Caribbean, 13, 146–150, 154–155, 157–160; in continental Africa, 142–147; globalization of, 141–142; Irish immigrants, 101, 104; Jewish performers, 39, 97–98, 101, 104–105, 140, 149
Modernism and the Harlem Renaissance, 68, 78, 82, 107, 110
Mordden, Ethan, 20
Mr. Lode of Kaol, 38, 63
My Green Hills of Jamaica, 211–212, 223–224

NAACP, 91, 171, 186–188
Negritude, 144, 180, 241
Negro World, 43, 85, 88, 89, 120, 186

New Negro, 34, 62, 63–64, 68, 92, 95, 106, 114, 171
"Nobody," 35, 39, 181
"No Nationality," 217–219, 232, 239

O'Neill, Eugene, 37, 184, 210

Pan-Africanism, 6, 8, 13, 15, 81, 91–92, 94, 99, 157, 160, 170, 174, 185–187, 206
Pan-Africanism from Within, 124
Peacock, Shane, 134, 161
Picong, 227–228, 233–235
Pleasures of Exile, 36
Pollack, Channing, 55
Price, Richard, 115
Primitivism, 23, 83, 100, 116, 144, 176, 216, 231, 233, 235
Prince Kojo, 119–121, 124, 128, 137

Rastafarian movement, 122, 158, 178
Reconstructing Womanhood, 193
"Ringtail," 228, 230
Rituals of Power and Rebellion, 148
Roaring Lion, 155
Robeson, Paul, 37, 210
Robinson, Cedric J., 185–187, 190, 193, 236
Rogers, Bill (Augustus Hinds), 154, 217, 221–223
Rogers, J. A., 54, 168
Rogin, Michael, 33, 39, 97–98, 100–104, 149
Rohlehr, Gordon, 156
Russ, Robert A., 209, 212–214
Rydell, Robert W., 164

Salome, 202–203
Sander, Reinhard, 125, 151
San Francisco Mid-Winter Exposition, 163–165
Schuyler, George, 86–89, 176, 186
Shuffle Along, 21–22, 176, 210, 214

Signifying Monkey, 12, 20, 95, 104, 107, 110, 112–113, 240
Slaves Today, 88, 176
Smith, Bessie, 146, 214
Smith, Eric Ledell, 140, 166, 182–183
Souls of Black Folk, The, 4, 6, 31, 66, 92, 132, 153, 180, 202
"Spectatorial Lust: The African Choir in England, 1891–1893," 142
Spence, Eulalie, 5, 73, 111
Sundquist, Eric, 97, 162, 172–174, 179
Swartz, Patti Capel, 209

Tarzan of the Apes, 82, 128, 131
Taussig, Michael, 67
Taylor, Patrick, 112–113
Terrible Honesty, 37
Tosches, Nick, 28, 145
Tovalou-Houenou, Prince Kojo, 119–121, 124, 128, 137
To Wake the Nations, 97, 162, 173
Trinidad, 34, 153, 216–218, 222–224, 227; "Little Renaissance," 150–154; "No Nationality," 217–219, 239
Tropic Death, 128
"Tropics in New York, The," 220–221, 223, 232
"Two Real Coons," 6, 28, 123–124

"Under the Bamboo Tree," 74, 274
Universal Negro Improvement Association (UNIA), 13, 17, 85–87, 89–92, 106, 112, 119, 124,126, 165, 188

Van Der Zee, James, 120
Vaudeville, 6, 37, 70, 124, 128, 133–134, 146, 154, 175
Veblen, Thorstein, 106
Vechten, Carl Van, 128, 177, 216, 238
"Vignettes of the Dusk," 126, 226–227

"W. E. B. Du Bois and Black Sovereignty," 185

Walcott, Derek, 152–153
Walker, Ada Overton, 2, 10, 32, 38, 81, 193–194, 200–203, 208; choreography, 23–24, 201; "Colored Men and Women on the Stage," 201; "cult of domesticity," 24, 236; death, 23–24; gender debate and, 201–204; "Opportunities the Stage Offers Intelligent and Talented Women," 201
Walker, George, 2, 17, 26–27, 28, 32–34, 42, 50, 65, 68, 70, 75, 79, 123, 167, 172, 175–177, 180, 192, 201–202, 208; death, 23; meeting with Bert Williams, 23; "The Negro on the American Stage," 165
Walrond, Eric, 9, 10, 43, 63, 73, 87, 111, 126–128, 221, 226–228
Washington, Booker T., 3, 12, 22, 27, 42, 46–49, 42, 51–52, 56, 68–69, 73–77, 81
Watkins-Owens, Irma, 94–95, 156–157
"West Indian Weed Woman," 221–223
"We Wear the Mask," 65–66, 153
"What the Twilight Says," 153
"What Were They Saying?: Black Women Playwrights of the Harlem Renaissance," 209
Where Dead Voices Gather, 28
Williams, Bert: and African Americans, 48–51; and Africans on display, 165, 167; birth and cultural origins, 5, 7–8, 46–47, 50, 54–55; "The Comic Side of Trouble," 52, 168–169; death, 20, 22; first use of blackface, 25; and integration of Broadway, 1–2; as last "darky," 32, 182; The Negro on Stage, 79–80; "Nobody," 35, 39, 181; real name, 139–140
Woll, Allen, 61
Womb of Space, The, 214

Ziegfeld, Florenz, 2, 18, 20, 35
Ziegfeld Follies, 2, 17–20, 35, 40, 43, 48

Louis Chude-Sokei is an associate professor
of literature at the University of California,
Santa Cruz.

Library of Congress Cataloging-in-Publication Data

Chude-Sokei, Louis Onuorah.

The last "darky" : Bert Williams, black-on-black minstrelsy,

and the African diaspora / Louis Chude-Sokei.

p. cm.

Includes bibliographical references and index.

ISBN 0-8223-3605-7 (cloth : alk. paper)

ISBN 0-8223-3643-X (pbk. : alk. paper)

1. Williams, Bert, 1874–1922—Criticism and interpretation.

2. Blackface entertainers—United States. 3. Minstrel shows—

United States—History—20th century. I. Title.

PN2287.W46C55 2005

792.702'8'092—dc22   2005015954